If You Can Keep It

Why We Nearly Lost It and How We Get It Back

Robin Koerner

To the Rabid Quill,

On Liberty!

Robin

If You Can Keep It: Why We Nearly Lost It and How We Get It Back

Print ISBN 978-1-941071-47-2
ebook ISBN 978-1-941071-48-9

STAIRWAY PRESS—SEATTLE

Cover Design by Guy Corp
http://grafixcorp.com
Cover Illustration by Rachel Koerner

STAIRWAY PRESS

www.StairwayPress.com
848 North Rainbow Blvd #5015
Las Vegas, NV 89107 USA

DEDICATION

For Edward Snowden –

who stepped out of his paradigm to help the rest of us step out of ours.

Table of Contents

ACKNOWLEDGEMENTS

SEVEN YEARS AGO, I'd have not believed that I would ever be sufficiently interested in politics to write a book about it. That I have done so stands as evidence of my good fortune in having in my life people who care as much as I do about the potential of humanity and the joy that comes when we exercise our natural rights in its actualization.

My first and deepest thanks go to Kristy Padgett, to whom I am grateful for very many things—but most of all here, for being unwavering in her belief that I had something of value to say to America, and in her consistency in not letting me believe my own excuses for not knuckling down and doing just that.

When I had knuckled down for long enough to produce something coherent and book-like, my good friend Daniel Smith cheerfully stepped up to edit its first version. It was some years later when he stepped up again to edit its last version. His work definitely improved my own.

It was Juliet Nail who read, and made extremely helpful suggestions concerning, the first manuscript that looked anything like the one you're holding. Her feedback helped me believe that the message in this book might actually be something that mainstream America needs.

I am especially grateful to KrisAnne Hall, a Constitutional attorney and extraordinary teacher, for sharing her legal expertise to help me craft a unique ending for this book.

At the very end of the writing process, Ismaine Ayouaz's unhesitating agreement to undertake the arduous task of formatting what was supposed to be the last draft—but ended up being the last few drafts—helped to ensure timely delivery to the publisher in useable form.

Meanwhile, my sister Rachel turned her talents to the front cover—and it's certainly the better for it.

The kind and consistent encouragement of Elias Mokole, Sarina Forbes and Katarina Korbelova have also helped me along the way.

With the support of those people, this book comes to you now. I am utterly grateful to all of them for enabling me to enjoy the very special privilege of bringing ideas that excite me to large enough numbers of people that they might just leave a small mark on a nation.

Before I could write this book, however, I had first to discover a passion of sufficient depth that it could push me through that often quite grueling task.

I am grateful to those who have fed that passion.

The ideas on which Chapter 1 is based are largely inspired by my work with www.WatchingAmerica.com, which has been run by hundreds of volunteers since its inception in late 2004. I am grateful to all of them (and especially its brilliant managing editors and senior editors) who have maintained and steadily improved that publication over the years.

Special thanks go to Glenn Cripe not only for sending me the very first reading list that pointed me in the philosophical direction in which I hope this book will broadly take you, but also for giving me the opportunity to travel the world from Brazil to Kyrgyzstan to teach the life-changing ideas that I discovered in the books on Glenn's list. That opportunity has helped me improve my own understanding of liberty while sharing its elevating power with others.

Two people are mentioned in the body of the book because of their pivotal role in bringing my own writing and thinking on liberty to a significant number of the American public. They are Israel Anderson, who in 2011 was the first person to see the strategic potential of my concept of the "Blue Republican," and helped put it in front of large numbers of people through social media, and Zak Carter who did the same through more conventional media—and was relentless in so doing. If not for those two, no one would have ever have known that I had anything truly original or efficacious to say. And if not for a single email kindly written by Dorian de Wind, I'd never have been given the platform on which I was able to present the "Blue Republican" idea—of which more in the book.

In the last few years, other people have provided the huge moral support and practical support that may yet enable the message of this book to be converted into a change in the political direction of our nation. I cannot list them all, but chief among them by a large margin are Paul Addis and Daniel Latrimurti.

To all of those named above, my personal thanks: you have made a large difference in my life, and in so doing, I hope, at least a small difference to the readers of this book.

In a somewhat different vein, I must acknowledge Dr. Ron Paul, who has helped millions of Americans, including me, see that America's political dichotomies (left vs. right, Liberal vs. Conservative, Democratic vs. Republican) really are false. I hope that in some small way this book does what he did so well: to tell the truth humbly, and in so doing to open minds.

I am genuinely honored that Jeffrey Tucker, a man whose love of liberty flows entirely from his deep humanity, took the time to read my work so closely—and then to write the most generous and thoughtful Foreword. If you take anything of value away from my work, I urge you to engage his.

When I graduated from university with a grade I had not dared expect, I sent my parents a card with a picture of a monkey on it, and the sentiment inside:

> *Thanks for helping this little monkey get to where he seems to have ended up.*

With this book, I think I may have finally done something of value with all that education they sacrificed so much to give me. So, Mum and Dad, thanks again for that: the Dedication to Edward Snowden notwithstanding, this one's for you.

FOREWORD

By Jeffrey Tucker

IN MODERN TIMES, the case for human liberty in its classical form has been radically, horribly, destructively misrepresented and hence misunderstood. It is not a plan for the socio-political order, imposed by intellectuals with an ideology. It is not an ethic of individualism that insists that dogs should eat dogs. It is not a partisan plot to skew the affairs of government for capital and against labor, or for any one group against any other group. It is not a slogan for a would-be junta wielding perfect knowledge of the way all things should work.

The case for liberty is for a social process that is free to discover the best social institutions to enliven and realize human dignity through choice and with love. In order for that to happen, we need what might be called, in the tradition of C.S. Lewis, mere liberty: the freedom to own, act, speak, think, and innovate. The exercise of such rights is incompatible with government management of the economy and the social order.

It seems rather simple, right? I think so. But brilliant ideas come in simple and effervescent packages. This is a good description of Robin Koerner's provocative and revisionist work, which I am humbled to introduce. It is a work of stunning erudition and sincerity. I also happen to agree with it. I've been struggling toward a similar thesis for a good part of my writing career, though I'm certain Robin has gone beyond even my most mature thought.

We need this book now. Too much is at stake for the cause of liberty to fail to expand its circle of friends. I've personally never met anyone who is against their own liberty. No one seeks to be a slave. No one wants all choice taken away, property stolen, and our bodies chained to a prescribed regime. To possess volition is part of what it means to be a living human being.

Our minds have to function—and what we think needs to be realizable. We seek to coordinate our choices with others in a way that benefits ourselves. We learn in the course of our lives that our own good is not incompatible with the good of others. A sign of a mature person and a developed society is that there is no separation between the good of one and the good of many.

If all this is true, how did it come to be that we are ruled by regimes that negate all the above? The modern state knows no limits to its power. There is no aspect of life into which it does not intrude. How has that affected us as individuals, as communities? It has taken away our liberty and hence part of our humanity. This is why the cause of liberty must be clear on what it opposes. We seek to end government as we know it. But that is not the whole of what we seek. We also favor something beautiful. Explaining what this looks like and the rhetorical apparatus that necessarily accompanies this is the greatest value of Koerner's book.

Three sections of this book gripped me especially. I'm intrigued at Koerner's deep analysis of prevailing political biases and how they reflect personal life conditions in an intractable way. This is a result of an intrusive state apparatus that everyone is seeking to control in their own interest. In absence of such an apparatus, political biases would still exist though their exercise would take different and socially constructive forms. The implication here is that it is absolutely necessary for the whole of society to be somehow converted to a libertarian vision in order that liberty is sustained. What we need is a minimum set of rules that reflect commonly held moral standards such as the golden rule. Again, liberty does not seek to displace cultural or religious heterogeneity but rather give it a new and productive life as a source of unity rather than division.

I also appreciate Koerner's extended explanation of money and its meaning in society. This is a major complaint against the free economy, that somehow it permits money to taint morality and beautiful aesthetics. He explains that money really is an organic outgrowth of human exchange, an essential institution that makes it easier to serve each other in a peaceful and rational way. People tend to think of money as crude and gritty and materialistic. In Koerner's rendering, money as an institution is a proxy for the realization of human aspirations.

The third aspect of the book that truly sweeps me away with its insight and depth is his section on liberty as a realization of a civilization of love. I know that time is short and that people don't read as carefully as they should. But this section deserves close study by every advocate of liberty. It will change the way you think and speak about the topic.

I have my own personal reasons for celebrating the appearance of this work. More than two years ago, writing my daily column, it occurred to me that libertarians might have picked up some bad habits in the course of their politicking. They might have a tendency toward a kind of reductionism, thinning out the core ideas to a single principle and applying it in ways that are contrary to the liberal spirit. I broke down camps within libertarianism into two archetypes: brutalist (named after the architectural school of thought) and humanitarianism. The essay was since translated into a dozen languages and prompted the greatest controversy of any of my mature writings. What I never had time to do was spell out what this humanitarian vision of liberty looks like in its fullest presentation. This is what Koerner's book has done: completed something that I only discerned in its barest outlines.

The cause of human liberty does not need another didactic treatise that proves beyond a shadow of a doubt that vast majority of humanity is living a lie and roiling in fallacious attachment to evil. What we need is a compelling case for why liberty can serve everyone right where we are today, regardless of life station, cultural preferences, language, or religion. We need writings that humanize what we favor. We need to understand that libertarianism is, at its root, liberal in spirit, inseparable from the historical forces that unleashed the most wonderful flowering of human dignity in the whole of human experience. This is what Koerner has done, and I absolutely celebrate the intellectual passion that led to this book's creation.

INTRODUCTION

Your Last Freedom

AMERICA HAS A grand founding narrative, according to which the nation was founded for the very purposes of life, liberty and the pursuit of happiness. Its government was instituted for, and justified by, the protection of these values. We Americans believe that we are a land of free people, a land of free enterprise, a land with a free press, and most of all, a land in which the individual is free to believe as he sees fit, and to express himself and act accordingly.

Our self-image is of the land of the free and the home of the brave.

But that old saw is rather hard to apply to the United States today. Consider just a few examples.

The right to due process is gone. Under the National Defense Authorization Act, an American can now be incarcerated indefinitely and without trial simply on suspicion of supporting terrorism alone. Who determines if your activities are suspect? Not a judge. Not an elected official. The Fifth Amendment has gone.

Americans are now killed by their own government without due process. With the killing of the American citizen, Al-Awlaki, by a drone, an American president assumed the power of life and death over citizens outside any legal process.

Your right to privacy is gone. Under the Patriot Act, an agent of the government does not need a judge to issue a search warrant before he invades your privacy—perhaps by searching your house or hacking your library records. He can write his own warrant and force his way in. Moreover, and even more reminiscent of 1984 than any of King George's abuses in the 18th century, government agencies now collect all of your emails, phone conversations and other electronic communications through technology that they have installed at hubs that belong to communications corporations. These are collected without your permission, and in spite of your not being suspected of a crime—to be listened to or read by the government at any time in the future. Such abuses make the fact that you cannot contract with a privately owned company to fly between privately owned airports in a privately owned plane without having the government take digital images of your naked body seem barely worthy of mention. And why even waste breath on the fact the TSA invades your privacy by performing what would be a physical assault if done by anyone else if you decline to let them collect those digital images of you? The Fourth Amendment is in shreds.

Just as you have no personal privacy, you have no economic or financial privacy. FinCEN is the Financial Crimes Enforcement Network. Under related legislation, banks are obliged to work for the government as spies on your financial affairs. If you make an unusual transaction at your bank—such as depositing $10,000 in cash—the bank will inform the government of the same by submitting a "Suspicious Activity Report" (SAR). Moreover, if you have a foreign account, you must, under threat of imprisonment, divulge to the government where all of your assets are. You must do so even if you file accurate tax returns, pay all of your taxes, and you are not suspected of any violation. To enjoy your liberty, you need not only a benign legal environment but also the capital that enables you to exercise your civil rights by acting on the choices you are legally allowed to make. Why, then, should the government need to know where your economic capacity is held—even after its gets its "fair" share?

Telling the truth can be a crime. Under the Patriot Act, if a federal agent writes his own warrant and serves it on you, don't tell your best friend what happened when she asks you why you are so upset. If you do so, you've committed a crime. And if, by the way, despite what you now know about FinCEN, you do deposit a large sum in your bank tomorrow, there's little point asking the bank if they went ahead and submitted that SAR: the bank won't tell you because it doesn't want to commit a crime, either. The First Amendment is gone. Did you think we needed it to protect disruptive or controversial speech? It turns out that now it does not even protect accurate and factual speech.

Under the National Defense Resources Preparedness Executive Order 13603[1], the federal government has claimed total power over every aspect of all American lives. The Executive claims for itself the privilege of abrogating any contract or agreement among private individuals and of dictating entire swathes of the economy—not only in an emergency situation, but also in peace time by delegating control of entire sectors of American life (such as "energy") to various government Secretaries. The entire Constitution has been ripped up by those whom it was written to constrain.

We are no longer a peaceful nation. We are a nation at almost perpetual war. The last decade has seen our nation participate directly and indirectly in myriad wars against protagonists who cannot harm us, and we continue to find new

---

1 http://www.whitehouse.gov/the-press-office/2012/03/16/executive-order-national-defense-resources-preparedness

theaters in which to operate militarily[2]. Bush's war in Iraq was justified by a false claim. Hundreds of thousands of lives have been lost in a country from which we were never threatened. But at least Bush went to Congress for permission. When Obama went into Libya, he called it "kinetic military action", rather than war, in an effort to avoid seeking from Congress the Constitutionally requisite permission for killing, through military force, yet more innocent non-Americans.

And then there is militarism, which is not quite the same thing as war. Whereas war refers to identifiable events, militarism is more of an outlook or a paradigm. Our very own Department of Defense funded a multi-million dollar study, headed up by Robert Pape, a professor at the University of Chicago, on the causes of suicide terrorism since it was first identified in the 1980s[3]. The study concentrated on suicide terrorism because that is 12 times more deadly than any other form of terrorism. The study found that in more than 95% of cases, the perpetrator was a resident of a nation that he or she regarded as a military occupier of his or her homeland. In other words, even those who appear to us to be religious fanatics do not kill themselves to kill us unless they perceive that we are militarily present where we have no right to be. Yet, we still put our military assets into foreign nations from which we are not threatened, when the same Department of Defense that organizes these operations commissioned the very study that has established that, by launching them, we are causing the very thing we claim to be fighting. Why, then, do we do it?

One of the least properly understood injustices in our nation is the systematic transfer of wealth to a select class of non-

---

[2]http://www.aljazeera.com/indepth/opinion/2012/09/2012916104846486602.html

[3] http://www.youtube.com/watch?v=X4HnIyClHEM

producers under special license of the government. As will be discussed at length in this book, our monetary system is designed to transfer real wealth from productive citizens to financial institutions in a process that benefits both political and economic elites. To a large extent, the "members" of those two elites are, of course, the same people. The privilege afforded to our banking sector makes the core of their business, to a first approximation, risk-free. Still, they manage to lose money, and when they do so, the same government that gives them the special privileges in the first place transfers to them more of their citizens' wealth through various forms of bailout.

The Rule of Law has clearly been replaced by the Rule of Men. The above examples of tyranny in American life all violate the Constitution, which is our Basic Law that articulates the foundational principles of the nation that all other laws must serve. The Rule of Law has always been the foil to the Rule of Men. But every one of the above examples is an example of our Lawmakers' putting themselves above the Law. As the Democratic Senator, Jim Clyburn, once said, "Most of what we do here [in Congress] is Unconstitutional."[4] Speaker of the House, Nancy Pelosi, put her contempt for the Law even more concisely when she responded to a calm question about the Constitutionality of arguably the most important law passed in the last decade, the Affordable Care Act, with the three words, "Are you serious?" [5]

Some of us are serious.

But too few, it seems.

How did We The People let this happen? Hundreds of books have been written about each of these divergences from freedom

---

[4] http://www.thedailybell.com/1108/Judge-Andrew-Napolitano-on-Chaotic-Courts-and-Unconstitutional-Justice-in-the-United-States.html

[5] http://www.youtube.com/watch?v=08uk99L8oqQ

in America—but there is little point detailing these problems if we don't understand how a nation of 320 million decent people who like being free can allow—or even cause—them to happen. Why the apparently inexorable slide to reduced liberty and the increased concentration of power by those who would lead us? Why is it so easy for "them" to perpetrate all of this on "us"? What makes us so compliant or passive? If we can find the root of that problem, we might actually be able to stop this rising tide of tyranny, and even turn it back.

Liberty, like charity, begins at home.

Arguably, modern Western culture's marker of the upper limit on tyranny can be found in George Orwell's aforementioned dystopic novel, 1984.

Set in a supra-national state called Oceania, the novel is concerned not with how tyranny arises, but with how a totalitarian state might operate once established. Accordingly, from the first line of the first page of the book, its main character, Winston, is completely oppressed: he has no privacy; no freedom of speech, no expectation of due process, no free access to information, and so on.

But Winston keeps one freedom until the very end of the book. It is a freedom that is so fundamental that it is the core of our very nature. It is so consistently used and so pervasive that we can't even see it. We don't think about the need to protect it or the value of exercising it, because it is so hard to wrest from us—even in a totalitarian regime like Oceania. That freedom is the freedom of the individual to observe for himself and to think for himself.

You might say that "observing" and "thinking" are not freedoms as much as they are simply inherent capabilities of human beings. But that would be a dichotomy so false as to be the exact opposite of the truth, because true freedom is inherent. It is as much a part of our humanity as are our hands or eyes. Indeed, the freedom to observe and think for ourselves is the first freedom we ever use and the last freedom we can count on having. In 1984, it is only at the very end of the book that Big Brother destroys that last freedom by destroying Winston's capacity to think for himself and to make sense of the data he receives from his own senses. Only at that point does the reader lose all hope for Winston and Oceania, because it is only at that point that the reader feels that Winston's oppression has finally become irreversible and that tyranny's triumph is complete.

All the while a man knows he is being oppressed, he always has reason to reject the oppression and the choice to fight back. As Goethe put it, "None are so enslaved as those who believe they are free".

Despite the fact that we have better access now to more information than ever about the nature of our political and our economic systems, and the activities and people that are involved in them, we as a people have not yet decided that we are oppressed, despite the above litany of eliminated rights. The only possible reason for that is that most of us have not yet "seen" things as they really are.

Why should that be so? Goethe again has the answer: "We see only what we know".

And if you know only one thing about knowing—or take only one thing from this book—it should be that single claim. Goethe did not say, "We know only what we see." Goethe was exactly right. What we already believe determines what we see. Those who can control what we believe, then, can blind us to our reality, allowing policy makers to make bad decisions in plain sight and get away with it.

And that is why, in politics and matters of civil society, Mark Twain was also right when he said, "It ain't what you don't know that gets you into trouble. It's what you know for sure that just ain't so."

This begs the question: what, then, determines what we know, even when it ain't so?

For at least three generations, most Americans have obtained their information about their country and the world through a pervasive media. 24-hour news channels abound on cable TV. Newspapers—albeit increasingly their online versions—still present first drafts of history that, at the very least, determine the topics of interest and the terms in which they are discussed.

Having the freedom to think and to believe as you choose—Winston's last freedom in 1984—will only serve us if we know how to exercise it.

This book is a primer in exercising that freedom.

In a book about how to consume food to stay healthy, you would expect to find a discussion of the nutritional value of what you eat, information about how your body processes what you consume, and information about how food is sold and marketed to you so that you can be a smarter consumer. In particular, it would point out the foods that have no nutritional value or are even harmful. Such a book would help you exercise your freedom to feed yourself in a way that best served you. It would be about food, the means of its production, and its effect on your body.

Analogously, this is a book about how to consume and process information to stay free. It will discuss the nutritional value (or otherwise) of the news you read or watch, how your mind processes the information you consume, and how information is sold and marketed to you, with the ultimate goal of making you a smarter consumer. In particular, it points out the false beliefs that are doing harm to you and your liberties. This book helps you exercise your freedom to inform yourself and think in ways that best serve you. It is about information, the means of its production, its effect on your mind, and, relatedly, its effect on our culture, which drives our politics.

The ultimate purpose of *If You Can Keep It* is to subvert the paradigms that subvert our freedom.

If we really inhabit the land of the free, then the invading armies of tyranny have metaphorically pushed us back to the water's edge. They have over-run our right to privacy, our right to due process, our right to free speech and even our right to life. They have most of the territory. We, the People, hold just a small piece of it—our freedom to think. It is a small proportion of the territory, but it is rich in resources if only we know how to extract them. We must regroup our forces on this small beachhead to counterattack, and eventually take back all of our freedoms—the very purpose of our nation. And if this land of the free is the home of the brave, we shall be up to the task.

CHAPTER 1

Mediography

IT IS EXTRAORDINARY that in a world in which all important information is delivered to the public through a set of institutions collectively called "The Media", the ways in which this public information, "the news", is produced and consumed, are a matter of so little popular discussion.

It is possible to study journalism at university, and no more learn about the nature of the media, information, knowledge production and acquisition and most importantly, how news content interacts with people's minds, than a carpenter at woodworking school learns about the thermal, mechanical and chemical nature of wood, and how a chair he makes holds up the behind that sits on it. A carpenter's art is to make things with wood, just as a journalist's art is to "make" articles out of information. But there is no requirement for journalists to have a philosophical understanding of what they are actually doing or an account of how their products act on the minds of those who read or hear them. And if journalists do not have such an understanding, then the public who consumes their output, certainly do not. All of us are the worse for it.

I'm not referring here just to understanding political bias in reporting, which is often obvious and gets many Americans on both the left and the right hot under the collar. Rather, I'm referring to more general and fundamental questions. Why do journalists write what they write? Why do producers of news deliver one news item over another? What determines how we, the readers and the watchers of their products, are changed (or not) by this news? Indeed, what really determines the news, and thence, what the public believes to be true about events that affect them? To answer these questions, we have to think about not only the media per se but how the human mind produces and receives information.

The facts-on-the-ground determine news content much less than we think they do. More so than any real events, prevailing paradigms, which can be cultural, national and political, not to mention the nature of media institutions, determine news content. These are the paradigms that govern not only the perspectives of both producers and consumers of news, but also the very information they are capable of perceiving and assimilating. This is a strong claim. To put it in other words, when we read the news, we are not only reading what has happened; we are reading who we are, and in particular, who the author is. By understanding why this is so, we can make our news much more accurate, honest and useful.

To fail to think critically and carefully about the media is to fail to think critically about perhaps the single greatest aspect of our culture that determines the choices we make for our nation and our planet—especially political choices. The Media constitute one of the most important power structures in the western world, and the filter for almost all of the information gained about everything on earth that we do not directly experience. To fail to understand how and why the media do what they do, and how their output interacts with people's minds is to misunderstand a huge part of modern existence and experience.

While a few academics ask the questions listed above in a discipline called the "Sociology of Media", the non-sophistication of the average news consumer is evidenced by the lack of a popularly used term for the mechanisms and effects of the production, communication and consumption of news. From here on, I'll use the term "Mediography" to mean just that—the study of the consumption and production of news, elucidating the interface between public information and human understanding.

News—public information about the world outside our immediate experience—is very often a matter of life and death, as it determines the context for political decisions through which human beings create their world. The field of Mediography, then, is at the intersection between the human mind and mass-information—and therefore underlies both our personal politics and global politics on the largest scale.

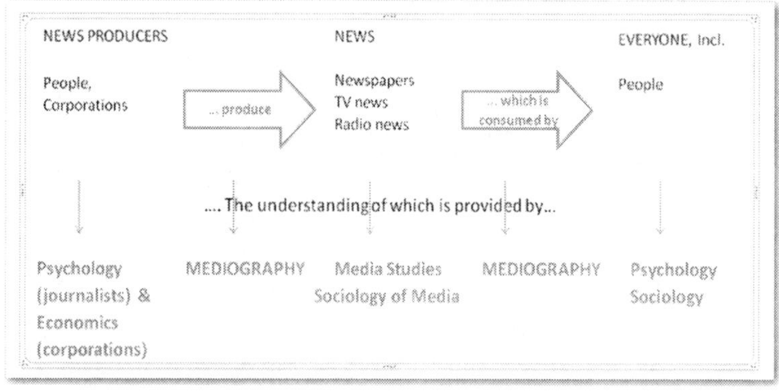

Your Paradigm Is Your World

When I was studying physics at the University of Cambridge (U.K.), I discovered that students of social and political science there are required to read a book that prima facie has nothing to do with politics at all.

It is called *The Structure of Scientific Revolutions* and was written by Thomas Kuhn, a historian of science, in 1962.

Following its publication, the book was immediately

recognized as a seminal work in the history and philosophy of science, but the importance of its fundamental idea to all fields of human knowledge is evident, for in it, Kuhn elucidates the idea of the Paradigm. A paradigm can be thought of as the set of concepts, and relationships among concepts, through which one understands the world. A paradigm is typically associated with its own language or vocabulary.

That our concepts determine how we interpret the world is obvious, but Kuhn said much more than that. He explained that our paradigms, or preconceptions in the broadest and deepest sense, govern how we perceive the world, not just how we interpret it. In other words, they determine how we see the world before our conscious mind can even work out what we are seeing. In other words, Goethe's line, "We see only what we know," is literally true. Most importantly, it is in the nature of paradigms that we aren't aware when they are "operating", and any paradigm will govern our perceptions in a way that reinforces that paradigm.

One of the most famous examples of this power of paradigms was an experiment conducted at Harvard University in 1949, called "the Perceptions of Incongruity experiment".

In this experiment, subjects were shown normal playing cards and asked to call out what they saw. This is easy to do and subjects would invariably identify the cards correctly. After a while, however, the experimenters would slip in "incongruous cards" in which the colors red and black were switched, so the subjects would be shown black hearts and diamonds and red clubs and spades.

What did the subjects see when shown those incongruous cards? According to what they called out, they did not see the incongruous cards, but normal playing cards—the cards they were expecting to see, without noticing the incongruity. For example, when they were shown a black six of hearts, they might call out simply "six of hearts" or "six of spades"—neither of which was correct. The important point is that the subjects didn't misunderstand or misinterpret anything—they actually misperceived something according to the paradigm in which they were operating—in this case, "the playing card paradigm", comprising everything they already know about playing cards.

Subjects would continue to fail to notice the incongruous cards, until they were displayed for longer and longer times. After a while, subjects would show a physiological reaction as they became uncomfortable, knowing somehow that something was wrong, but not being conscious of what. Only later, when they had been forced to look at a number of incongruous cards for a very long time did they "get" what was going on and see what they were looking at.

Paradigms exist in all areas of human life—cultural, religious, political, scientific, and even linguistic. Words represent the basic concepts through which we see the world. For example, English-speakers use the notion home without a thought, but it is a particularly Anglo notion, which does not quite mean residence, house, domicile etc., and which cannot be translated exactly into another language. This inability to translate between paradigms is called incommensurability, to use Kuhn's word. This fact would be incidental and abstract if we did not live in a world in which incommensurability, which more prosaically might be called a mismatch among different people's preconceptions, is the sine qua non of political distrust and global conflict.

The example of the English word "home" is very simple. It is an example of different paradigms' not including the same word or concept. But consider another aspect of incommensurability—when what is apparently the same word has different meanings in different paradigms. The Chinese word for "should" is yinggai (pronounced "ing-guy"). You can correctly translate between "should" and "ying gai" without any evident problem. However, at some point if you live in China or are a very close student of

Chinese, you will eventually discover that "should" in Chinese does not have the connotations of moral obligation that the English word does. In Chinese, "should" more closely indicates practical and political obligation: Neither the Chinese language nor its culture incorporates the Western notion of natural moral law. It certainly has no such notion in its religion, since—which reinforces the point—the Chinese do not really have something that Westerners would even recognize as religion. When I was learning Chinese and discovered the "should omission", it answered in one fell swoop about a third of all the questions I had about the differences between Chinese and Western cultures in which I had lived.

This fundamental fact about Chinese culture, evident in its language, plays out whenever we in the West marvel at their apparent lack of concern for human rights either in their own country or abroad. It is not that the Chinese have the same moral considerations but behave worse than we do. They just don't have the same (cultural, religious etc.) basis of the idea of human rights. This means of course, when we in the West get a concession out of the Chinese in this area, we have generally not newly convinced them of some moral good, but rather, they see the value of accommodating our point of view in maintaining a good relationship and harmony with those across the table from them. Harmony and relationship are two notions that are very strong in the Chinese paradigm, but they are not based in what someone from the Judeo-Christian culture would regard as an absolute morality. A Western observer may see a certain Chinese behavior as more or less moral, since morality is a notion that a Westerner cannot help but apply in politics, but in "seeing" Chinese behavior in this way, we see something that doesn't exist. And in reporting Chinese behavior in this way, we are promulgating a fundamental misunderstanding, and perforce, division. This particular difference is a perfect example of paradigmatic differences that have huge consequences for world politics. Understanding it is critical to the success of any strategic negotiation with the Chinese, and of how, in the case of the USA for example, any competition for global dominance might play out in this century.

Consider an example of this paradigm-effect in an important American news item about the Middle East. In early November '06, the Drudge Report ran a headline, "Iran Fires Missile that can Reach Israel". Was this headline factually accurate? Yes. Was it deliberately biased? No. But was it misleading? Thoroughly.

A map of the Middle East will reveal that any missile that can reach Israel from Iran can reach much of the Arab world. Someone with a more sophisticated understanding of the Middle East than that of the average American reader would appreciate that historic Arab-Persian tension is as important to the geopolitics of the region as Israeli-Muslim tensions. In other words, the (political) meaning of the ability of Iran to fire that missile is totally missed by Drudge's headline, which therefore may be accurate technically, but has no explanatory power. Not only does it not increase the reader's understanding of the situation in the Middle East, but also, by reinforcing the prevailing Western paradigm that the Israeli-Muslim dynamic is the main geopolitical cause in the region, it contributes positively to misunderstanding. This kind of paradigmatic filtering is more important than any superficial bias the media may have toward the left or the right, about which we hear so much, and it is the bias of assumptions unquestioned, and even unseen, by both left and right.

Other ways of writing the Drudge headline would be "Iran Fires Missile with Range of 1500 miles" or "Iran Fires Missile that Can Reach Most Arabs and Israel", but Drudge's paradigm is incomplete, such that even without intentional bias, his paradigm, rather than the facts themselves, determines the presentation of the story.

How important is this phenomenon? To what extent does the paradigm of the news producer govern the news? It is a function of the complexity of what is being reported: the simpler the story, and the less complex its context, the more an accurate report will usefully represent the reported events. For example, "Cat Gets Stuck in Tree" is an isolated incident. It does not depend on any important geopolitical currents in the area, and it will not have difficult-to-predict consequences. It does not affect the perceptions of many people nor does it run up against people's politics or prejudices. A story like the Iranian missile story, however, is quite different. It depends on many things, exists in a rich context about which the news producer or consumer is likely to have some opinions. These opinions may relate to completely unconscious ideals and beliefs bound up with his or her identity, but in all cases will be limited by the knowledge that the news producer or consumer already has about the event. The meaning of the events in the story will in fact depend on many things about which the news producer is simply ignorant. Accordingly, the more complex or subtle the context of a story, the more the prevailing paradigm, rather than the events in themselves, determines what goes into a news report.

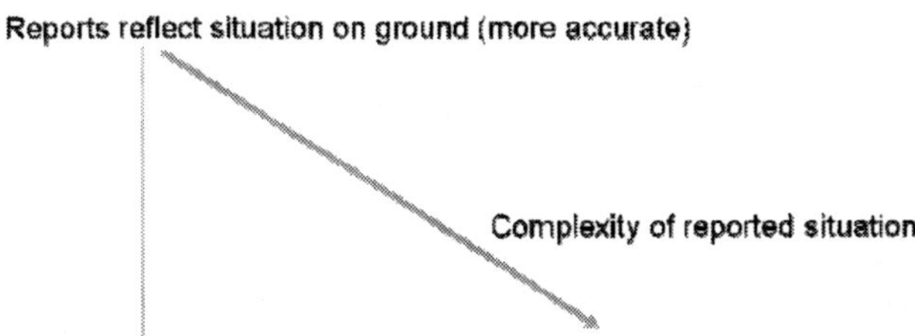

A reader of news, like a producer of news, brings his or her paradigm to bear on the content of a news report. In the main, news is consumed by an audience whose culture is that of the news producer. For example,

Fox, CNBC and CNN's cable news channels in the U.S. are staffed by Americans. One could say that the "production paradigm" is largely the same as the "consumption paradigm".

To understand what I mean, take a look at the following image and phrase. This was one of the many graphics that appeared on the internet immediately after the terrorist attacks against London on 7th July 2005—England's 9/11 in some respects.

I have asked many Americans if they understand it, and not one has so far, but any Brit will understand it immediately (and usually break a smile when she does). The purpose of the graphic is to show resilience in the face of terrorist attack. But for Americans, it must be translated. Its meaning is as follows. Drinking tea is quintessentially British. When terrorists destroy London, we respond by turning in their general direction—distracted, as it were, by the ruckus—but we continue to drink our tea. Note that we don't turn in their "actual" direction, because that would indicate greater success of the terrorists in distracting us. In other words, "We are not going to give you the satisfaction of a reaction or let you win by altering our behaviors in even the tiniest ways".

None of that is made explicit in the graphic, but its creator, obviously a Brit, operates in the same cultural paradigm as all the Brits who might see it. The paradigm is simultaneously so deep and subtle that the word "tea" and the understatement of "general direction" suffice to convey the quality of unruffled-ability that is fundamental to the British character. Only very particular aspects of the British paradigm (the power of understatement, the national characteristic of resilience, and the central place of tea in British culture) give this graphic any meaning. For most Americans, who have a very different cultural context, it is utterly meaningless. This relationship between meaning and cultural context is critical to the proper understanding of many reported events.

In general, when a news report does not contain all the information that is required to understand fully the reported events, the context, and therefore the meaning, must somehow be supplied by the reader. Accordingly, the impact of both the news producer's and the news consumer's paradigms must be considered before information in the media about issues that affect us, and, therefore, those issues themselves, can be understood.

We must consider the impact of both the news producer's and the news consumer's paradigms if we are going to have a sophisticated take on the information we gain everyday about issues that affect us, and therefore, on those issues themselves.

The extent to which a piece of writing requires the reader to attribute his own meaning to a piece of text is related to the type of text. Mathematics, for example, is the most reader-proof language, and mathematical texts leave no room for interpretation or disagreement. Anyone who understands the symbols of mathematics, regardless of any perspectives they may bring to an article, is a passive recipient of the meaning of a mathematical paper. Toward the other end of the spectrum is poetry. While poetry is referential (representing or indicating something outside itself, out there "in the real world"), the experience of poetry clearly depends as much on the reader, her experiences, upbringing, culture, perhaps even politics and taste, as on the words themselves. At the furthest extreme, we could perhaps place abstract art, which many people would say is not even referential, and elicits a response which can in no way be inter-subjectively agreed upon by viewers, but is very personal to each viewer.

We might suggest the following list. Items further along the arrow convey less objective meaning, and the effect on the consumer is more determined by the consumer than the content.

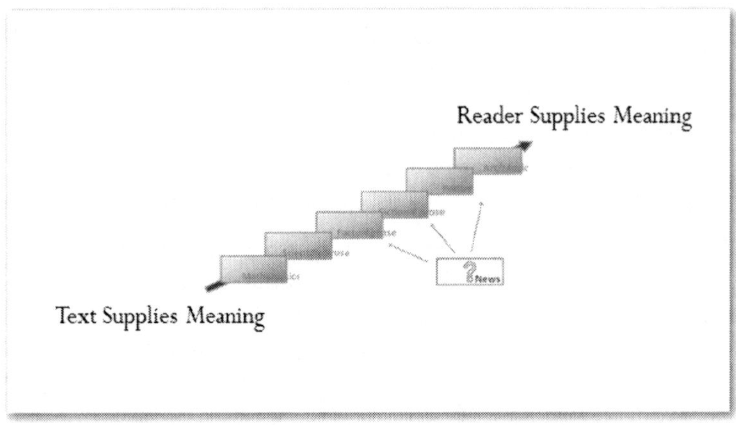

Where should the average cable news report be put on this scale?

Prima facie, a news report is factual prose. But people do not tend to react to the evening news like they do to an "objective" feature article in a quality journal, or a documentary about natural history, both of which are actually factual prose. Immediate reactions to news vary at least as much as those to poetry. And different people can find diametrically opposite meaning in the same report.

What does it tell us that there are as many responses to supposedly factual reports as there are to poetry? The fact clearly supports the earlier point that most of the meaning of a story or meaning that underlies a story, is not in the selected and stated facts, but in a much larger context in which the facts of the report have meaning, have cause, and have effect—and about which various readers may have greatly diverging beliefs.

Intuitively, we know this: even as we read our news, we know its incompleteness and inadequacy. What we think we know about the larger context, which for complex world events is largely related to our own political and cultural prejudices as well as our background knowledge of the topic, determines both our reaction and the interpretation that we believe the article supports. Again, of course, our paradigms cause us to interpret reported facts in a way that reinforces our paradigms.

We should consider the wide range of reactions of different people to the same report of a particular event as empirical evidence for the above claim that news reports are limited in two fundamental ways: a) they present a very small fraction of the relevant truth about a complex situation they are reporting on; b) they are responsible for a very small fraction of the response of a reader to the report.

To understand why this is the case, we must think about how news effectively samples complex data.

We can represent a complex situation by this star.

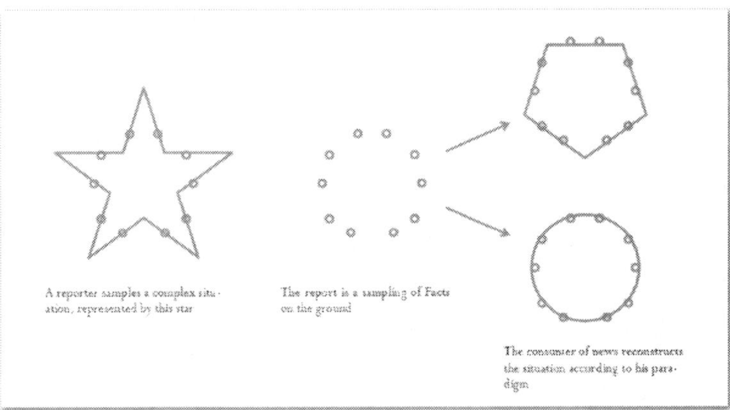

This is an idealization of how we project a reality onto the news we get. It illustrates how we have no way of determining what the reported situation really is. Even if our projected reality "fits" the information, we can't immediately determine if our projections are close to any objective truth.

In the example of the star, any argument between those who interpret the situation as a pentagon, and those who interpret it as a circle is an argument between news consumers' paradigms. It is not an argument about reality, which is here neither a pentagon nor a circle.

This raises an obvious question. Before we get to any practical questions of how best to report events, how do we get ourselves unstuck from this philosophical problem and free ourselves from the apparent limits on the accuracy and usefulness of news?

There is no way of judging between paradigms from within them. And there is very little practical way for a reader to test his interpretation of the news about an event against the event itself, because the only information about the event is in the news... it's a chicken-and-egg problem.

But it is not hopeless. Scientists, about whom Kuhn originally wrote his "Structure of Scientific Revolutions", have faced this problem since before science was even named.[6] With limited data, revealed not in news reports, but in experimental reports, scientists have to "choose" between views of the world, or theories. The process is analogous to that by which politicians and private citizens use news to choose between political views of the world, including perhaps, views on the Iraq war, the drug war, the welfare state and whether the next Congress should be Republican or Democrat.

How do scientists get out of their current prevailing paradigm, and change it when their own perceptions are being determined by the current prevailing paradigm? Whatever the answer, it is one all consumers of news need apply if we are to understand our country better and make better choices for ourselves.

---

[6] When the Jesuits told Galileo that they did not need to look through his telescope since they already knew the earth did not move around the sun, the paradigm of "science" itself did not exist! At least the Jesuits were explicit about their own paradigmatic assumptions, which is more than we can say for many of us today. In any case, in the field of human knowledge, those Jesuits started as we have gone on.

First off, scientists never believe they have the truth. Even though they are collectively responsible for the field of human endeavor that arguably has done as much to improve our lives than any other, they are fundamentally agnostic. Whenever you hear someone say, "it has been scientifically proven that…", chances are that person is not a scientist. If you ever hear the same in an advertisement, don't buy the product. The path of science is the path toward truth. But like all paths, it can be moving toward the destination only if it hasn't yet arrived there. Each step along the way is an ever closer approximation to truth. The progress of science logically depends on the belief that truth has not yet been achieved. If anyone believed that any field of science had found its truth, that field would be finished and the scientists out of a job. That has never happened.

In science, where reported data are only accepted when corroborated much more thoroughly than almost anything in any newspaper, researchers understand that a single new fact can, without any previously recognized facts' being found to be wrong, totally change the underlying theory that the data as a whole support.

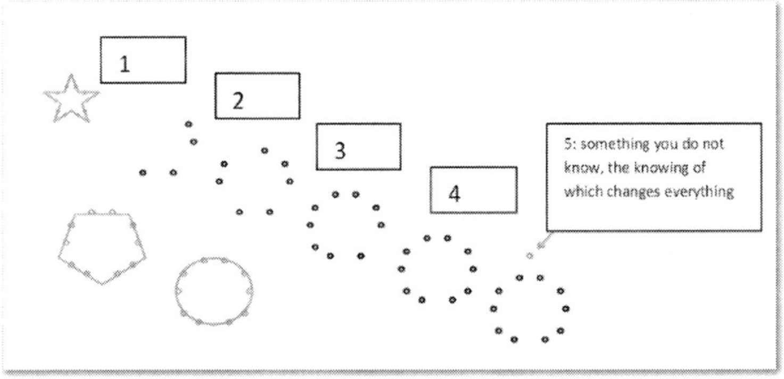

As reports come in, we accumulate data and engage in an ongoing debate about what the underlying reality is. Scientists conduct such debates knowing that at any moment a single fact could make the very debate wrong. In this example, as the data come in, the underlying reality could be a pentagon or a circle…right up to the last piece of data, which changes everything. The red datum is the first clue that the reality is neither. Those with minds truly open to truth are never scared of that something they do not know, the knowing of which can change everything.[7]

Scientists are not only open to these red data points: they actively look for them. Science proceeds by scientists' trying to prove themselves wrong as fast as possible. This is the opposite of how individuals develop their political views and how, often, countries conduct foreign policy. In most fields of human endeavor, progress rarely occurs without making something or someone wrong.

We may not be able to persuade our politicians to operate in this way, but we would have more right to demand it if we could operate this way ourselves. And we get the opportunity to do that whenever we read or hear the news. We maintain our own openness to truth by reading not to prove to ourselves that we were right all along; not to see how the article fits with our own beliefs about the world, but to try to find actively how the information in the article makes wrong something we currently believe.

This speaks to another fundamental fact about science. Facts can never prove a theory; they can only support one or disprove one. For example, parts one to four in the above figure support the pentagon and circle theories. They do not prove either one. A single datum in part 5, however, disproves both of these theories, but does not prove any other.

The example also shows how easily we can delude ourselves

---

[7] This is one of my favorite quotable expressions from Neale Donald Walsch, who I hope would be happy to see its use here.

into believing that any of our media coverage is "balanced" and that "balance" is a virtue. In a world in which the data are interpreted as a pentagon by some and a circle by others, any debate between the two seems balanced. But the idea that we have heard a balanced discussion is particularly dangerous to understanding. It makes us lazy. If we've heard both sides, we are lulled into thinking that we must have heard the truth in one of them—or at least as some combination of the sides; of course, when it comes to complex human affairs, that is almost never the case. There is usually, somewhere, a single hard-to-find truth, but it has a hundred sides—not two, not Republican or Democrat, not American or French, not Christian or secular, and not liberal or conservative. We suffer intellectually and culturally when we do not force ourselves to come up with new positions or possibilities that don't fit the current spectrum of opinion, defined typically by everything two sides agree on—often unstated—when they appear to disagree. Human beings tend to display the kind of creativity required to get out of our own self-created dichotomies and disagreements to find a truth that falls outside them, only when our current positions (pentagons and circles in the figure) fails dramatically (such as in part 5 in the figure), and especially when our own limited perceptions cause us to suffer (as happened in the USA on 9-11-01).[8]

How we read the news is in some ways more important than how scientists read their papers and experimental reports, because whether someone believes the earth goes around the sun or the sun around the earth does not determine how he behaves toward others. However, what we believe about weapons of mass

---

[8] For the record, this is not to say we are in any way morally responsible for 9-11. It is to say only that if we had been able to see some big things in the world that we didn't even know existed, let alone mattered, we may have acted differently, pre-emptively, to have saved ourselves from that tragedy.

destruction in a foreign country, abortion and even whether tax cuts reduce or increase governmental revenue, are all matters of life and death.

The American Media

As Americans, we tend to think that we have access to global news. The fact that we do not becomes evident when we ask the question, what is news?

Today's news corporations certainly have global reach and technology allows them to find and convey information on the actions of most of the people whom it targets in most of the world. But knowledge of actions and events only helps us to understand the world when we also know how these actions and events are perceived. America did not invade Iraq because Iraq had weapons of mass destruction, but because America perceived that Iraq had them. Nothing fundamentally changed in Iraq between the 2004 election of a Republican president and the 2006 rejection of the Republicans in Congress. Only perceptions changed. Clearly, Charles Maurice de Talleyrand-Périgord, arguably history's greatest believer in Realpolitik, espoused an eternal truth when some 200 years ago he stated, "In politics, what is believed is more important than what is real."

It is important to realize just how useless news is when it excludes information about the perceptions of affected parties. The fact that perceptions are often wrong, incomplete or biased, does not make them any less facts of a situation. Consider a simple example.

Imagine a scene in which a gentleman in a car is looking across the passenger seat through an open window at a woman dressed as policewoman. The man says, "I love you". Imagine the car was pulled up in a residential area in the evening. Now imagine you knew exactly where this was occurring. Imagine you had precise details of the car, of the surrounding area, and even the weather. You can know all of that information and know nothing about what is really going on in the scene and therefore, nothing about what will happen next.

Perhaps the man has been pulled over for a traffic violation; is in an inebriated state and is inappropriately trying to distract the policewoman. If so, he might be about to spend the night in the local jail. Or perhaps the man is off to a late-night business meeting, telling his wife that he loves her as she's about to leave, dressed up as a cop, for a Halloween party. Even an accurate and complete report of all visible aspects of that scene could not tell you which, if either, is the correct interpretation.

Therefore, pure descriptions of events—even including the actions of the people involved—tell us nothing useful. Rather, the perceptions and assumptions of the parties who cause or are affected by events really determine the meaning, or essence, of those events. By the meaning of an event, I mean its causes and its likely or possible effects. If that is true for such a simple scene as in the example above, how much truer is it for the type of complex political situation that is the stuff of the front page of the New York Times and the lead story on CNN's Situation Room?

Any kind of "global news coverage" that is true to its stated purpose of informing the public has to cover global events and global perceptions of those events. By that definition, cable television and our newspapers of record do not offer global news.

Given the incommensurability of paradigms, described above, the only way to understand another's perceptions of an event or the world at large is to begin by recognizing that one's own paradigm—cultural, political, linguistic—simply may not include the concepts that can accurately describe the perceptions and experiences of others. The only approach to truly global news, therefore, is to let others tell you their perceptions of the same events that you see, and to try to "get into their head"—despite differences of language, culture, upbringing, values, childhood experiences etc.

I lived in California on-and-off a few years ago. As a Brit, brought up on the BBC, I discovered the British press in bookshops in Orange County. I started hanging out in the coffee shop at Borders with the foreign newspapers as a response to the feeling that I couldn't get world news on the TV here in the States.

First, finding information about the non-English speaking world was simply difficult. Second, most of the commentary on such networks as CNN, Fox, ABC etc…would leave me asking, "why don't they address X?" —where X would invariably seem like an obvious question. Most disappointing were the panel discussions, which always involved Americans only and, usually, Americans whose views fit quite neatly into the prevailing American ideologies, Conservative and Liberal, such that most of what was said would be predictable and lacking genuine insight.

I was all the more stunned by this state of affairs after discovering the wonderful C-Span which presents so much information and such a range of thought on so many critical issues, presenting for all Americans largely unmediated, the workings of their own country's administration, other countries' administrations, global agencies, commentary from all over the world, and conferences with some of the world's most informed people—with myriad backgrounds, perspectives and even nationalities—on some of the most pressing topics or our time.

Nevertheless, it was in the country that invented C-Span that I was left shocked one afternoon as I watched an episode of "Crossfire" during the run-up to the Iraq war, in which a Republican Congresswoman was presented with the results of a global survey of tens of thousands of people, who were asked, "Who is the greatest threat to world peace?" According to the polled citizens of many nations from Europe, through the Middle East to Asia and the Americas, George W. Bush beat Kim Jong-il and Saddam Hussein to that title. Given the sheer number of respondents and the credibility of the polling firm, the poll data were more valid than most of the poll data that US political parties use to track the favorability of their candidates, but the Congresswoman said without any consideration of the implications of the results, “That’s just not a credible poll,” and she was done with it.

Without wishing to assert the correctness of the opinion so overwhelmingly held by the respondents, that Bush was at that time the world’s largest threat to world peace, there are many good reasons for the result, which could have usefully been addressed.

- The US is alone in having the ability to project power around the world and invade foreign countries.
- The US was alone in declaring its desire to invade a foreign country.
- The US had just invaded a foreign country. At the time of the poll, the US spent more on weapons than the rest of the world put together.
- The US was upgrading its nuclear arsenal, contravening the spirit of the nuclear non-proliferation treaty.
- The US is the only country to have attacked another with a nuclear weapon.
- The US felt more threatened than any other country after 9-11.
- The US had used unusually bellicose rhetoric that set them against those who did not explicitly agree with them.
- The US preferred not to talk to dangerous regimes in a bid to make them in any way less dangerous.

- The US has invaded more foreign countries than any other since the second world war.
- The US media and political establishment were producing disparaging statements about countries who were vociferously seeking a non-military solution to some of the world's present problems.

The obvious bogeymen, such has Saddam Hussein and Kim Jong-il, were not producing rhetoric about invading even countries on their borders, let alone anywhere else in the world.

These other dangerous regimes simply did not have the physical capability of threatening world peace on a scale that the US could.

All of the items in the above list were known at the time of the particular Crossfire episode. The poll could certainly have been said to be "credible", to use the Congresswoman's word. Whether or not the respondents were in any sense right about the threat represented by President Bush, there were myriad critical issues that were worthy of being addressed and made the findings of the survey "reasonable".

Of course, to many outside the U.S., the comment of the Congresswoman belied something even more disturbing than ignorance—the arrogance of implying that opinions are not credible simply by virtue of their being different from one's own. While this is par-for-the-course in American political punditry, we should never get comfortable with it.

A couple of years after that "Crossfire" episode, data exist regarding how world peace has been affected by the leaders about whom that poll asked its question. Remember, the poll did not ask readers who was the most "evil". That would be a moral question, and one would expect that Bush would not have outscored Kim Jong-Il or Saddam Hussein in answer to it. The question in the poll was, rather, a practical one, "Who is the greatest threat to world peace". What metric could best be used to measure such a thing? A simple measure would be the number of people whose deaths were a predictable consequence of the actions of these men. To the best of anyone's determination, Bush's actions in Iraq unlocked the chaos from which has followed three times as many deaths as were caused by Hiroshima and Nagasaki together. This number is about an order of magnitude greater than those caused by actions of Saddam and Kim. Of course, in the case of Bush, we should also ask "How many lives has his actions saved?" That is a fair question, which can only be answered by serious analysis. Whichever way we cut it, the rest of the world, it seems, was not wrong when they identified Bush—as a matter of fact and not morality or intention—as a threat to world peace.

The Human Paradigm

For the sake of understanding the media, we can split all news into actions and perceptions, ours and others', and represent the world in a powerful 2x2 matrix.

		PERCEPTIONS WE	*PERCEPTIONS* THEY
ACTIONS	WE	What **we** think about what **we** do	What **they** think about what **we** do
ACTIONS	THEY	What **we** think about what **they** do	What **they** think about what **they** do

When we look at the world this way, we see that the so-called "global media" in the U.S. operate in only the two left boxes.

They will tell you about what we, Americans or at the very least, English speakers, think about what we and others do. The American paradigm is the paradigm of only 5% of the world's population, and is the paradigm of none of the people affected by some of the most important issues reported in the news, such as the Israeli-Palestine conflict, the crisis in Darfur, the operations of Al Qaeda in the Middle East. And even more importantly for our choices as Americans, it is not the paradigm of the people who are affected most by many areas of American policy, such as the keeping of foreign military bases, American military interventions, the imposing of trade tariffs on imports to the U.S., American charity to poor nations, among many others.

To access global perceptions of global events, one needs to read the foreign-language press. Doing so was more-or-less impossible over two years ago, but in 2005, with the availability of WatchingAmerica.com, which translates foreign news articles about the United States, "global media" has begun to be redefined. Watching America offers a unique window into the effects of events on the minds of others, offering access to reporting that has an explanatory power beyond anything that is filtered through domestic news institutions.

News stories only explain (or help a consumer understand) an event when they communicate something about the right-most two boxes in the matrix, because no event happens in a vacuum. Rather, earlier events cause later events as people perceive and respond to them in a manner determined by their interpretation of those events. Understanding others' perceptions, then, is critical to understanding the meaning of any reported event in the news. Without an understanding of meaning in this way, the information about the event per se is entirely useless. In the earlier example of Drudge's headline, "Iran fires missile that can reach Israel", the problem was that nothing is communicated about the over-arching context of this fact—that many Arabs fear Persians and it is their perception (Israelis' perceptions notwithstanding) of Iran's achievement that determines the full meaning of the firing of that missile.

As long as we fail to see the world through the eyes of others, we suffer from "not knowing what we don't know". The above matrix is a generalization. It divides the world into "Us" and "Them" but there is always more than one "Them" (at least Persians, Arabs and Israelis, in the story about Iran's missile). One of the greatest limitations of obtaining all one's news from the American press is that you have no way even of recognizing who "They" are. In the Middle East for example, we may know about Israelis and Muslims, but any news from that region is next to useless if we know nothing about historic tapestry of Persians, Arabs, Sunnis, Shiites, Jews, Christians etc. The only way to find out what you don't know, is to read the stories about a region from that region, because those stories necessarily present not only the facts on the ground, observed up close, but also the perceptions and responses of those more immediately affected by them, which perceptions are likely to be those that underlie the dynamics of the situation, and will therefore determine the effects and causes of the events reported.

Robert McNamara, Secretary of Defense under Kennedy and Johnson (1961—1968), and therefore during much of the Vietnam War, made the following remark in the documentary, "The Fog of War", which directly illustrates the massive importance of this point, on which thousands of lives sometimes depend.

In the Cuban missile crisis, I think we did put ourselves in the skin of the Soviets. In the case of Vietnam, we didn't know them well enough to empathize, and there was total misunderstanding as a result. They believed that we had simply replaced the French as a colonial power and we were seeking to subject South and North Vietnam to our colonial interests, which was absolutely absurd. And we, we saw Vietnam as an element of the cold war—not what they saw it as, [which was] a civil war.

The Vietnam War is believed to have taken close to five million lives.

Later in the same documentary, if any clarification were needed, McNamara emphasizes,

We must try to put ourselves inside their skin, and look at us through their eyes—just to understand the thoughts that lie behind their decisions and their actions.

That latter statement is true of any situation that involves more than one human being and has high stakes.

In a story published in Yedioth Ahronoth[9], an Israeli commentator, Moshe Elad, a former colonel in the IDF who had held senior posts in the Palestinian Territories and in Lebanon, wrote the following.

> *[A]n American basketball player on his way to play in Israel was asked whether he's afraid to come such a short time after the [Lebanon] war. "War?" He said. "It's been going on for five years now."*

This is how it is for the average American. For them, the Middle East is just one big swamp comprising Israel, Lebanon, the Palestinian territories, and Iraq.

He is right of course, because that basketball player's view of the Middle East is from a long distance, and anything seen from a distance is seen in less detail than the same thing seen up close, and from a distance, nothing in the minds and hearts of the protagonists can be easily observed.

Truly global media—in the right-hand boxes in the above matrix—can show us who "they" really are, which is of course a prerequisite to understanding what "they" experience and why "they" do what "they" do. We should turn to the global media, not

---

[9] http://watchingamerica.com/yediothahronoth000001.shtml

because it is any more accurate than our own in the U.S., but because they can fill out our picture of events that involve "them", whoever they may be, helping us see their causes and potential effects.

For the middle east, then we could expand "They" in our matrix above, in this way.

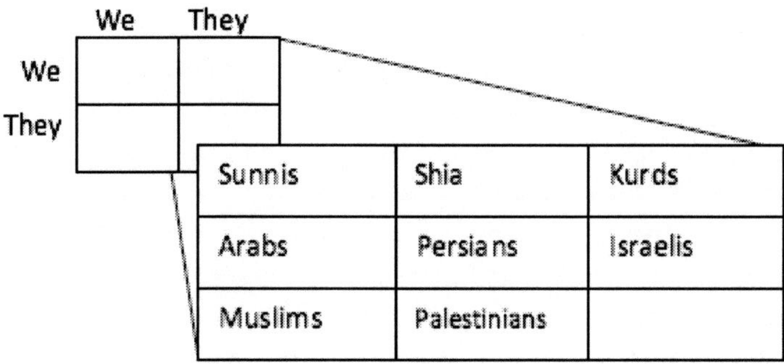

An excerpt from the New York Times shows the consequences of mistaking the American media alone for a truly "global" media.

Take Representative Terry Everett, a seven-term Alabama Republican who is vice chairman of the House intelligence subcommittee on technical and tactical intelligence.
Do you know the difference between a Sunni and a Shiite? I asked him a few weeks ago.

Mr. Everett responded with a low chuckle. He thought for a moment:

> *One's in one location, another's in another location. No, to be honest with you, I don't know. I thought it was differences in their religion, different families or something.*

To his credit, he asked me to explain the differences. I told him briefly about the schism that developed after the death of the Prophet Muhammad, and how Iraq and Iran are majority Shiite nations while the rest of the Muslim world is mostly Sunni. "Now that you've explained it to me", he replied, "what occurs to me is that it makes what we're doing over there extremely difficult, not only in Iraq but that whole area". [10]

There is such a thing, then, as deadly ignorance.

Such ignorance would be impossible in a country in which global coverage truly was global in the way described, if we were humble enough to appreciate that we didn't understand a person—let alone an entire nation or region—until we had listened to them. We can listen to American news about the Middle East and understand nothing about the divisions between Sunnis and Shia, Arabs and Persians, Baathists and the Iraqi people, but it would be impossible to remain in complete ignorance if we had read the media of any one of these groups.

What We Need to Know About Them, Whoever They Are

While the most fundamental differences among us are realized in our paradigms, our humanity is shared, and basic motivations and fundamental emotions are felt by all. They may manifest differently from culture to culture, with different factors' being recognized as causes of particular experiences or states of mind. Simply, if you're an Israeli, you may fear Palestinian suicide

---

[10] Jeff Stein, http://www.nytimes.com/2006/10/17/opinion/17stein.html?_r=1&oref=login

bombers. If you're a Palestinian, you may fear Israeli missile strikes, but they have in common the experience of fear.

If you had the time to read over a few months or years thousands of articles from any country, you would begin to get some understanding of an underlying political and cultural narrative, complete with roles and characters. In America, like anywhere else, the narrative that plays out page by page, cable news channel by cable news channel, day by day, affects the reader.

Consider the myriad news stories penned and screened in the years since 9/11. Many of them broadly tell of a narrative that includes the following concepts roles.

Irrational Aggressors	Terrorists
Feared Political Actors	Muslim Extremists
Motivation of Aggressors	Hate freedom
Public Enemy No. 1	bin Laden
Dissenting Group	Liberals
Historic Justification	9-11

Here's a passage from a newspaper, with some of these words in it, explaining part of this narrative.

As a consequence of *Islamic terrorism*, and most importantly, the disappearance of certain legal protections, this country has been caught in a vicious circle of *fear* and *security*. This circle of fear took hold after *Al-Qaeda...brought down the Twin Towers.*

Which paper could that be from? The New York Times, The Los Angeles Times, or perhaps the Boston Globe?

Actually, it was from an Iraqi publication, but with some of the key words switched. Here is the original:

> *As a consequence of the American occupation of Iraq, and most importantly, the disappearance of*

> *the rule of law, this country has been caught in a vicious circle of violence and international terrorism. This circle of violence took hold after American forces … invaded Iraq. Iraq of Tomorrow, Iraq (translated)*[11]

In fact, we can extend the above table to include the same roles in the prevailing Middle-Eastern Muslim narrative.

ROLE	U.S.	Middle East
Irrational Aggressors	Terrorists	Zionists
Feared Political Actors	Muslim Extremists	Americans
Motivation of Aggressors	Hate freedom	Support Israel / Hegemony
Public Enemy No. 1	bin Laden	George Bush
Dissenting Group	Liberals	Secularists
Historic Justification	9-11	Israel-Palestine / Attack on Iraq

In other words, if you deconstruct two superficially opposing narratives, you will often find that to a large extent they have the same structure, indicating that the first paradigm we need to be conscious of in interpreting news about ourselves and others is simply the human paradigm, including our emotional make-up and basic motivations, which may determine the meaning of a story more than any particular events.

Systematic Media Biases

In the U.S., political partisans make much of media bias, as Liberals often point to its corporate ownership, while Conservatives often point to the tendency of journalists, and certainly publicly funded media, to be Liberal.

---

[11] http://www.watchingamerica.com/iraqoftomorrow000002.shtml

Such biases exist and are worthy of discussion, but they distract from more important, systematic biases that are exhibited by nearly all media institutions, everywhere, and especially television media. We must be aware of them so that we can allow for the sizes and shapes of the blind spots of these institutions' mirrors on the world.

Before listing these biases, I should say that, as someone who has been running a 350-person organization that collates and translates news and views about the USA from all over the world, I have come to believe that unless you are willing to look at unconventional news sources, you will learn more about the world from talking to people who are directly involved in the events in which you are interested, and by reading books about them, than you will by listening to or reading coverage by the usual suspects of American media.

Probably, the very best way to begin to understand a place, its prevailing themes and its important events and issues, is to learn the necessary language and get on a plane. After all, the media are like the surface of the ocean: you can learn something about its surface by looking at its surface, but nothing about the nature of the entire ocean, which extends far beneath, in literally another dimension.

Bias Toward What is Easily Seen

The media report what can be observed, because most journalism is not investigative. While this seems both obvious and necessary, this fact alone creates the most important bias in news coverage. Often what is not happening but could have happened (the counterfactual) is at least as important in interpreting events and decisions, and understanding their effects, as what actually happened, and can be seen to have happened. For example, we cannot judge the effectiveness of the recent economic stimulus packages, even by the standards of those that promoted them, if we do not know what would have happened in their absence, or put another way, what they prevented from occurring.

This is not an academic concern, but a profoundly practical one. Like the economic stimulus, the war in Iraq cannot be judged morally except in the light of what would have happened in the absence of that war. News organizations should be concerned with such things because whether the actual outcomes of events and decisions match those that were expected from them is certainly newsworthy—especially when the events or decisions were controversial. For example, how many jobs will be lost as a result of the siphoning off of earnings to pay off the debts run up in the bailouts? Without consideration of that question, any commentary on the effects of the bailouts on employment, for example, is meaningless. Moreover, without consideration of that question, the media fail to give us the information required to judge honestly those on either side of that particular debate or those who decided upon and implemented the policy.

The importance of the counterfactual in commentary usually demands no more than a broad understanding of the subject areas that certain events touch on.

The bias toward the seen, and away from the unseen (the counterfactual) affects the media's presentation of all events—whether they be causes or effects—and causes public information, the media, to tend to promote interventionist policies.

Consider the story of the broken window, due to the economist Frederic Bastiat, a 19th century French economist. I rewrite it in full here.

> *Have you ever witnessed the anger of the good shopkeeper, James B., when his careless son happened to break a square of glass? If you have been present at such a scene, you will most assuredly bear witness to the fact, that every one of the spectators, were there even thirty of them, by*

common consent apparently, offered the unfortunate owner this invariable consolation—"It is an ill wind that blows nobody good. Everybody must live, and what would become of the glaziers if panes of glass were never broken?"

Now, this form of condolence contains an entire theory, which it will be well to show up in this simple case, seeing that it is precisely the same as that which, unhappily, regulates the greater part of our economical institutions.

Suppose it cost six francs to repair the damage, and you say that the accident brings six francs to the glazier's trade—that it encourages that trade to the amount of six francs—I grant it; I have not a word to say against it; you reason justly. The glazier comes, performs his task, receives his six francs, rubs his hands, and, in his heart, blesses the careless child. All this is that which is seen.

But if, on the other hand, you come to the conclusion, as is too often the case, that it is a good thing to break windows, that it causes money to circulate, and that the encouragement of industry in general will be the result of it, you will oblige me to call out, "Stop there! Your theory is confined to that which is seen; it takes no account of that which is not seen."

It is not seen that as our shopkeeper has spent six francs upon one thing, he cannot spend them upon another. It is not seen that if he had not had a window to replace, he would, perhaps, have replaced his old shoes, or added another book to his library. In short, he would have employed his six francs in some way, which this accident has prevented.

Let us take a view of industry in general, as affected by this circumstance. The window being broken, the glazier's trade is encouraged to the amount of six francs; this is that which is seen. If the window had not been broken, the shoemaker's trade (or some other) would have been encouraged to the amount of six francs; this is that which is not seen.

And if that which is not seen is taken into consideration, because it is a negative fact, as well as that which is seen, because it is a positive fact, it will be understood that neither industry in general, nor the sum total of national labour, is affected, whether windows are broken or not.

Now let us consider James B. himself. In the former supposition, that of the window being broken, he spends six francs, and has neither more nor less than he had before, the enjoyment of a window.

In the second, where we suppose the window not to have been broken, he would have spent six francs on shoes, and would have had at the same time the enjoyment of a pair of shoes and of a window.

Now, as James B. forms a part of society, we must come to the conclusion, that, taking it altogether, and making an estimate of its enjoyments and its labours, it has lost the value of the broken window.

When we arrive at this unexpected conclusion: "Society loses the value of things which are uselessly destroyed;" and we must assent to a maxim which will make the hair of protectionists stand on end— To break, to spoil, to waste, is not to encourage national labour; or, more briefly, "destruction is not profit."

Bastiat told this story to show the nonsense of one theory, and to promote another. If it seems abstract, consider that the logic of the spectators, who suggest that the breaking of windows is a good thing as it keeps glaziers in business, is the exact same logic as the American administration applied in establishing the "Cash for Clunkers" program. Let's have some fun and rewrite Bastiat's piece some words switched out.

> *It is an ill wind that blows nobody good. Everybody must live, and what would become of the automakers if old cars were never scrapped?*
>
> *Now, this assertion contains an entire theory, which it will be well to show up in this simple case, seeing that it is precisely the same as that which, unhappily, regulates the greater part of our economical institutions.*
>
> *Suppose it costs ten thousand dollars to buy the new car, and you say that the scrapping brings ten thousand dollars to the automakers—that it encourages that trade to the amount of ten thousand dollars—I grant it; I have not a word to say against it; you reason justly. The automaker produces the car, sells the car, receives its ten grand, smiles broadly, and, in his heart, blesses the Obama administration. All this is that which is seen.*
>
> *But if, on the other hand, you come to the conclusion, as is too often the case, that it is a good thing to break cars, that it causes money to circulate, and that the encouragement of industry in general will be the result of it, you will oblige me to call out, "Stop there! Your theory is confined to that which is seen; it takes no account of that which is*

not seen."

It is not seen that as our car buyer has spent ten grand upon one thing, he cannot spend them upon another. It is not seen that if he had not had to replace his car, he would, perhaps, have replaced his old kitchen, or bought a few more suits. In short, he would have employed his ten grand in some way, which this scheme prevented. And if in fact James B is not paying for the car himself, but enjoying some subsidy from his fellow citizens, then they too are unable to spend that money to put toward the replacement of their old kitchen, or to buy a few more suits.

Let us take a view of industry in general, as affected by this circumstance. The car being scrapped, the automaker's trade is encouraged to the amount of ten grand; this is that which is seen. If the window had not been broken, the kitchen seller's trade (or some other) would have been encouraged to the amount of ten grand; this is that which is not seen.

And if that which is not seen is taken into consideration, because it is a negative fact, as well as that which is seen, because it is a positive fact, it will be understood that neither industry in general, nor the sum total of national labor, is affected, whether cars are scrapped or not.

Now let us consider James B. himself. In the former supposition, that of the car being scrapped, he spends ten grand, and has neither more nor less than he had before, the enjoyment of a car. True, he has a new car and not an old one, but he also loses much more, since he in fact has replaced an old car that may have been paid or had only a few

> *payments left, with a new obligation to pay car payments for years to come, diverting that money away from other purchases or the security of paying down debt etc.*
>
> *In the second, where we suppose the car not to have been replaced, he would have spent ten grand on a new kitchen, for example, and would have had at the same time the enjoyment of a new kitchen and a car.*
>
> *Now, as James B. forms a part of society, we must come to the conclusion, that, taking it altogether, and making an estimate of its enjoyments and its labors, it has lost the value of the scrapped car.*
>
> *When we arrive at this unexpected conclusion: "Society loses the value of things which are uselessly destroyed;" and we must assent to a maxim which will make the hair of protectionists stand on end— To break, to spoil, to waste, is not to encourage national labor; or, more briefly, "destruction is not profit."*

The point of this historical and economic diversion in a chapter about mediography is that in reporting what is seen—the broken window and the work to the glazier, or the scrapped automobile and the work to the automaker—the report is distorted by its incompleteness to an extent that would lead an unsuspecting reader to a judgment that might even be the opposite of what is the case.

Such distortion can be avoided in only two ways—by reporting the event itself (Cash for Clunkers, to take a modern example), without mentioning any of its proposed or apparent immediate effects, or by reporting it with a complete indication of both its seen (someone gets a new car, the automaker keeps a job, and the autoparts supplier keeps a job etc.) and its unseen effects (that money diverted from the buyer of the car from other purchases, the kitchen-maker loses a job, the financial burden on the family through car payments, and the lost future productivity as future tax dollars are diverted to pay for the debt that was raised to pay for the program).

Of course, it is much easier for a news organization to present what is immediately visible than to work to find and elucidate what has been prevented, and to do the hard work necessary to identify effects that are not immediately obvious because they are things that were prevented from occurring. The problem is the media equivalent of the wife who sees her husband looking under a street lamp for her car keys, while his car is parked far away. She asks him how he could have lost his keys in that location—so far from the car and the house. He says he didn't, but he's looking there because that is where the light is.

We hear much from the political right of liberal bias in the American media. If there is any, it is not so much a "liberal" bias as an "interventionist" one, in one subtle respect: if the media tend to present what is immediately seen, then they give those who wish to do something rather than nothing a greater platform to justify their actions in terms of their intended effects, which are invariably visible and positive, while the negative, unseen, effects of their actions are never reported.

The primary causes of most events are the decisions of human beings, and even the causes of large events are often the decisions of a relatively small number of human beings. Usually, political decision-makers are responding to information and goals that are not public knowledge, according to certain tendencies of their character or values they hold. Absent the information they used and knowledge of their goals, any causal explanation of an event is necessarily wrong. The most general problem of the media is that they are almost "never in the room" when the relevant decisions are made and so they are left with two alternatives in their presentation of events. The first is to stick only to the visible facts and, knowing they do not have access to information about their causes, say absolutely nothing about them, taking care to attribute no agency to anything. The problem with this first alternative is that, obviously, it's of no use in helping the reader understand the meaning or true context of an event. Such presentations do not make news organizations seem knowledgeable or very useful, nor are they very easy to read.

Sticking to visible facts without imputing intention, cause or agency is hard to do, as becomes evident when you consider that this would mean that we'd never see the following expressions.

> *Well more than half of the deficit was caused by the ongoing economic crisis.*

A crisis describes a state of affairs, characterized by many events, values of various metrics and human decisions. It cannot cause anything. It can only refer to events that may cause other events.

> *Washington doesn't believe that…*

Washington is not a human mind. Therefore, it does not believe.

> *America doesn't want to see Israel take such an action.*

Who is America? Who is Israel?

> *The middle class is taking a stand against this.*

The middle class, also not being a person, cannot be a pure causal agent. It may refer to a collection of causal agents, whose decisions, in some complex way that must be justified, have some overall effect that is being indicated by the story, but also other unknown effects that might or might not bear on the one that is being explained.

So almost always, the media go for the second alternative, which is to make some meaning (cause and effect), out of whatever facts are available. We are programmed to make sense of the world in patterns. This is what Nassim Taleb has popularized recently in his now-famous books on the financial markets as the Narrative Fallacy. In the case of the media, it involves attributing causes to entities that have no causal power, except weakly, when they are considered in a decision made by a human being or series of human beings. In other words, the media bring their bias toward seen events to the narrative fallacy to imply false explanations of the events they are reporting upon. In this way, they can tell a story when they have only a bunch of facts, despite their fact that they don't know the true story (because they weren't in the room) or when, in fact, there isn't one. (Sometimes things that seem causally related aren't related at all.)

Taleb describes one of the simplest manifestations of this informational Tourette's syndrome in the business press's insistence on telling us that every move in the stock market happened because of some particular event, which is thus purported to be its cause, such as in such comments as "oil stocks moved up slightly on Chinese growth figures", which means anything only if it means that the Chinese growth figures were the sole cause, or majority cause, or at least, leading cause of the move in prices. This is usually nonsense because a) none of these is the case, b) none of these could be determined to be the case, even if it were, c) even if this was a cause, it would not explain most of the event, d) even if the publication of Chinese growth figures were causally related to the price move, they can be so only via the will of traders who, within a complex system, choose therefore to take some action, and may have multiple reasons for doing so, e) in any case, the action of those traders "directly opposes" the action of other traders who are on the other end of the trades, and presumably have other reasons for so being, and f), most importantly, the move in the stocks of interest may be within the normal fluctuations of the market "noise", such that any assigning of cause is necessarily pointless.

The need to appear to explain, rather than just to report facts, underlies a set of epistemological errors that prevail in news coverage. News organizations will tend to assert causes of events that 1) are visible, 2) are proximate to the event, 3) involve agents that are not even causal agents (like "America" or "the Left"), or 4) are causally insignificant even if they could be causal agents in the situation of interest.

A remarkable story illustrates the failure of the media when they combine the narrative fallacy with lack of information. Before I tell it, I must provide some background.

On 7 May 1999, the Americans under NATO bombed the Chinese embassy in Belgrade. The USA claimed that the bombing was a result of using a set of outdated maps, and that the bombers thought they were hitting the Federal Republic of Yugoslavia's weapons procurement department. The Chinese were understandably upset, and demanded an apology. The U.S. offered an apology, but Chinese-U.S. relations were badly affected. The bombing was front-page news all over the world, and many column inches of ink were used up on it. The Western press pretty much accepted the story that it was an accident. The Chinese press didn't, and their story was that the Americans were at fault for not coming clean.[12] In fact, no media anywhere found out and reported the truth, which I found out 10 years later.

My story begins a few days after the bombing, when I was still a teenager, and with my parents at a large party held by

---

[12] See, for example: http://english.peopledaily.com.cn/90001/90776/6654193.html

friends of our family. The father of the family whose party we were enjoying was of significant rank in the British Army, posted to Germany and working in the Signal Corps. Since the Chinese embassy story was very much a hot topic, we talked about it, and he told me he was perplexed by it. He said he knew that it was impossible that the Americans could be using bad maps—that the information is so accurate, and the fail-safes are so standard, that there has to be some other story, but he didn't know what it could be.

I never thought much again about that story until I was in Calgary, Canada, a decade later.

Having problems with my laptop, I called Hewlett-Packard to make use of my on-site repair warranty, and a day or two later, an engineer came to where I was staying.

He had to pull my entire machine apart, and fit a new system board and a couple of other parts—a process which takes the better part of two hours. Unable to use my computer while it was in pieces, I took a seat at the end of the table where the engineer worked and we got talking. He was a very interesting fellow and the conversation was fascinating. We got to talking about the nature of our work, how satisfying we find it, and our hopes for our respective futures. In the course of this conversation, at my enquiry, he told me about the most interesting day at work he'd ever had.

I should say that this point that based on my 90 minutes or so of conversation with this man, I believe he was not prone to drama, and tended to choose his words carefully. I have no reason to disbelieve the following story.

On his most interesting day at work, this hardware engineer was told that he was to collect whatever forms of ID he had and make himself available at a particular location to the North East of Calgary. The requirement regarding "whatever forms of ID" was bizarre, and so the engineer pressed for further information and was given none. He gathered whatever forms of ID he had at home and went to the specified location.

The location of the job was an American military base. At the entrance to the base, he was informed that he was required to repair a printing device. Since the location was highly sensitive, under normal circumstances, he was told, he would have to undergo extensive security-clearance protocols before entering, but since this was an urgent repair, and there was not time for that procedure, an accompanying four star general would serve as his security clearance. He was instructed that when told to look left or right as he walked through the base, he was to do so.

As the engineer conducted the repair, the four-star general stood by him at all times. They became quite comfortable with each other, and talked to pass the time. During that conversation, they discussed the bombing of the Chinese embassy in Belgrade, and the general told him that the bombing was not an accident at all. In fact, the opposite was true: the embassy had been the target of more precision-guided ordinance than almost any other target before that time, because a few weeks earlier, an American stealth plane was downed over Serbia and the Serbians were picking it apart and delivering its components to the Chinese in their embassy, who were storing them in the basement of the building. The Chinese knew that the Americans knew what they were doing, but would not stop. America responded by destroying the embassy, and presumably the bits of bomber that were hidden in its basement.

I asked the engineer if he had checked the story. He hadn't but was confident that I'd find information about the downed American warplane if I looked for it. Sure enough, five and a half weeks earlier, on March 28th, an F 117 Stealth fighter was downed outside Belgrade.[13]

This story fits the data.[14] Even if you choose not to believe it, it fits the data at least as well as any story that prevailed in the media at the time or since. As the cause, or if you prefer, possible cause, it was missed because the news outlets went with a cause of the embassy bombing that unlike this one, was visible—the war over Yugoslavia, with the chaos, and thus generalized potential for error, that people associate with war—and proximate—faulty maps—rather than six weeks earlier in another location. That this was the official explanation of the American government made it all the easier to promulgate.

The media were not in the room when the decision to bomb the Chinese embassy was made, so were not exposed to the true cause. The media also did not have the information on which the deciders in the room were basing their decisions, and so, again, were not exposed to the true cause. The Western media defaulted to their paradigm of trust in the moral rightness of the West, and generally accepted the story that the bombing was an accident. The Chinese media largely defaulted to their paradigm that the thing was fishy and that the Americans had some other motive. The Chinese media were half-right, since the event wasn't an accident, but they were wrong in thinking that the original causative agents were the Americans alone, when it was the Chinese who were the first to behave in a questionable manner (given that they were not in conflict with the USA at the time and

---

[13] For example, http://kosova.org/post/US-F-117-Stealth-Fighter-Is-Downed-in-Yugoslavia.aspx,
http://www.defense.gov/news/newsarticle.aspx?id=41992

[14] Coincidentally, at the time of editing this text, some degree of confirmation of this story was provided by:
http://www.guardian.co.uk/world/2011/jan/23/china-stealth-fighter-us-technology

had no right to the American property).

The same factors were at work as the American news companies presented to us the financial crisis. Although, after a few years of so doing, some of them moved beyond the idea that "greedy bankers are responsible", which is the obvious cause because it is most proximate to the collapse, the real (traceable) causes escaped most anchors and commentators. "Greedy bankers" were the first cause to be presented in the media, because they are visible, for sure, but also because they are superficially most closely associated with the crisis—they were in the right time at the right place, and certainly had their hands on many of the levers. Maybe they were caught holding the bloody knife, but an explanation of events requires us to ask whether anyone else paid for the hit, to stretch the analogy. Importantly, while those who are superficially closest to an event may be its most proximate cause, they also may be the least important of all its causes. This was likely the case in the financial crisis, as we shall see in Ch. 4, when we examine the United States' identity as the Land of Opportunity.

Much has been, and is being, written about the crisis. Although many of its most proximate causes can be identified in the last decade, other direct causes include decisions that were made as far back as 1913 and 1971. [15]

It may seem pathological to trace causes so far back, but it is not, because those causes (including establishment of the Fed, and elimination of the gold standard) were necessary causes (meaning without which current events in their present form would be impossible). The fact that these causes can be undone even now makes them genuinely newsworthy. Failing to trace causes back

---

[15] Some readers will immediately know the significance of these dates, and why I mention them here. If you are one of them, you and I share, at least in part, a particular paradigm of U.S. economic history.

far enough leaves us trying to understand a problem based on certain "givens" when, in fact, the "givens" are not "given" at all—but can be changed, preventing a situation from occurring in the future. This is important because if the apparent "given" is a direct cause of a problem, however distant it may appear, then any solution to the problem that fails to address this cause will be nothing more than a treatment of symptoms. Moreover, in politics and economics, just as in medicine, so-called solutions that treat symptoms but ignore causes are likely to have unintended consequences, which may make matters worse.

In the case of the financial crisis, many people are concerned about the likelihood of massive inflation in the next few years, as the money created out of thin air by the Federal Reserve feeds into our economy, pushing up the prices of everything. If this happens, politicians and the media will again have us focusing on visible and proximate causes—such as greedy shopkeepers who are gouging these consumers. The media will present plenty of commentators to speak about these things, and we will lap it up. However, if today's "inflationists" are right, then the media will be wrong, and the ultimate cause will have been the printing of money by the Fed years earlier, a necessary condition of which was the elimination of the gold standard a generation before that. The people who made the decisions that originally caused the events will not be nearby when the consequences hit, and that is why the media won't find them, and we, the citizens, will therefore not find out about them.

The difficulty of accurate and useful reporting increases as the systems being reported upon become more complex, as complex systems are characterized by outcomes that depend extremely sensitively on particular variables. This property is exemplified by the now-proverbial butterfly that flaps its wings in Peru and causes a hurricane in India. In such systems, while it may be possible to say that certain variables affect particular outcomes, it is generally impossible to know enough about a variable or how exactly it affects outcomes to be able to identify it as the cause of a particular observation. This certainly applies in the case of the aforementioned attempt to explain why a market moves in a particular way, or why a member of a political party takes a particular decision. Non-linearity, then, subverts explanation, and so the media will always tend to eliminate it from their presentations of events. In so doing, news reports inadvertently imply that causes of events are much simpler than they often are.

Decisions that Shape the World Are Made Privately by Individuals

One of the most common reasons why the media fail to present the true causes and context of events is that most important decisions that shape our world are made by relatively small cadres. Recent examples of life-altering events that have been in the news and shaped the lives of millions of people include the 9/11 attacks, the wars in Iraq and Afghanistan, the setting of artificially low interest rates by the Fed, the printing of U.S. dollars and the bailouts to banks. In history, they include the decision to establish the Federal Reserve, and later to come off the gold standard, the decision to invade Vietnam, the original decision by the USA to invade Cuba, and the decision of Stanislav Yevgrafovich Petrov that the American nuclear missile launch he detected on the Russian defense system that he was operating was a system malfunction and not a real launch. Petrov, as it happened, literally saved the world, but you didn't hear about it because there were no media in the room.

The psychologies and perceptions of a few minds therefore disproportionately determine events, and are mostly invisible to the media. How the world looks to these persons in elite positions, with their own interests, almost always with much more information than is available to the media, differs from how the world looks to us. As the media are unable to present, let alone interpret, information it doesn't have, facts presented in the media are almost always insufficient to be able correctly to interpret the real cause or potential of an event, and opinions formed by trying to make sense of massively inadequate information are necessarily wrong, because the actual decision is being made in a different world from that believed by everyone else to exist.

In the metaphor from earlier in this chapter, while the world thinks a situation is a pentagon or a circle, the decider is likely to have extra information that tells him that it is in fact a star or, at least, something other than a circle or pentagon.

Restated, events alone don't determine events in the absence of minds, which is precisely why the right-hand column of the 2x2 matrix a few pages back, is so important. Events happen when earlier events are considered by a few people, often political and business leaders, and senior public servants, who then make decisions that cause those events. Therefore, to be able truly to understand a situation, the personal motivations of these people and the information available to them must be accurately known.

The Profit Motive

Apart from the limitations of prevailing cultural, linguistic and political paradigms, already described, most media organizations are limited by specific and explicit interest. In the case of many of the foreign media, especially in parts of the world where some of the most challenging conflicts are faced, these limitations are state controls. In extreme cases like North Korea, there are no media except that produced directly by the government. Most media in the West are free of direct state control, but the corporate interest is to profit, and therefore to advertisers, rather than truth or moral leadership. This agenda, legally enforced (as it is illegal for a board of a public company to take business decisions that are not in the interest of its shareholders), becomes more important as the number of news corporations declines with media consolidation.

There is nothing inherently wrong with the profit motive, and certainly, corporations driven by giving their customers what they want should be free to thrive. However, it is incumbent on us as consumers of their product to be aware that they profit by presenting to their customers a product that makes them feel good, as they see, hear and favorably interpret information from members of the political team—usually Conservative or Liberal, as we shall explore later—with which they identify.

Moderation and Moderates Are Under-Represented

Voices of moderation (often the voices of peace in situations of conflict or potential conflict) are under-represented and extreme voices are over-represented in all sectors of the media. There are a number of reasons for this. Calls for peace and the end of harmful activities are not news, nor are they particularly newsworthy. Animus and posturing, of any stripe, sell more than commonsense. A provoked consumer is an engaged consumer. For these and other reasons, reported content tends to be written from the ends of a prevailing spectrum of views about an issue, rather than the middle, and reports on a conflict situation tend to reflect the positions that are at odds with each other, over facts or opinions that do not support either side of the conflict.

Interestingly, this effect is evident at Watching America.com: the site links to articles of various positions, left and right, liberal and conservative, pro and anti-American…and everything in between, from well over a hundred countries. Some of the most enlightening and surprising articles, and indeed, the most well-written, are not extreme, and are valuable precisely because they don't support any prevailing political view in the USA. But it is not the articles with a high quality of writing, originality of content, or even great insight that are the most linked or even the most read. Rather, it is the articles that most passionately support the views of what might be called the hard left and hard right of American politics that gain the most attention—often regardless of the quality of the arguments made.

Furthermore, those who are most passionate about a particular view tend to have the greatest interest in spending more energy than others in pushing their views out through the media. These are the people who are fighting hardest for something. Accordingly, once again, those whose are less active, perhaps because they have more moderate views, and are more content with the status quo are therefore under-represented, while more extreme positions are relatively over-represented.

Mistaking Semantics for Reality

At any given time, the media of any modern culture will be airing, and thus perpetuating, one or more prevailing debates. The media represent a public forum for opinions to be offered, challenged and developed. However, a close reading of media from a range of countries will reveal that all are guilty of debates that appear to be about something important in reality, but are in fact entirely semantic. For example, for weeks after the Israeli campaign against Hezbollah, the Lebanese media were full of segments about whether Hezbollah "won" in that country. This is as much a debate about what to call something, rather than an attempt to understand better what in fact happened, and its implications. It is not dissimilar to the debate in 2006 and 2007 in the USA over whether we were "winning in Iraq"—again a debate about what to call what little we know about a situation (in the absence of almost all truly relevant data), the outcome of which tells us nothing factual, but usually serves only to promote one side of a political argument over another.

Dissent and Those Who Stand Outside Paradigms

In any country's media, those few who do share the prevailing paradigms may not be completely absent. Since paradigms are imperfect, if ubiquitous, and tend to reduce our ability to see unmediated truth (inasmuch as that term can mean anything), dissenting voices may even be disproportionately likely to capture something that is both true and important that is being missed by the mainstream, merely because it is the combination of truth and importance that almost always provides the psychological motivation for dissent concerning issues or beliefs of the day.

In the Middle East, for example, Wafa Sultan, an Arab psychiatrist, stands boldly outside her prevailing cultural paradigm. When asked the extent to which America is to blame for Arab ills, she explains that the Arab choice is not between antipathy toward the West and violent opposition to the West, but between either of those two—and remaining culturally and economically backward—and standing back and taking ownership of their own part in causing their own situation, and thereby giving themselves the potential to become a 21st century culture with global credibility. She is very often seen on Arabic news shows as a foil to the myriad Islamic clerics who are put up against her.

Of course, this is not to say that all dissent is accurate, or even that mainstream debates are always vacuous or misinformed, but rather that dissent, in all media, tends as a matter of systemic bias (even logical necessity), to be a good place to begin searching for truth that the prevailing paradigm has an interest in not addressing. If the dissenting voice does not present a truth, it is at least very likely to shine light on that part of a prevailing or mainstream paradigm that may be at odds with facts on the ground.

This "main stream" of which the mainstream media are a part

is the same "main stream" in which most readers and listeners live. Since a cable news channel or newspaper must speak to a sufficiently large audience to survive, there is a tendency (for the news producers) to speak from the mainstream to the mainstream (of news consumers). While on the surface, this tendency seems to contradict the tendency for extremes to get greater play, it does not, since the "extremes" are really those that are recognized, defined, and thus legitimized by the mainstream. In other words, they are often opposing views within a paradigm or opposing sub-paradigms that share fundamental, often unspoken, assumptions with each other, and can both be identified within an over-arching paradigm. As a specific example, we hear a lot about the Left and Right, or Democrat and Republican, on American news. Superficially, Left and Right are "opposing paradigms". But they exist within an over-arching paradigm in which assumptions about the American identity and American politics are shared. We will be considering this phenomenon in the next few chapters, and we will explore first problems with the paradigms of Left and Right as they limit our media coverage of events and our understanding of American politics, and thereafter, the most ubiquitous omissions and errors in our over-riding paradigm—simply, the "American paradigm".

There's mainstream boring (which is most of what we read and see on the news), mainstream extreme (which is most of where the media hype is), and then there's non-mainstream, which may be perceived as off-the-wall.

Necessarily, the bias toward the mainstream, including political or cultural "opponents" that comprise it, is a bias against the presentation of all those truths that start off as heresy or an extreme minority view—which, as you'll realize if you stop for a moment to consider, covers most truths worth knowing. Examples include the idea that the earth moves around the sun (Copernicus and Galileo), that lives could be saved by having doctors wash their hands between handling dead bodies and delivering babies (Ignaz Semmelweis). When, in 1543, Copernicus first propounded the heliocentric view of the universe, he did so in the last year of his life for fear, many believe, of condemnation. Indeed, when Galileo empirically verified Copernicus' theory about a century later, he was put under house arrest. When, in 1847, Semmelweis was able to reduce the mortality from childbirth at his hospital in Vienna to under 2% from a much higher figure, he was roundly ridiculed by the Viennese medical establishment of which he was a part.

Consider that there are "true statements" that are well established and everyone knows. These are not newsworthy. The newsworthy truths are the new truths—those that are not generally known but are just becoming known or are known to just one or a few people who may be concentrating on a particular subject or investigation.

When such new truths are not in line with received wisdom, or consistent with a prevailing paradigm, they are "heretical" to one field or another. In this sense, most important truth starts off as heresy—a proposition that must be rejected, because acceptance would challenge so much of a prevailing paradigm that, in some cases, even people's identities (and often careers) could be threatened. Accordingly, why would a news outlet risk ridicule or alienation of an audience by presenting such content? They generally don't, and so very much of what would importantly extend human knowledge goes completely unreported by those whom we rely on to find things out and report them to us.

Consider a present-day example, involving Ron Paul, a Congressman from Texas, and Peter Schiff, a broker and author from Connecticut. These are two men who successfully predicted the outcomes of monetary policy and housing policy in the USA for years. In the case of Schiff, the predictions were highly consistent and highly specific. For years, Ron Paul got little coverage, and Schiff was laughed off various news shows. Their arguments about what was about to happen in the U.S. economy are the same today as they were then. Before the current recession, they were heretics, and few media outlets paid attention to them. Now, events have brought their formerly off-the-wall views if not into the mainstream, then at least much closer to it. We'll be returning to Peter Schiff later.

Everyone Has an Interest in Their Own Status Quo (or The Benefits of Not Being Too Close to a Story)

With respect to personal relationships, it's easier for someone on the outside of a situation to see things as they are and tell them like they are, than it is for those in the relationship on the inside of the situation. The same is true of the media: it's easier for the media on the outside of a situation or culture to call it as it is than for those who are or could be affected by the event that is being observed or reported.

Specifically, reporters or writers at non-American media outlets, for example, do not have an obvious personal and vested interest that things in the U.S. should be one way or another, so to that extent at least, they can call American issues like they see them. In contrast, and referring to personal life to strengthen the point, I may have a personal interest in not making a particular observation about something in my life or something that could affect me directly (including my own economic problems, my favored political party, my leaders and much else), because once I admit to it, I may have to act on that observation, and that action could be difficult or costly. Most people tend not even to do the things that would make them happy if doing so would be painful in the short run.[16] For this reason, American journalists, being human, have a natural tendency not to see certain things as they are, if the consequences for them (or their readership, which often has broadly the same interests) are too great or disruptive.

News Outlets with Audiences that Are Unsympathetic to the Establishment Are Usually More Useful

As the Left pointed out often during the Bush Presidency, the apparent naïve acceptance by Fox News of most of what came out of the White House made a joke of Fox as a News organization. As an outlet that wanted to support that administration, Fox was well served by not asking the questions that could expose bad decision making, even when bad decisions appeared obvious to many Americans. Given their studied lack of curiosity, Fox failed consistently as a provider of information.

However, now the world is very different. We live in Obama's America now, and Fox News is no longer pointless. Indeed, the opposite is true. The issues that will overwhelmingly determine the experience of this nation over the next generation, such as the aforementioned fiscal crisis and the accompanying transfer of wealth from American citizens to the government, are at the time of writing being tackled by Fox more closely than by its competitors. This is not to say that they are being tackled by Fox in a particularly studied way, or that more than just a minority of shows are tackling these issues, but they are at least being tackled on that network.[17] Fox, of course, has its info-

---

[16] This is oftentimes manifest in the common choice of security over happiness, seen in so many lives.

[17] For example, "Freedom Watch" on Fox was one of the few shows that covers real events, policies and economic decisions that affect or will affect the lives of

taining pundits. Until relatively recently, Glenn Beck, a presenter who makes himself an easy target with his emotional and sometimes sloppy expositions, was a good example. Beck is not a paragon of investigative journalism, but at least he attempts to relate issues of interest to his (large) audiences to both present and historical decisions to which they do not superficially appear to be related. In this sense, credit is due to him for making an original attempt to nudge Americans to look toward context in understanding the meaning of events. Ironically, the value he can provide in this regard would be greatest for the very people who are least interested in listening to him.

The take-home point here is that it is always easier for an anti-establishment news network to reveal news-worthy truth. Important, actionable truths in the political sphere typically concern policies or events that are going wrong or motivations that are wrong (which are for that reason alone the most news-worthy). A network that knows that its audience is less sympathetic to the prevailing political establishment is served better by presenting facts that put in a bad light those whose decisions bear most strongly on our current situation. Moreover, these are invariably the facts that we should require our media to do more work to uncover, precisely because they are the facts that the powerful interests tend to want to keep from us. Under the Obama administration, Fox is such a network. Under the Bush administration, Fox was the opposite of one.

---

all Americans but are hardly touched by other networks. Most importantly, they are presented from a perspective that does not assume that the establishment Republican or Democrat perspective of an issue is any more worthy of consideration than any other. And, as we shall see in the next chapter, there are others.

The Media Have an Awful Track Record at Identifying Awful Track Records

The latter part of this chapter has included a number of reasons why the effectiveness of the media as conveyors of true and useful information is limited. These are mostly systematic biases. The media don't publicize these limitations, nor do they do anything to overcome them by preferring commentators who have a track record of accuracy in a particular field of interest.

It makes sense that the media should give more airtime to those whose hands are on levers of power than on those whose hands are not, since only in understanding what those people think or intend can we understand what is likely to happen or even why those people believe what they believe—whether they are right or wrong. That said, audiences might be well served from a media bias toward truth that is manifest in favoring those commentators who have a track record of accuracy over those who do not—or, at the very least, in monitoring reporting on the accuracy of the previous assertions made by those they put on air. As already mentioned, and as we will revisit later, the present financial crisis is fertile ground for examples. In the years leading up to 2008, hundreds of people in the media made comments about why the U.S. economy was just fine. A few did not. Why do we still hear from the hundreds and not more from the few? In other words, why do we hear more from the schools of thought that have more people rather than those that have more often been proven correct? And if we must hear from the former group, why do their commentaries not come with a ticker-tape informational health warning, such as, "This commentator previously predicted that house prices in the U.S. never could fall because they never have in the past."

This is the fundamental reason why the "fairness doctrine", which some legislators would like to bring back in the USA, would completely defeat its stated purpose. It biases media against truth in two ways. Someone has to decide what view constitutes the opposite of another view, and therefore to decide the terms of a debate. (If you've heard from a Democrat legislator and a Republican legislator on some economic issue, have you really heard all equally valid opinions on the issue, or even two opinions that will necessarily point up the greatest principle that may be at stake? The answer is almost always no.) In saying A must be opposed by B in public media, we reduce the likelihood that the media will look to V, X, Y or Z, who may not share the unstated and often shared assumptions and interests of A and B.

Moreover, such a doctrine allows legislators to define fair in matters of opinion. Yet, in a nation whose Constitution includes the First Amendment, all speech is fair.

Getting Out of the Home Paradigm: The Benefits to Americans of the Foreign Media

In the light of some of the philosophical arguments above, I'd like to make a few brief comments about the one obvious place Americans can go to try to get through the limitations imposed on them by their own paradigms, and their media. What follows would be true for anyone in any country, as it's not only Americans who can benefit from foreign perspectives.

The most obvious benefit of reading the foreign media is that, like the American national and local press, the foreign press is "on the ground" in the place on which it reports. We've briefly mentioned this already. When it comes to any situation that has some causes or effects outside the USA, then, some other press is closest to the action. The comments above about the benefit of distance from an event notwithstanding, simply by virtue of closeness to the events, a section of the foreign press will often present facts that have not been noted by our American media, which they missed simply because of distance.

Also, since the foreign media reports are written from the

paradigm that prevails in the region of those reported events, they are directly able to speak to the perceptions (right hand-side of the 2x2 matrix) in a way that cannot be done at a distance. Indeed, they must speak to the perceptions of the news consumers for whom the content is originally created or else they will not appear credible to their audience. Therefore, as outsiders, we will always come to better understand the perceptual (including political, psychological, cultural etc.) context of the events if we read the foreign press coverage of their own issues. This is especially true for American news consumers since much foreign coverage presented in the U.S. is provided by American commentators who are employed by American news corporations. It is exceedingly rare to see a foreign journalist reporting on something unless it is a natural disaster story. Unlike in the British Broadcasting Corporation, for example, political reporting of foreign events by foreigners is almost absent.

The greater range of information provided by foreign media helps better challenge both our own leaders and our own media. This "keeping us honest" effect is stronger than the way in which our own media keep our own leaders honest, since the different paradigms abroad allow information that is not even considered by our own media to slip through, and this information may cause us to challenge our own leaders in a manner that our own media cannot. In other words, foreign media may challenge assumptions that are shared by all American media, but which our media may not even be aware of making.

Taken together, one's own media and the foreign media illuminate our humanity by showing, often subtly, how people in very different frames of reference are similar, and in some respects, even the same. The ideas that on the one hand, all people are fundamentally the same, and on the other, that cultures make people so fundamentally different that true mutual understanding is impossible, have been debated for hundreds of years.

Often, limited by our own preconceptions and our distance from a problem, we ask, "How can we solve this or that problem over there?" This is the stuff of foreign policy, which often turns elections and the course of nations. Unsurprisingly, the press "over there" have answers to such questions that are sometimes much more compelling than our own answers. A couple of articles from a far flung region can be worth hundreds of pundits on our own national television.

The foreign press therefore provides information and perspectives that can provide us with a much greater context for assessing the veracity and biases of our own news channels and newspapers. When the range of the political leanings of U.S. news producers is placed on a spectrum of global opinion about issues pertinent to the U.S., American debate will sometimes be shown to be, at best, uninformed or insufficient, and, at worst, meaningless. In all parts of the world, op-eds tend to address the very things caused in whole or in part by American policies that antagonize their local populations, and they discuss the elements of their experience that we must know about in order to have any influence. In recent times, America has in many parts of the world come up against the eternal truth that it is impossible simultaneously to influence and to antagonize. Properly understood, then, foreign news reports, now available to all through such sites as Watching America, are more-or-less manuals for our State Department.

Much of the resistance that some people have to foreign views is, in fact, understandable resistance to the most extreme views, sometimes distasteful, hate-filled or unhinged, that appear in the foreign media. The value of such aggressive writing, however, is not in its accuracy, or even in its intent, but in its crystallization of the extremes of perception between which more mainstream views fall, and with which political processes, and attempts to influence, must deal.

One of the most important advantages a foreign reporter

always has over a domestic reporter in writing about a domestic event, is that the domestic media institution cannot report without contributing in one way or another to the political debate in their home country. Potential accusations of having taken a political position can be very dangerous as they can affect perceived integrity, audience figures, and revenues. As a specific example, Le Monde in France can say things about the U.S. that are much less likely to alienate Le Monde from its own French audience than the same comments by CNN or the New York Times in relation to their audiences.

Different cultures shine different colored lights on their own events and ours, as they have different histories and cultural experiences against which, by comparison and contrast, to assess events. In so doing, their media often identify different causes and effects of decisions and actions, and therefore different patterns of behavior and policy that elucidate otherwise un-noticed intentions and motivations. Even if they are wrong, they are rarely useless.

Pictures and Paradigms

Paradigmatic limitations affect more than just the textual content of news reports, whether written or spoken. They also determine what images we do and, more often, do not see in our media.

Recent history has shown that the old cliché that a picture is worth a thousand words is true in the media. In both Vietnam and Abu Ghraib, a few pictures touched public opinion more than had millions of words in hundreds of articles that had actually argued the very disconcerting truths that the pictures immediately revealed.

There is good reason for this. Words always present cognitive claims, or propositions. They can therefore be argued with or disagreed with. To use words is invariably to assert something. "The car is blue" or "the blue car" are both assertions. Even a qualifier such as "It seems to me that..." does not really prevent whatever follows it from being an assertion, inviting agreement or disagreement. And it is always possible to dispute an assertion, or simply deny its validity based on its apparent incompleteness, or the lack of credibility of the source. We've already considered how we tend to resist data that do not fit our paradigms. More obviously, we also tend to disagree with arguments when we see that they come from a perspective that we have already decided we don't like, or sometimes simply because they are made in a vernacular that suggests a frame of reference or set of opinions that might threaten our own views.

Photographs and film footage are not arguments or even assertions in this sense. They show "something that was there" and in that respect differ from reported facts, which are filtered through and are selected by the paradigm of a reporter or a news institution whose veracity and motivations can be challenged, or whose imputed agenda easily dismissed.

For this reason, photographs have a way of breaking through or challenging a paradigm in a way a textual or verbal report cannot, by presenting visual information without interpretation, and in a manner that deprives the viewer of the opportunity to attribute its details to any mediating intent or agenda. Of course, a photographer gets to choose and frame her subject, but she does not get to create the scene as a writer does, or even choose the "general topic" to which the image speaks.

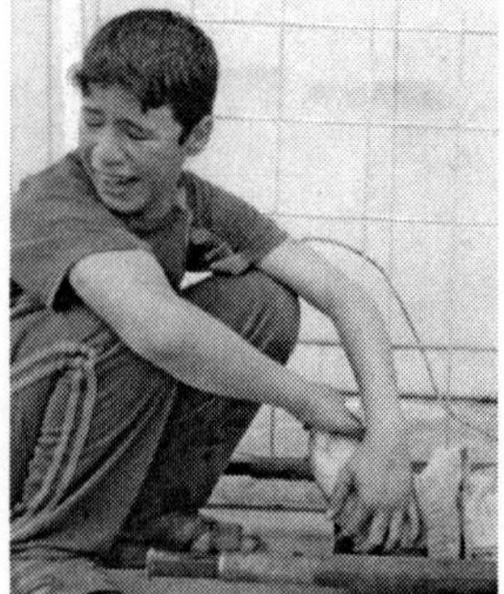

This picture is of an Iraqi boy whose father was killed in Iraq. The picture does not reveal how he was killed, but it communicates the situation in Iraq in a way that text cannot, because it shows immediately the human experience that is being caused. It does not make a case, and so does not invite cognitive resistance, even as it does trigger basic human repulsion or emotional resistance. To discount the importance of what is portrayed is more difficult than discounting the importance of a particular article or textual statement of it. As humans, we connect to the human being portrayed here in a way we cannot connect to a text.

We will consider later the idea of the "American paradigm" and how it limits the American media. Many amazing photographs that are available to American mainstream media institutions are not used because our media do not want to risk the strong responses of their audiences, whether of disgust, revulsion or whatever else. The photograph above was freely obtained over the American Yahoo! public newswire. Such pictures, hard to fit into the American framing of the Iraq war, at least before the elections of 2006, were very typical of pictures displayed in non-American media, but conspicuous by their absence from American newspapers and television screens.

While photographs are typically the most powerful images, precisely because they are not created and they present visual data without human alteration (except in cases of fraud), cartoons also have a special power for those who are truly interested in getting into the two right-hand boxes in the 2x2 matrix.

Arguments about policy that are based only on information that is provided by media from only the left two boxes in the matrix are usually arguments about what someone somewhere should do, as determined by the arguer and removed from anyone else's experience of a situation. As we've shown in this chapter, though, global affairs are determined not just by actions and events, but also by how they are perceived—for right or wrong.

Political cartoons[18] often directly display those perceptions in a way that prose does not. Unlike a photograph, their content, like prose, is completely produced by the author, and so can "be argued with", but like a photograph, they don't directly assert—while nevertheless implying something very powerfully. Restated, cartoons present perception as a perception and not an argument. The perception can be rejected as wrong, but the fact of the perception—and a perception is a fact—is just there, conveyed with a clarity that benefits from making no effort to persuade.

[18] Figure (from Al Khaleej, U.A.E.): An answer to one of the questions prompted by 9-11. The question in the bubble is, 'Why Do You Hate Us?'. The critical point is that the cartoon does not state the answer. It is the answer.

CHAPTER 2

The False Dichotomy of American Politics (or Left is Good and Right is Right)

"The Fundamental Suspicion"

PARADIGMS ARE VERY powerful. Even if we can recognize intellectually that those who operate in different paradigms see the world in a different way (since their concepts determine their perceptions), most of us cannot shake a particular feeling about people who operate in different paradigms. We could call this feeling a "fundamental suspicion", and it profoundly affects America today.

This suspicion is not a conscious thought; it is subconscious—more like "a feeling in the bones". It is the feeling of being unable to imagine what it must be like to be someone who holds a fundamentally different worldview from our own. Like a stone in one's shoe, it is hard to ignore. Most importantly, it prevents us from trusting the motives of those who have these different worldviews, and from freeing ourselves from the idea that there just must be some unknown, perhaps unknowable cause that prevents those who see things "wrongly" from seeing what they would surely see if only they weren't prevented, pathologically, by that cause.

To understand this "fundamental suspicion', consider some examples.

With respect to politics, many on the left just can't get past the feeling that their opponents must be driven by something other than goodwill; that there is some damage or emotional need, probably unconscious, that causes their opponents to have their reactionary views that seem to be untouched by the basic human desire to support one's fellow man. Similarly, many on the right just can't get past the suspicion that their opponents must be driven by a sense of moral superiority that places themselves above others as they seek to impose their policies on others for their own good.

With respect to religion, many atheists have a fundamental suspicion that religious people must, in some small part of their brain or heart, just know that their beliefs are not reasonable, and so must be motivated by some hidden psychological need or lack of development. This works the other way too: many religious people have a fundamental suspicion that no one can really believe that everything around us had no first cause. If such an atheist and such a religionist were in debate, the former might be filtering everything he hears through his unconscious feeling that his interlocutor really needs a psychological crutch, while the latter might be unconsciously filtering everything through her unconscious feeling that her interlocutor just doesn't want to face the possibility that something might be true that would impose an unwanted moral discipline on his life.

In the realm of culture, many non-Americans look out from their cultural paradigms toward America, and can't shake their fundamental suspicion that no one in America can really believe that the right to own a gun is about freedom when there are so many more gun homicides in the USA than in any developed country where there is no right to bear arms—so whatever the true, unstated motivation is, it is probably sinister. These fundamental suspicions are easy to spot within American culture, too: you can usually find them wherever there are culture warriors. For example, many pro-lifers just can't get past this sneaking suspicion that a human life is obviously a human life from the moment it is "created", by simple definition, so it simply must be the case that pro-choice advocates are bordering on evil if they can put any interest before the life of an innocent person. On the other side, it is just so obvious to pro-choice advocates that any normal person would pull a living child out of a burning laboratory before they would take ten test tubes that contain fertilized embryos that they just can't shake their sneaking suspicion that pro-lifers are disconnected from reality.

In all cases, this "fundamental suspicion" constitutes a deep psychological obstacle to understanding the other side of any debate that matters, as it precedes and filters all content that does not fit our current paradigm.

Another Experiment about Paradigms

During the run-up to the 2004 presidential election, 30 men—half self-described as "strong" Republicans and half as "strong" Democrats—agreed to undergo an fMRI bran scan, while assessing statements by both George W. Bush and John Kerry in which the candidates clearly contradicted themselves. Not surprisingly, Republican subjects were as critical of Kerry as Democratic subjects were of Bush, yet both groups give their own candidate a pass.

The neuroimaging results, however, revealed that the part of the brain most associated with reasoning—the dorsolateral prefrontal cortex—was quiescent. Most active were the orbital frontal cortex, which is involved in the processing of emotions; the anterior cingulate, which is associated with conflict resolution; the posterior cingulate, which is concerned with making judgments about moral accountability; and—once subjects had arrived at a conclusion that made them emotionally comfortable—the ventral striatum, which is related to reward and pleasure.

Westen, who was responsible for the experiment, is quoted in an Emory University press release as saying, "We did not see any increased activation of the parts of the brain normally engaged during reasoning. What we saw instead was a network of emotion circuits lighting up, including circuits hypothesized to be involved in regulating emotion, and circuits known to be involved in resolving conflicts."

Interestingly, neural circuits engaged in rewarding selective behaviors were activated. "Essentially, it appears as if partisans twirl the cognitive kaleidoscope until they get the conclusions they want, and then they get massively reinforced for it, with the elimination of negative emotional states and activation of positive ones," Westen said.

The implications of Westen's work are huge, because they show us that our political responses and opinions are determined primarily by the political team or group with which we identify, and as a corollary, its relationship and opposition to, the "other" team (especially if there are only two, as is the case with the main political parties in the USA).

There are of course many self-identified political teams or groups in the USA, but according to Rasmussen, as of June 2010, over 68% of American adults identify with one or other of the main teams—Republican or Democrat. Therefore, a large majority believe in a political language and set of assumptions that are largely defined by opposition to another language and set of assumptions. Currently, American political debates, whatever else may be true about them, are dominated by this oppositional structure and the assumptions and perceptions of the opposing paradigms.

Our Politics Are Our Paradigms

What are the implications of this? First, when we think we are doing politics or talking about political issues, we are mostly not talking about, or making decisions about, any actual events on the ground. Moreover, we are unlikely to be assimilating new information as events occur, and testing our system of political beliefs against that information, modifying them as necessary.

Rather, when we are talking politically, we are usually talking from, and expressing, paradigms. These paradigms are used, shaped and defined mostly by the media. Nearly all of the uses of the terms "Republican", "Democrat", "Left" or "Right" to which a citizen is exposed are heard or read in the media. Remember, the media constitute the only institution that has enough reach to bring millions of the population into a common discourse. Therefore, they necessarily reinforce the paradigms from which political discussion proceeds. We could say that the media don't merely present our politics to us: they determine the very conceptual tools with which individuals can think and act politically. The media affect politics by determining the concepts and vocabulary used in our political discourse more powerfully than they do by making editorial choices, or even by choosing a particular editorial angle over another.

Politics can be intuitively defined as our discursive responses to perceived events and facts about our society and economy. Politics therefore includes choices made in response to events which affect what subsequent events and facts will have most impact on us in the future, in a kind of vicious or virtuous cycle.

Since the media supply the concepts of which our discursive responses comprise, when we are discussing the media, we are engaging in politics every bit as much as if we were discussing abortion, gun rights, the war in Iraq, or the national debt. Similarly, when we teach ourselves to recognize our paradigms and how they shape the information we consume in the media, we are doing politics, too.

I'll make an even stronger claim. In discussing the media, we are doing politics at a deeper level than we may be when we are discussing any of the above list of usual subjects, because to discuss the media is to discuss the agency that maintains the paradigms that govern our political thinking on all of these topics.

I have already framed mediography as the epistemology of the media and public discourse—a kind of public epistemology. Thus defined, mediography is inherently political. We could call it subconscious politics or meta-politics: if "conscious politics" are the opinions we hold about the things we think we see around us (and our actions in response), then "subconscious politics" is the structure of, and concepts used in, the discourse that shapes those opinions, responses and actions. Since this subconscious politics is determined largely by what is not seen, and even by what our paradigms prevent us from seeing without special effort, it has much more power over us than "conscious politics".

Whether or not you go along with my big claim for the importance of mediography, it is surely impossible to understand American politics, or the American media's coverage thereof, without understanding the two ill-defined paradigms called the political Left and the political Right—or Liberal and Conservative.

Turn on any news channel in the USA and you may hear one or both of these words many times an hour. This is peculiar to the American media. The media in other countries do not tend to refer to two political wings, or teams, in quite the oppositional way in which they are used here in the USA. First off, their use by the American media is problematic in the simple but critical respect that neither is clearly defined. But the more serious problem is that the very structure of the political Left and the political Right, or Liberal and Conservative, rests on two false assumptions, which are

- Liberal and Conservative are in some way opposites, or at least dichotomous.
- Socialists and neo-cons and/or the religious right, being the most extreme liberals and conservatives respectively, are the most extremely opposed.
- Liberal and Conservative cover the spectrum of political perspectives (they "exhaust the political space").

To understand better these paradigms, and why they disserve us, we need to look briefly at history—and especially the history of the word "liberal".

Classical Liberalism

Before the word Liberal (capital "L") was used in the USA to describe progressives and others on the left, and often affiliated with the Democratic Party, the word was used without a capital "L" in the term "classical liberalism", which, we shall show, is the root of that thread in modern Liberalism that also appears, surprisingly enough, in modern Conservatism.

Classical liberalism grew in the West in the 19th century. The opening paragraph of its Wikipedia entry includes the sentence:

> *[Classical liberalism] is committed to the ideal of limited government and liberty of individuals including freedom of religion, speech, press, assembly, and free markets.*

Already we see something interesting. Limited government and free markets are more often associated with modern Conservatives. Freedom of speech, press and assembly are more often associated with modern Liberals. Freedom of religion is perhaps associated equally with both. The notion "individual liberty" is fundamental to both Liberals and Conservatives, who admittedly emphasize different areas of its application.

Two of the most important modern expositors of classical liberalism include Frederic Bastiat, mentioned in Chapter 1, and Friedrich von Hayek. The works of both of these men were fundamentally concerned with preventing tyranny and the unfair treatment of one or some groups at the hands of one or many others. These are decidedly modern Liberal concerns. But in this pursuit, both of these authors, and others in the tradition, explain why well-intentioned interventions by politicians in what would otherwise be the outcomes of the free choices of individuals are almost always self-defeating. They believed that such interventions tended to fail even when the choices of individuals appeared to lead to a society in which some were significantly worse off than others. They wrote that such interventions almost always result in loss of freedom without a justifying improvement in whatever social or economic metric is intended to be improved. Nowadays, such statements appear to support a laissez-faire political economy, and so sound more Conservative than Liberal.

We may say that the classical liberals were concerned with a just society—a passion of the modern Left—but in pursuing it, talked a lot about the importance of economic liberties—a passion of the modern Right.

These authors wrote often to warn us of the need to be on guard against the rise of tyrannical regimes at home. Hayek, for example, used Hitler's Nazis as the foil for some of his arguments in the Road to Serfdom. In the last century, we see classical liberal authors cited as influences by conservative politicians, such as Reagan and Thatcher.

To an American today, familiar with the Left vs. Right divide, and in the wake of an economic collapse that many believe is a result of run-away laissez fair capitalism, the link between social and economic justice on the one hand, and private economic liberty, approximated by the term "free-market capitalism" on the other, is far from certain and looking weaker than ever. While a deep analysis of that link is beyond the scope of this book, it has been elucidated very well by the authors already named and many others. Suffice to say for now that this link between social/economic justice and individual liberty is related to all of the following fundamental principles of classical liberalism.

- There must always be a bias to limit the reach of government because it is the single monopoly of force in our society.
- Private property is a natural right because without it we have no means of keeping the fruits of our labors or, therefore, of being able to increase our happiness through our own efforts, or of being able to protect ourselves against anyone who would harm or tyrannize us.
- When government acts for some alleged social good—usually redistributive—we tend only to see the immediate benefit (usually to some subset of the population) for which the action was taken. We do not see the social or economic cost born by others, which is often in the form of a good that is prevented from being done and is therefore unseen. (For me, this idea, conveyed by the brilliant Frederic Bastiat in The Seen and Unseen is one of

the most compelling arguments for the need for economic liberty in pursuit of societal fairness.)

- Democracy alone does not protect people. The Tyranny of Democracy refers to a situation where a majority can democratically vote for policies that benefit them at the expense of a minority. A progressive tax, especially when a large minority or a majority do not pay it at all, could be considered an example, even though many liberally minded people do not regard this in the same way they regard theft. Think, therefore, about a population in which all women, representing 51% of the voting public, vote for a tax that affects only men. Nothing in a democracy protects against this. Only the republican idea of unalienable rights of the individual does so, and once that idea is admitted, and we have protected against the "male tax" (!), how then do we justify, for example, the systematic transfer of wealth from those without children to those with (which happens in the USA, the UK, and many other democracies)? If you are not persuaded, consider that some of the taxpayers who may be subsidizing other people's children may themselves be without children because they believe they cannot afford to bring up a child properly.
- All giving to Peter takes from Paul eventually. Since all redistribution is an act of force in that it is conducted by the threat of imprisonment etc., the

moral burden on those that would redistribute is great, and the bar for justification must be set high.

- The Rule of Law must prevail because only Law enforced equally against all can ultimately protect against the possibility of the arbitrary Rule of Men. Protection against the unlawfully or unfairly wielded power of some men is generally considered a primary concern of modern Liberals, whereas modern Conservatives are more strongly associated with law and order. Both concerns are in the classical liberal tradition and bear interestingly on the current debates in the USA about illegal immigration.
- Governmental attempts to help people generally distort incentives and/or create moral hazard, incentivizing behaviors that cause more pain or loss in the future.
- True freedoms are "freedoms from", not "freedoms to". The American Constitutional rights of "life, liberty and the pursuit of happiness" are freedoms from having one's life taken, having one's actions limited (when they do not harm others), and the fruits of one's labors (property) removed. In contrast, any freedoms that are "freedoms to" are not fundamental freedoms, since they must be granted by a powerful entity (e.g. government), which, if it has the power to grant them, has the power to remove them. The Founders made it very

clear that some freedoms are not alienable precisely because they are granted by no authority on earth.

The above considerations are reflected in the following comment of Milton Friedman:

> *In my opinion, a society that aims for equality before liberty will end up with neither equality nor liberty. And a society that aims first for liberty will not end up with equality but will end up to a closer approach to equality than any other kind of system than has even been developed. Now, that conclusion is based both on evidence from history, and also, I believe, on reasoning, which—if you try to follow through the implications of aiming first at equality—will become clear to you. You can only aim at equality by giving some people the right to take things from others. And what ultimately happens when you aim at equality is that A and B shall decide what C shall do for D.*

This is a wonderful summary of classical liberal thought—not only for the obvious reason that it shows the dangers of sacrificing liberty up-front in the pursuit of such a social good as equality, but also because it provides a means of falsifying the classical liberal position—by historical evidence: whether Friedman's claim is right is, after all, only testable against history.

The purpose of this exposition of classical liberalism is to show that its components exist in modern (American) Liberalism and Conservatism. This will help us understand what drives these paradigms and how they differ. It will also clarify the contrast between how Liberalism and Conservatism are in fact related to each other and how they are presented as relating to each other in the media. This examination will help us unpack the two false assumptions about the American Left and Right with which I started this chapter.

Milton Friedman is considered today to be more of a conservative than a liberal. And yet his own justification of his position is in terms of liberty and equality—two things that modern Conservatives and Liberals would say are important metrics for understanding the quality of a society, even though the two groups would disagree on the extent to which one or the other should be pursued. Now, a Liberal could object to Friedman's saying that liberty should be pursued over equality, and that is why Friedman cannot claim liberal sensibilities. But read Friedman's quote carefully. The reason that Friedman says that liberty must be pursued is empirical—not ideological. The claim is that as a matter of fact, evidenced by history, pursuit of equality leads to lack of liberty and equality—both of which, by implication, are favorable, and could be used to justify the pursuit of the other. On the other hand, also as a matter of fact, evidenced by history, the pursuit of liberty leads not only to liberty but as close as has ever been achieved to equality.[19]

In the above quotation, Friedman indicates his values, or moral intentions, as being pro-liberty and pro-equality. It certainly involves a kind of utilitarian (greatest-good-for-the-greatest-number) social moral calculus, which is the stuff of modern Liberal politics. Simultaneously, Friedman indicates an empirical recognition that liberty is the vehicle for getting there.

The quote was taken from a lecture series in which Friedman

---

[19] To avoid misunderstanding, let us acknowledge the banal response that poor soviet countries achieved greater equality at the expense of liberty, and allow that Friedman is reasonably assuming that most of his listeners would not seek to argue for any of the regimes that had achieved very high equality through poverty and the elimination of most individual liberties in a police state. Almost all Americans of whatever political persuasion would agree that in such states, the loss of liberty clearly exceeds the gain in equality.

expounded the positions for which he is well known—that liberty includes economic liberty as well as social civil liberty, according to a model that we broadly call capitalism. This is not an argument for corporatism, which is today confused with capitalism, but could not be much further from it, as we shall discuss later. More succinctly, Friedman, like many others, has the moral concerns of the left because they are good, but the policies of the right because they work.

By now, readers on the moderate left may be feeling decidedly uneasy because they can think of plenty of people with views they despise on the right and may believe that those extreme rightists just don't care about social justice or fairness at all. And no doubt, many on the moderate right will be able to think of people on the left whose views they despise and feel that I am being much too generous to those extreme leftists. They may believe that those extreme leftists just don't care about liberty at all.

Extreme leftists and rightists certainly exist, but I do not believe they are the majority; nor are they the ones I want to talk about.

Most Liberals are not socialists who put no premium on individual liberty, and think they know what is best for everyone else economically, and would force their knowing on others for their own good. Similarly, most Conservatives are not the social conservatives or religious rightists who put no premium on individual liberty, but think that they know what is best for everyone else in their bedrooms or places of worship and would force their knowing on others for their own good.

Rather, most of us—on the left and the right—share some of the basic respect-thy-neighbor principles of classical liberalism. For that reason, and to understand American politics more accurately, I want to reject this divide....

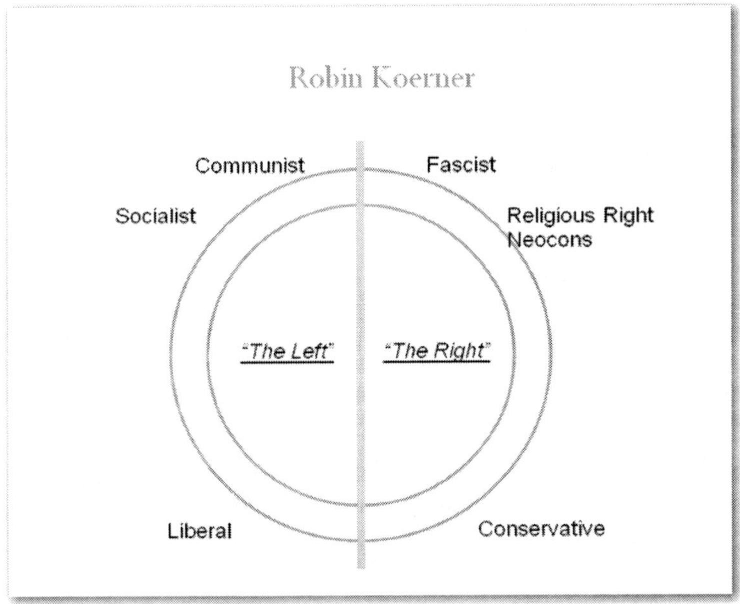

… and create this new one:

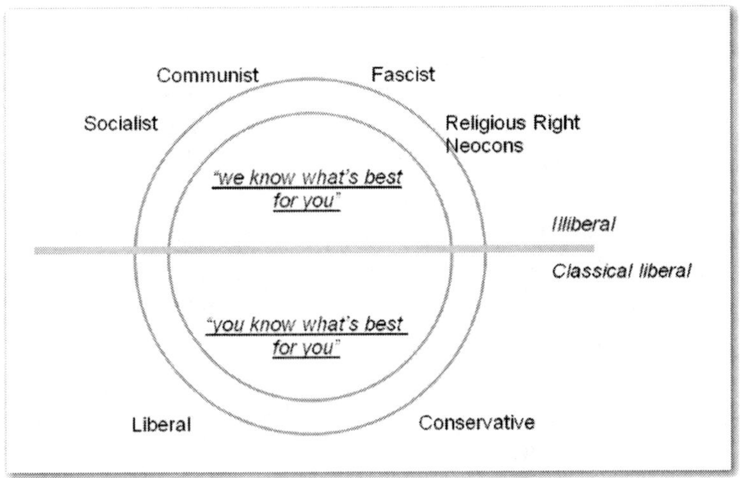

This newly defined political paradigm will help us not only understand our nation's politics more accurately; as we shall explore in the final chapter, it will also help to meet America's most serious challenges more effectively, and as a more unified nation.

A New Spectrum and the Asymmetry of Left and Right

The fundamental difference in American politics is not between the non-extreme left and the non-extreme right, even though the only political position you ever hear of is Left vs Right. Rather, it is between, on the one hand, the moderate left and right (or dare I say, "thinking left and right"?), who share a love of liberty and social justice, but just don't realize it (for reasons we'll see in a moment), and, on the other hand, the extreme left and right, who share a belief that they know what is "best" for everyone. Their difference is that "best" means "economically fairest" to those on the far left, and "morally right" to those on the far right. Nevertheless, both groups share the sense that their moral rightness over-rides others' individual liberty, which, to the rest of us, is something worth preserving in its own right.

Surely a belief in the primacy of individual freedom would appear to be a large enough principle for defining political groupings? But if so, how can it be that those on the moderate left, for example, see those on the moderate right as their opponents, rather than those on the extreme left? And similarly, how can it be that those on the moderate right see those on the moderate left as their opponents, rather than those on the extreme right? The answer is impossible to see until you can step outside of the left/right dichotomy so beloved of our political commentators. And it is inextricably bound up with the false assumption that left and right oppose each other.

The words "left" and "right" are opposites. And once we identify, even slightly, with one, it is hard to understand the other except as an opposite—not only because the words are antonyms, but because there is no adjective of the same class that is in any way "between" left and right. At least black and white, while opposite, are not the only colors. In a world where our political positions were assigned colors, and you identified as "politically black", and thus naturally resisted views deemed "politically white", you would at least be open to the possibility of politically grey, red, blue, green, yellow etc. But there is no analogy when we specify politics using the terms "left" and "right". Moreover, not only are "left" and "right" opposites; even in their common usage, they define an entire space: each refers to everything on one side of a single line. In that sense they are exhaustive and symmetrical opposites.

And it is that apparent symmetry—that opposition—which leads us astray.

The truth is, Left and Right are not symmetric, and they do not entirely oppose each other. The school of thought called classical liberalism can help us to understand why.

Intending Doesn't Make It So

Broadly, Liberals support Liberal policies because they believe that they do good, in that they directly reflect and help to realize a fair or good society. In this sense, if a policy enshrines the moral goal, it achieves its primary purpose, regardless of its secondary consequences. One might say, then, to a Liberal, policies as tools for changing society contain their moral intent explicitly. To a Liberal, that's what politics is for: why even do politics if not to make society more just? Naturally and reasonably, Liberals judge Conservative policies by those standards and, perceiving an absence of moral goals enshrined in Conservative policies or Conservative language that includes nothing explicitly about a fairer society, they are likely to assume that Conservatives have different intentions. Since the Liberal knows that his intentions are good, the Conservatives must be bad.

Notice how this interpretation of the Right by the Left is based on an unconscious assumption of symmetry between Left and Right, and that each side of the political divide can be sensibly judged by the standards of the other.

In fact, Conservatives tend to support Conservative policies not because they believe those policies directly enshrine a moral good per se, but because they work, in that they are mostly likely to bring about the best possible society—a la Friedman. In other words, they prefer policy that will have good outcomes to legislating fairness directly. They generally expect the best possible outcomes in the long run by refusing to interfere with the principles that, to them, precede politics.

The asymmetry between Left and Right lies in the fact that Conservatives don't share with Liberals the unstated assumption that a policy can directly produce fairness or any other social value without causing harm elsewhere. Rather, they dispute the very assumption that politics is the sphere in which good can be engineered. They see the outcomes of policy as removed from the intentions behind its implementation. Rather, they are determined by causes and effects that are related to human action and by incentives that are so complex that we need to be modest about our power to achieve the effects we seek. Many, like Friedman, would have us look to history to see what have been the actual effects of well-intentioned policy in the past. That is not to say that history does not include abundant examples of good things done by the hand of government, but on balance, the Conservative thinks most things would have been better left alone, once all the unintended consequences have been accounted for. Therefore, the Conservative observes that a good intention behind a policy does very little to determine the quality of its outcome, and only outcome can ultimately justify policy—

whereas for a Liberal, it is the good intention that justifies the policy because it is embodied directly in the policy.

To illustrate the point, consider the speech given by David Cameron, elected Prime Minister of the U.K. in 2010, in his last party conference before the election. Seeking to oust the left-of-center Labour party, which, like the American Democrats includes those who would be called political progressives, he said:

> *Next year, Gordon Brown [Labour prime minister] will spend more money on the interest on our debt than on schools. More than on law and order, more than on child poverty.*
>
> *So I say to the Labour Party and the trades unions: just tell me what is compassionate, what is progressive about spending more on debt interest than on helping the poorest children in our country?*

The general point is clear. Often in politics, to pursue socially good, even "progressive" ends, like good schools, a country will inadvertently put itself in a situation that eventually subverts those ends. In this case, Britain had borrowed largely to pay for huge public programs, but now must pay more on servicing that debt than it will pay on the public goods mentioned.

In another part of his speech, Cameron tackles welfare:

> *Just think of the signals we send out. To the family struggling to raise children, pay a mortgage, hold down a job.*
>
> *Stay together and we'll give you less; split up and we give you more.'*
>
> *To the young mum working part time, trying to earn something extra for her family "from every extra pound you earn we'll take back 96 pence."*
>
> *Yes, 96 pence.*

> *Let me say that again, slowly.*
>
> *In Gordon Brown's Britain, if you're a single mother with two kids earning £150 a week the withdrawal of benefits and the additional taxes mean that for every extra pound you earn, you keep just 4 pence.*
>
> *What kind of incentive is that? Thirty years ago this party won an election fighting against 98 per cent tax rates on the richest. Today I want us to show even more anger about 96 per cent tax rates on the poorest.*

The point here is that those benefits to which Cameron was referring were all passed by parliament with the good intention of improving the lives of those in poverty, giving them a cushion and therefore an opportunity with which they can take back economic control of their lives and improve their standard of living. The unseen consequences, though, were the creation of an extraordinarily regressive effective tax that would stop any rational mother who must weigh up the earning of more money, minus the huge withdrawal of government benefits, with the spending time with her child from choosing to go back to work. If she is keeping four cents in every dollar she earns as her benefits are withdrawn, it makes no sense to work. The policy therefore keeps her out of work, dependent on benefits and therefore without any real opportunity to take back control of her life.

So what does a Conservative see, when he looks at a Liberal policy that he disagrees with? Since the Conservative tends not to formulate policy out of good intent, he does not see in Liberal policies bad intent. Rather, he sees misunderstanding or lack of knowledge or both. So to a Liberal, the Conservative is on the wrong end of the good-bad axis, whereas to a Conservative, the Liberal is on the wrong end of the right-wrong axis! The lack of symmetry between Conservative and Liberal politics is thus revealed.

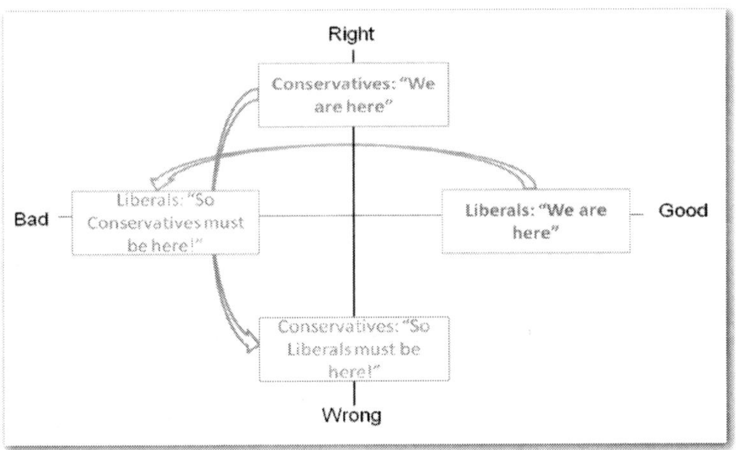

This is why the left and right so often talk past each other. They respond not just to each other's policies, but to something they assume about their opponents as they try to understand the policies without being in their opponents' heads. In other words, the perpetuation of this false divide in our political discourse is a specific example of what goes wrong when we do not pay heed to the 2x2 matrix in the first chapter. When it comes to Right vs. Left, we can effectively respond to our opponents when we understand not only how they perceive their own actions, but also how they mistakenly perceive ours. Those perceptions are as much political facts as are actual policy.

Just as Newton's classical mechanics and Einstein's Relativity are "incommensurate paradigms" to use Kuhn's term, American Liberalism and American Conservatism are "incommensurate paradigms"—meaning that they cannot be fully expressed in the language of, and based on the assumptions of, the other.

The paradigms can be transcended, however, by the recognition that while the Left seeks to measure good policy by whether principles of Liberty and Fairness are evident in their

formulation, the Right seeks to measure good policy by whether principles of Liberty and Fairness are evident in their effects.
In summary,

The Left – Moral	**The Right** – Empirical
• "These policies are right" (moral intent, focused on the means)	• "These policies work" (empirical understanding, focused on the ends)
- therefore -	*- therefore -*
• Opponents have wrong intent	• Opponents have wrong understanding
- therefore -	*- therefore -*
• The Right is bad	• The Left is wrong.

Seeing this asymmetry between the right and left is of critical importance, as it reveals the golden nugget of shared sensibility of the moderate Left and the moderate Right. It shines a light on which elements of both Left and Right are actually at odds with the principles of liberty and social justice (used in a pure sense, not as a code word for social engineering) that lie at the heart of both the American Left and the American Right—on the Left as the driving intentions in the formulation of policy, and on the Right as the metrics for measuring the practical outcome of policy.

In taking up this political ecumenism, we must be aware of the different operating assumptions of the left and right. The left assumes that the power of government makes it the most effective entity for doing good, while the right assumes that the power of the government makes it the most effective entity for doing damage. It is certainly a fact that all law that is not in the spirit of old English "common law" is an expression of government force and so skepticism is the correct starting position. When the right fails to articulate this skepticism in relation to a particular policy debate, it can appear to the left as heartless or intransigent.

As a concrete example, consider a speech given by Donald Berwick about the US healthcare system to a British audience, whose healthcare is delivered by the government-funded and run NHS (National Health Service). Obama appointed Berwick in 2010 to the position of Administrator of the Centers of Medicare and Medicaid Services.

Berwick said:

> *So you could have had a simpler, less ambitious, less troubled plan than the NHS. You could have had the American Plan. You could have been spending 17% of your GDP to make healthcare unaffordable as a human right, instead of spending 9% and guaranteeing it as a human right. You could have kept your system in fragments and encouraged supply-driven demand instead of making tough choices and planning supply. You could have made hospitals and specialists, and not general practice, your mainstay. You could have obscured. You could have obliterated accountability and left it to the invisible hand of the market instead of holding your politicians ultimately accountable for getting the NHS sorted. You could have let an unaccountable system play out in the darkness of private enterprise instead of accepting that a politically accountable system must act in the harsh and the sometimes very unfair daylight of the press, public debate and political campaigning. You could have had a monstrous insurance industry of claims and rules and paper pushing instead of using your tax base to provide a single route of finance. You could have*

> *protected the wealthy and the well instead of recognizing that the sick people tend to be poorer and that poor people tend to be sicker. And that any healthcare funding plan that is just, equitable, civilized and humane must, must, redistribute wealth from the richer among us to the poorer and the less fortunate. Excellent healthcare is by definition redistributional. Britain, you chose well.*

A good Liberal will respond to this positively. On the surface, the paragraph comprises statements of fact, marshaled to point out the failures of the American healthcare system. Except for the last couple of sentences, there may be nothing at all in this speech that is false or unreasonable. But look closely at how the statements are chosen, and the erroneous assumption with which the speech is infused, which is that the described problems that are indicated are caused by private enterprise rather than government intervention. The italicized sentences in the above are real problems of the American healthcare system that the Liberal is concerned with fixing and that Berwick is wrongly presenting as a result of the free market at work. The underlined sentences are those places where Berwick makes incorrect assumptions explicit. Every one of the italicized statements is, in fact, caused by bad, incoherent government involvement, or the absence of a free market. That is not to say that Berwick is in fact wrong that Britain's socialized system of healthcare produces better outcomes than the system today in the USA, or that Britain benefited from the government takeover of healthcare provision in the 1940s, both of which claims may be true without supporting Berwick's understanding of why America needs to follow Britain's lead to get out of the peculiar problem it has created in its own healthcare industry.

While a thorough treatment of the problems of American healthcare is beyond the scope of this book, set against Berwick's speech, we should point out the following.

Most of that 17% of health spending in the USA is not in any form of private market, but is government spending through Medicaid and Medicare.

The fundamental mechanism by which free markets affordably deliver goods to people is by giving those people incentive to look for value by weighing the lowest possible price for a service against the highest quality of that service. It is a bizarre government law that incentivizes employers to provide health insurance (to gain tax benefits) that means that users of health services have no incentive to shop for low prices at the point of consumption: they (indirectly) and their employer (directly) have already paid for the service through insurance and so the cost of the service is completely irrelevant to the consumer at the time of delivery. Therefore, the ONE market mechanism for keeping down prices to levels that are determined chiefly by the cost of producing and delivering the service is eliminated. For this reason alone, the healthcare industry—before the passing of the new healthcare laws—was the least free market industry in the entire United States. Therefore, Berwick's claim that the invisible hand of the free market is the cause of the problems in American healthcare is not just wrong. It is the opposite of the truth. Again, though, we should be clear. Berwick is sincere: he operates in a paradigm that assumes that legislation from good intentions is the primary driver of good results. Once he makes that assumption, the lack of good results in the American healthcare system is per se evidence to him that lack of government action—and therefore, the presence of the only thing that exists in its absence, the free market—must be responsible for the mess America's healthcare system is in.

As is well known, insurance companies are prevented from competing across state lines, another aspect of the American healthcare system that prevents any kind of free market from working. Insurance companies are certainly blameworthy in the ill-treatment of many Americans, but the lack of operation of the free-market, which would give patients access to the services of competitors, prevents victims from voting with their feet.

There are many other points that can be brought against Berwick, most of which have been explicated extensively by the opponents of Obama's efforts to reform healthcare. But the above few are enough at least to illustrate the detrimental effect of the political paradigm on political perspective.

If you identify as a Liberal and don't accept the foregoing, then accept for now that there may be at least a strong case that the interests of those who suffer from the mess of America's healthcare system will only be maximally served by looking at real data and discerning the effects of government (of which there are many) from the effects of market action (of which there are fewer) in the health sector.

A moderate Conservative who might make the above objections to Berwick would be taking issue with Berwick's factual claims—some explicitly but most implicitly—about the causes of outcomes. Moreover, a Conservative would see the outcomes of bad government involvement in American healthcare as typical of the effects of government involvement in the meeting of any important human needs. But to a Liberal, the Conservative's saying "No" to the changes the Left wishes to make, is to say "No" not only to those changes, but to those humane instincts that motivate the Liberal's desire to impose those changes. (Hence, "Those Republicans just don't care about the uninsured.") The Liberal, then, can rightly demand of the Conservative, "Well, if you really do care, what would you do?" And the Conservative answer, which will be motivated by the desire to deliver the best outcome possible, will probably start with an absence of attempts by legal force to deliver an ideal outcome, based on the belief that this mechanism, all things being equal, is the most likely to fail.

So we have a situation in which the humane Liberal has a

problem of trust in the Conservative. In the case of healthcare, their question is, "if these Conservatives really care about everyone's healthcare, why are they happy to have a system that does not guarantee delivery to all?". And the best Conservative answer is a version of Friedman's answer, above: negatively, the attempt to guarantee provision will fail, based on evidence of government involvement in various fields, in various countries, at various times, and positively, this fact should not be surprising anyway since (as the classical liberals never stopped pointing out), free individuals in free association can act in their best interest more effectively than can a system planned by removed individuals that, even were they geniuses, depends on a) the imposition of the system by law (and therefore force) and b) the elimination or prevention of any communitarian solutions to the social or economic problem that is to be solved.

There is another philosophical difference that, when forgotten, separates the Liberal from the Conservative: The Right's preferred mechanism for the delivery of economic and social good works precisely because people act not out of good "liberal" intention but out of a self-interest that expresses no such intention.

With this in mind, let's return to Berwick's error. Berwick claims that excellent healthcare is necessarily redistributive. Again, if you start with a system in which access is artificially restricted—which will always hurt the poor the most—then the delivery of the service to all, by definition, involves a redistribution. But Berwick means that the provision of this service depends on forced redistribution, and in that he is wrong, as can be seen by considering the fact that even the poorest Americans have access to affordable food—as critical as healthcare, obviously—which is distributed to them in a matter that satisfies their needs almost completely. Not only is the food-coverage of Americans practically 100% complete without the guarantee of food provision by force of law, but also attempts to guarantee that complete provision of food to all Americans have failed everywhere they have ever been attempted. In the way that matters then, the Conservative would argue that the end that Berwick is seeking—the distribution of the service (uniform in that everyone has enough food to live) in a manner that decouples it from the distribution of wealth (which is completely non-uniform, varying massively among individuals)—is at odds with the method that Berwick believes will get us there, which is forced provision of that service. Certainly, the USA has foodstamps, but the system that makes healthy food affordable for all has developed in the absence of forced provision.[20] In the USA today, you may have 100 times more money than I do, but we both can afford 100% of the food we need, and that is the point. In socialist states, and still in countries whose farmers suffer from tariffs imposed on their goods, governmental control of production invariably limits access to food.

We can now see why Conservatives and Liberals so often appear intractably opposed even though they do not need to be. If each group understands the other as sharing a desire to maximize a social good within their own paradigm, necessarily incomplete like one's own, then ideological debates, (emotionally charged by clashes between good motivation and imputed bad motivation, and between understanding and perceived naiveté) can be diffused, and the political question of "which side is right?" becomes reframed as a practical question of "how best do we

---

[20] One may still object that some people are in poverty, and government assistance is required to get it to them. As we shall see in the next chapter, this is not because the production or delivery of food in a free market is too expensive, but that other systemic problems with our system of money and inflation have made the poorest Americans artificially poor. Finally, an argument that government welfare is ineffective is not to argue that welfare should not be available through communitarian approaches, for example, as we will also consider later.

achieve?".

For a Liberal or a Conservative to agree with the foregoing, she does not need to change her fundamental beliefs about what is "so" or what is "right", but just to acknowledge that apparent political division arises from incompleteness of knowledge, or more accurately, a failure to recognize the incompleteness of one's knowledge—especially about the paradigm of one's opponents.

We Cannot Imagine What We Have Never Seen

Why is it so hard for us to see this, to break free of our paradigms, to come up with whole new political approaches? Why do we mistake our partial knowledge for complete knowledge—a mistake made more likely by a lack of political imagination? It is hard because we can't imagine what we have never seen, and we cannot easily think in a way we have never thought.

Although we think we are divided left vs. right, we all live in one country in which the most important large-scale social and political programs are delivered in only one way—through the force of federal law, by people who are motivated by salary, rather than by an interest in improving the outcomes of the programs that they help to deliver.

All developed Western democracies are basically social democracies. The term implies that what is done in the name of society is a kind of collective compromise or perhaps even a distillation of the best intentions and practices of a nation. But the term is entirely misleading, because none of us, left or right, can significantly influence the most important social or economic programs that operate in our communities. The implementation of social and economic programs is entirely non-democratic because the "demos" (people) have no "kratos" (power) in those programs. They cannot directly see the good they do, or the evil. They cannot see the effects on the people from whom resources are taken, and the effects on those to whom they are given. They do not choose what works in their communities and what has already failed. We cannot see these effects because for many possible reasons: we may be far from them; they may be evident only over long periods, or, as we considered in Chapter 1, the most important effects may even be those that cannot be seen in principle, because they are those things that have been prevented from happening.

If citizens had more direct experience of the complexity of the effects of policy on individual lives in their own communities, including, critically, the unintended and unobvious consequences, and had any way to feed that experience back into improvements to the policy, then the crass mode of left. vs. right argumentation would lose its power as soon as its failure to say very much about the outcomes of policy, and help in its creative improvement, became evident.

Most Westerners have never seen what universal healthcare provision looks like without a government, and so we cannot imagine it. Similarly, in the West, the last people who saw the provision of economic safety nets by local communities died a long time ago. When somebody points out that government is not the only institution that can provide a good to an entire society, it is easy to agree in principle, even though we may not know what the alternatives could look like. However, an even more important point is much less obvious: where the government is not observably acting, we are not necessarily seeing the results of the collective actions of individuals' making a free choice, and we are very unlikely to be seeing the operations of a free market. That's important because people often default to government action having decided that voluntary action, or market action, cannot deliver a particular social or economic good.

As we shall see in the next chapter, the government (and banks) have their greatest effect on our lives in ways that are the least visible, and should be equally offensive to the both political left and right, who, after all, have something in common: we don't know what we don't know and there are some things that are hidden from all of us.

No One Has a Monopoly on Empiricism

In the Bush years, the term "reality-based community" began to be seen increasingly to describe the moderate left. The term was coined by the left to distinguish their approach, quite fairly, from the neo-cons. Their reasonable point was that the neocon right-wing (not the small-government right I have been referring to) was formulating policy apparently based on an overarching grand design, (as articulated for example, in the Project for the New American Century). This design, it seemed, was being implemented globally at the cost of many hundreds of thousands of lives in such countries as Iraq and elsewhere. Since the policies did not appear to take us closer even to the stated grand design, to the moderate left and, later, we would find out, to many of the moderate right, the neocon project seemed to be carried out in spite of reality—rather than as an engagement with it.

The term "Reality-based" community, then, was a good name for moderate Liberals who wanted to formulate policy in response to America's current situation and as the effects of its current and recent policies. As the term implies, this type of politics is indeed decidedly empirical, looking to events, including the responses of other political actors to events and America's actions. This results-orientation on the Left during the Bush years sounds more like the approach I assigned to the moderate right above. What are we to make of this?

First, to repeat, those on the moderate left share a purpose with those on the moderate right. This purpose is in contrast with the shared purpose of neocons or socialists, which is to deny the primacy of individual liberty for a so-called "greater good". Second, there is a difference between left empiricism and right empiricism. While both empiricisms are worthy of the name, the left tends to believe that a practical political response is one formulated in the light of the evidence of the here-and-now, while the right tends to believe that a practical response is one formulated in the light of the accumulated evidence of history.

The immediate and obvious objection is that the left, through the likes of Marx etc., has a tradition of highly historical interpretations of the political. But they hold little sway now in American political life, being decidedly mechanistic and nineteenth-century. Moreover, this kind of leftist historiography is completely unlike the discourse of the modern moderate left in the USA.

In moderate politics, the left is being empirical when it formulates legislation or looks for state action that is directly targeted against a problem that is presently observable. From this perspective, they may see the right as decidedly non-empirical, because they resist such action, seeming to the left to deny the existence of the observable problem, or at the very least, to deny its importance. To the left, this can smack of not just a lack of empiricism or a refusal to be reality-based, but of a certain moral indifference. Again, this would be an erroneous conclusion born of incommensurate paradigms: in such cases, the right is being highly empirical in its resistance to legislation or policy, because it seeks to draw on an empirical understanding—even if induced from historical data—of not just the practical situation that is to be dealt with now, but the outcomes of governmental (as opposed to voluntary) approaches taken to such problems before and elsewhere. "Reality-based", then, while fairly used by many on the moderate left, is perhaps a term worth fighting for by the right.

CHAPTER 3

Land of the Free?

UNDERSTANDING THE AMERICAN Left and Right is critical to our being able to lift ourselves out of the political boxes that determine our perceptions. It can help us see commonality where we saw none before and, hopefully, find ways to move a divided country forward together. Most importantly, since our paradigms dictate the news we hear and the way we read it, seeing through the left/right division can help us to leave behind the paradigms and assumptions we bring to the media that report to us about our country, and be better able to see through them to the facts on the ground and the real American story.

But the most pervasive paradigms are not those associated with our political tribes, but with our very identity as Americans.

The assumptions that most strongly determine the direction of our nation may be those associated with paradigms that are shared by all Americans—not those associated with only the political paradigms of the Left or the Right. These are the paradigms that, within typical American discourse and thought at least, have no opposites.

What, then, could be said to constitute "the American paradigm"?

What concepts are so much part of our identity that they are found throughout our social and political history; can be found in the very justification for our existence as a nation, declared in the Declaration of Independence; written into the legal foundation of our nation, as in our Constitution; referred to informally throughout our culture, are impossible explicitly to dishonor by those in power; set the standards for our national heroes, set the standards by which we judge other nations; form the moral themes of our movies; are challenged and resolved in our TV dramas, and would, for all these reasons (and more) be the answer given by the majority of Americans to the question, "Who are we?"

We all know the answer.

We are, we aspire to be, or at the very least we think of ourselves as, The Land of the Free and The Land of Opportunity.

The first epithet refers broadly to civil and social freedoms and rights; the second refers broadly to our economic freedoms and an environment that rewards both entrepreneurism and effort.

How great is the gap between this dual-pillared American paradigm and American reality in the early 21st century? In this chapter, we'll consider the first of those pillars—the United States as the Land of the Free; in the next, we'll consider the second—the United States as the Land of Opportunity.

How We Won the War on Terror (9-11-01 to 12-1-11)—A Satire

On 1 Dec. 2011, American citizens celebrated in the streets as their government snatched final victory in the War on Terror—through a maneuver that used legislative brilliance rather than bullets.

The moment of victory came when 61 Senators passed a

version of the National Defense Authorization Act for Fiscal year 2012[21] that allows the indefinite military detention on American soil of American citizens who are merely suspected of having connections to terrorism.

To understand the genius of this legislation, some background is necessary. The Patriot Act, passed before the dust of the collapsed World Trade Center had settled, had already removed the fourth amendment rights of Americans to privacy, allowing federal authorities access to the private affairs of individuals without any court oversight. That act had also removed their rights under the first amendment to free speech, by making it illegal, for example, for one American to tell another that he has been served with a warrant under the Patriot Act—not, of course, a warrant issued by a court, but by a federal officer who can now write his own warrants without any judicial oversight.

What Senators McCain (R, Arizona) and Levin (D, Michigan), and those who voted for the legislation that they sponsored, cleverly realized, however, is that since the terrorists are attacking America for its freedoms and "way of life", the only sure way to win the war is to eliminate all of those freedoms and way of life so that the terrorists will have no further reason to fight. (This is why the comprehensive laws that already exist in the USA that make the aiding and abetting of any terrorist organization or activity a crime, but leave untouched the inalienable rights of American citizens, simply do not suffice.)

For that reason, on 1 December 2011, an amendment to the aforementioned National Defense Authorization Act that would seek to preserve the very last freedom of Americans—to receive due process, including the right to a trial by jury, as required in the Constitution, before being detained by the state—was

[21] http://www.opencongress.org/bill/112-h1540/show

defeated, ensuring that no American freedom, and therefore no reason for the terrorists to hate America—any longer existed. Now, and thankfully for those who wish to defend the American values of peace and freedom, Americans can be detained by the military without trial or limitation.

The achievement of the U.S. Congress is all the greater in the light of the United States' own Department of Defense study[22], headed by Robert Pape of the University of Chicago, that collected and analyzed huge amounts of data on suicide terrorism—which is 12 times more dangerous than other forms of terrorism when measured by the number of people killed per incident. In this U.S. government study, speakers of the local languages of the families of suicide bombers were sent to speak with family members of the terrorists to gain as much information as possible about the context and the people involved, and the database thus obtained on suicide terrorism is, as far as we know, the most comprehensive in the world.

The most astonishing conclusion of this work, however, was that 95 percent of all suicide terrorist attacks—going back to the 1980s—are against countries that the terrorist regards as occupying (in the sense of a military presence) physical territory that the terrorist regards as a homeland. This 95 percent figure includes attacks by all those radical Islamic groups who have attacked Israel and the USA. It explains why the U.S., for example, has only suffered such attacks (such as on 9/11/2001), from citizens of countries in which it has a military presence: as the DOD study points out, we were attacked by Saudis on 9-11, but not Iranians, Sudanese or representatives of other countries with a large radical Islamist contingent, and Saudi Arabia is the country that plays host to American military forces.

Thankfully, though, McCain and Levin—and the majority of

[22] http://www.youtube.com/watch?v=X4HnIyClHEM

the U.S. Congress—know better than to listen to their own military, whose studies are clearly distorted by their desire to understand their enemy so as to minimize the loss of life of soldiers, airmen, sailors and marines. Since understanding the true nature of the threat to the USA puts the country on the slippery slope to confining its actions to those that would actually counter, and possibly, therefore, defeat it, removing the need for this new martial law, the National Defense Authorization Act has been carefully written with absolutely no mechanism restoring American rights when the terrorists put down their arms, as they are bound to do when they realize that their reason to fight has been—just as many Americans can now be—"disappeared".

This "locking in" of the elimination of the Bill of Rights will certainly help Americans sleep better in the knowledge that the war on terror, now won, will not begin again should the USA slip back, in a moment of weakness, to the freedoms that caused the foreign haters to take up arms against the United States in the first place.

There are, however, a few reports of fringe elements in the USA, most of whom seem naively enthralled by outmoded political ideologies such as Constitutionalism, and the "just war doctrine" (an outdated idea, rooted in the Judaic and Christian traditions, that wars are just if they increase the safety of the combatants, have a defined goal and are winnable), who are not joining the victory parades.

In interviews and social media, they have been repeating what appear superficially to be anachronistic pleas, but may in fact be something much more sinister—expressions of terrorist sympathies. Most of them seem to be a version of the idea that if America gives up its Bill of Rights for safety, that not only will the terrorists have won, but that America, itself, handed them the victory.

Indeed, one wrote, "If the government is going to protect my life, it must first leave my life full of the liberties that make it worth protecting." [23] Although such extremist sentiments could obviously become dangerous were they to take hold more widely, there is little danger of that, as the federal authorities already have their eyes on the dangerous elements who are most likely to share them—including people who manufacture coins out of precious metal[24], own weather-proofed ammunition[25], may be missing a finger or two, or—perhaps the most dangerous of all—those who typically have seven days of food in their home.

We should be glad that we no longer have to wait for the smoking gun to come in the form of a terrorist food hoarder's giant mushroom[26]: the National Defense Authorization Act now permits the feds to lock her up forever on suspicion alone, without all the difficulties that attend a trial.

Post 9-11: The Politics of Fear

There are hundreds of good books about the loss of basic liberties in America today, and there are thousands of compromises of those liberties that are suffered by Americans that really do warrant all those pages and all that ink. I mentioned a few in "Your Last Freedom". I'm not going to rehearse them all here, but take for granted that you, the reader, have a deep sense that the compromises of every one of the rights in the Bill of Rights are both pervasive and deep. If you need a refresher, scan the relevant part of that opening chapter again.

There is little doubt that some of the most egregious eliminations of our basic rights—such as the right to privacy

---

23 http://www.huffingtonpost.com/robin-koerner/a-decade-after-911-time-t_b_957236.html

24 http://www.fbi.gov/charlotte/press-releases/2011/defendant-convicted-of-minting-his-own-currency

25 http://www.youtube.com/watch?v=anjVgWNzQnk

26 http://www.cnn.com/2003/US/01/10/wbr.smoking.gun/index.html

(including the right to have our personal effects, and that includes our data neither searched nor seized), the right to due legal process before forfeiting our property or even life to the state; the general right to be left alone as long as we harm no one else—have been perpetrated against the People since 9/11.

For that reason, and because my permanent residency in the United States has been entirely since the terrible events of that day, I will confine my brief observations in this area to this most recent period.

The politics of our nation since 9/11 have been the politics of fear.

Because of fear that one of us is a terrorist, we've allowed our intelligence services to listen into our private conversations; because of fear of terrorists from abroad, we have killed innocent people in foreign nations (supposedly to protect ourselves here); because of fear that our planes will get blown up, we let government agents put their hands on our children's crotches and look at our naked bodies, and because of fear that the economy will implode, we've given trillions of dollars to organizations that have brought us to that point.

None of it feels very brave or free. None of it feels very American.

Nations confident of their strength don't seek fights. The most powerful nations win without firing a shot. Nations confident of their security and the ability of their agents to maintain it don't compromise the dignity or legal rights of its citizens. Nations confident that the innovativeness and entrepreneurism of its people can provide prosperity don't reward bad custodians of financial resources to "save the system."

America has surely been a great nation. But with true greatness—true power—comes self-confidence. What has happened to the America that the world used to love, even if in some quarters, grudgingly? It was always American self-confidence, justified largely by the examples we set regarding the treatment of our people and, during our grander historical moments, other people, on which our leadership depended. We were respected and powerful to the extent that other nations wanted to be like us—to have our prosperity, our freedom and our openness.

In the light of all of that, we would do well to ask, who have we become today and who do we appear to be?

Minimizing risk at reasonable cost is the action of a sensible man or nation. Trying to eliminate all risk at any cost—not only financial, but also of principle—is the action of a man or nation that has become obsessive, compulsive, scared, or all three.

A few years ago, a friend of mine returned from a tour in Iraq as a proud American soldier to be required at Seattle airport to remove his shoes and equipment and be screened in the full fashion. The treatment shocked him as it was his first encounter with it and gave the lie to what he believed was his purpose a day earlier on the streets of Baghdad. Simply, how could he have been fighting over there to protect American liberties and values if they were being compromised away with so little fight at home?

The rest of us might ask how we so easily take away the Fourth Amendment right of that soldier, who a day earlier had put his life on the line for our Fourth Amendment (and other) right(s). We could ask a similar question about the First Amendment right of a Vietnam vet who is now a member of the tea party and is on a government agency list as a potential troublemaker for that reason, or, to push the point further, the inalienable right of the small businessman to pursue happiness and be treated equally with all others if his taxes are being used to bail out the bank that holds his mortgage but made poorer business decisions than he did.

The use of force—whether legal or military—always reveals a failure of some other, preferable means. If our sons and daughters in uniform are truly fighting for American freedoms, then those freedoms must all still exist at home uncompromised:

inasmuch as we give them up at home, those men and women cannot be fighting to protect them, just as a matter of simple logic. Those of us who are fortunate enough to stay at home while our soldiers fight abroad, demean their service if we are too lazy not to speak out in opposition when our leaders compromise our Constitutional rights (always for our own good). And if, worse, we support those compromises out of our own fear, then we meet our soldiers' bravery with our own cowardice.

In the last century, America led the free world by being the indispensable nation that others sought to emulate. But obsessive, scared nations, like obsessive scared people, are not models for anyone. America had led the free world by persuasion, based on a moral authority that came with the rights and prosperity that its legal and economic systems provided for its people. As our nation has ceased to trust in those rights and the system that has provided its prosperity, we have given up moral authority and persuasive power. That is why so many of our attempts to make ourselves safer will fail in their stated purpose.

The national shock of 9/11 is, at the time of publication, about 14 years behind us. We can afford by now to take a deep breath. If anyone attacks us, we'll still be able to respond with the greatest military force in the history of the world. If anyone should infiltrate us, we have some of the most honorable men and women and the best technological means to find them, and a justice system, older than the country itself, to deal with them. If we face a recession, we can take our losses and come back with the ingenuity and effort of an entrepreneurial and serious population. If another nation should grow its economy in leaps and bounds, we can say "good luck" to them, because we know we can do that too.

We call our country the land of the free and the home of the brave. But who, honestly, is feeling brave and free today?

Can America get its swagger back—for the good of the world, let alone ourselves?

Being the America that we were founded to be is a choice. We can swagger without shouting. We can carry the big stick and not be the first to use it. And we can instinctively say "Hell, no" each time anyone would take it upon themselves to take even one of our liberties away to make us "safer" or for any other purpose.

I wonder how many Americans would voluntarily fly in a commercial jet in which passengers did not go through today's imaging scanners or the full pat-down at the airport, but went only through the security procedures that were in place on Sept. 10, 2001? All passengers would know, along with any potential terrorist, that our flight is marginally less secure.

The risk of attack would, I suppose, be marginally higher than it would be on those planes whose passengers had gone through today's procedures. But since it is about nine times less than the risk of dying by suffocation in my own bed, I would take the odds to make the statement that as an American, following Franklin, I will not give up my liberty for my safety; that I want America back; that I would rather have the Bill of Rights than the extra 0.0001 percent reduction in the probability of being blown out of the sky. I bet there would be millions like me.

There is no such thing as certainty. If you don't want uncertainty, then you don't want life. Americans have always embraced uncertainty and taken life by the scruff of the neck. The real question is, "if I am to take a risk, for what is the risk worth taking?"

If the government is going to protect my life, it must first leave my life full of the liberties that make it worth protecting. And in the USA, when those two things are in tension (and they rarely are, despite what we are told), it should be up to the individual to decide on the balance.

If we so choose, we have the power to make the last 14 years of fear, wars, invasions of privacy, bailouts etc. the exception to the rule of American history, rather than the new normal. It would be the choice to be changed by not what comes at us but what comes from us.

9/11 was a historically unprecedented shock and we acted accordingly. We were shaken. No shame in that. But at any time, we can choose to take stock at what we have collectively done to our nation and determine whether it has served us and will serve our children. We may disagree on what we find but I'd wager that many will say that we have compromised away more of our own identity than any terrorist attack ever did take or ever could take.

On that day, terrorists took approximately 3,000 lives. The loss was severe; we should learn its lessons of sensible precaution and humility. Each one of those lost souls was—is—an infinity, and we should never forget them. It goes without saying that the relevant agencies should be fully resourced to protect us, and their work supported—right up to the point that America is in danger of no longer being American.

Yet, fewer lives were taken on 9/11 than are lost in one month on American roads. Everything else that we may have lost since then in our so-called "war against terrorism", we have consented to lose.

In fear and shock, we may have given the terrorists more of what they really wanted, by making ourselves poorer in both treasure and liberty.

Osama Bin Laden said:

> *All we have to do is send two mujahidin...to raise a small piece of cloth on which is written 'al-Qaeda' in order to make the generals race there, to cause America to suffer human, economic and political losses.*

While some of the expenditures of treasure may have been wise, were all of those of liberty, too?

To remain the land of the free and the home of the brave, America must see where it has fallen short of its promise to itself and choose to be itself again. Indeed, to honor the memories of our countrymen lost on 9/11, we must choose to become more truly American than we have ever been.

How will we know when we've done that? At the very least, we will have more civil liberties than we did on 10 Sept 2001—not fewer; and we will be less frightened—not more.

Privacy vs. Security—a False Dichotomy

The Fourth Amendment prohibits unreasonable searches and seizures and requires any warrant to be judicially sanctioned and supported by probable cause. It was adopted in response to the abuse of the writ of assistance, a type of general search warrant issued by the British government in pre-Revolutionary America.

It refers to the natural right that has arguably been the most pervasively abused by the US government these last few years, through such executive agencies as the NSA. In fact, the abuse of this right could not be more perfect if the actions of the NSA were actually calculated to violate the amendment as completely as possible: government agents now search records about your activities (such as the phone calls you make, when and to whom) that involve only you and other private persons or companies (such as your friends or your phone network provider); they store (seize) that data and they do it all without probable cause concerning your guilt in a crime, and they do it all under a more general search warrant than even the British government deployed in the 18th century.

We have fallen far.

Why? The answer again relates to fear.

There is really only one argument in support of mass surveillance by the State: increased security can be bought with reduced privacy.

That claim begs the question: "how much privacy buys how much security?"

It is almost impossible to imagine how two completely different abstractions—security and liberty—could be compared, when idiomatically, we can't even compare apples and oranges, so we should be very uneasy that an entire political age has been built on just such a comparison.

But, since our leaders insist on making it, and it is the only one they ever make for extinguishing our civil rights, and in particular our privacy, let's run with it ...

To the defenders of the surveillance state, security means "saving American lives". That is why Feinstein and her ilk justify governmental surveillance with statements like, "the NSA's bulk collection of metadata might have prevented 9/11".

That only makes sense as a justification if the privacy of all Americans is of less value than 2996 innocent American lives. Of course, it's not just our privacy that has been sacrificed: our freedom of speech and our right to due process have been sacrificed by the same laws, and with the same justification, that paved the way to systematic and secret violation of privacy. So what the likes of Feinstein are really saying is that the American way of life has less value than 2996 innocent lives.

Moreover, most of the same people in government who advocate sacrificing the American way of life (liberty) to save American lives (security) support the sacrificing of American lives to save the American way of life.

This inconsistency goes beyond the moral: it verges on the mathematical.

To date, the American government has, in the War of on Terror, sacrificed nearly 7000 American lives and somewhere between a hundred thousand and a million non-American lives to "protect" (so we are told) the American way of life.[27]

Our way of life, of which our privacy is an important part,

---

[27] http://en.wikipedia.org/wiki/War_on_Terror

cannot simultaneously be worth fewer than the 2996 American lives lost on 9/11 and more than the approx. 7000 American service personnel and hundreds of thousands of innocents we have killed abroad.[28]

Assuming Feinstein and friends are not being deliberately disingenuous, what she must really mean is that the surveillance state, and the War on Terror of which it is a part, would not just have saved 2996 Americans on 9-11, but that they are saving more American lives than, all the Americans we have lost through fighting "the War on Terror", plus the non-American lives taken by our actions (presumably and somewhat sickeningly weighted by some factor that makes each one worth less than a "saved American"), plus whatever value we might give to the American way of life, which includes our privacy (measured, for mathematical consistency) in terms of a number of lives.

Indeed, precisely this ability to quantify is assumed when Obama tells us of the need to "balance" or "weigh up" our security against our liberty.

Since no one is arguing that killing innocent foreigners makes us any safer, but our government has killed huge numbers of them, it is apparent that the more closely an innocent non-American life is valued to an innocent American one, the more American lives must be saved by the sacrifice of liberty to reach this so-called balance between liberty and security.

Our leaders keep getting away with this nonsense because, as far as I know, not one politician or journalist has yet asked two obvious questions on which this entire trade-off of security and liberty depends. 1) How many American lives is the American way of life worth, and 2) how many innocent non-American lives have the same value as an innocent American life?

There is only one pair of answers that is mathematically and

---

[28] http://en.wikipedia.org/wiki/United_States_military_casualti...

morally consistent with the Bush/Obama/Feinstein case for eliminating basic civil rights, including privacy, as part of the War on Terror: the value of a non-American life must be de minimus, and the value of American liberty must be approximately zero.

Either the math is wrong. Or the morality is wrong. Or both.

So much for the variables. What about the logical inconsistency: if liberty must be sacrificed to save American lives, how can sacrificing lives for liberty possibly be justified? If there are mathemagical numbers that can resolve that paradox, let's have them.

Denis Diderot, one of the most famous thinkers of the Enlightenment, rightly remarked, "In order to shake a hypothesis, it is sometimes not necessary to do anything more than push it as far as it will go."

An internally inconsistent hypothesis doesn't need to be set up against a competing one to be shown to be false. It simply collapses under the weight of its own contradiction when examined closely. So let's push the buy-security-with-liberty hypothesis as far as it will go.

And because I believe in competition, I'll offer up my own base-case strategy for preserving American liberty and lives.

It's in two parts, and it's really complicated.

Here goes.

1) Don't give up any liberties. 2) Don't put Americans in harm's way.

Now, I am aware that this kind of extremist politics may not keep all Americans safe in a utopia of liberty: after all, 9-11 happened. But I do know that if you don't give up any of your liberty, then you still have all of your liberty (I'm definitely going to beat Feinstein and Obama on logic) and that making others feel secure does more for one's own security than doing the opposite.

Perhaps I am wrong—and if I am, the NSA will be the people to prove it.

After all, they're the guys with all the data.

Do Unto Others…

Later in the book, we shall discuss in depth the Declaration of Independence, the Constitution and their origins.

For the purposes of this chapter, I'd like to make just one observation about them. The philosophical basis of the Constitution of our nation is that life, liberty and the pursuit of happiness are natural rights, meaning that they inhere in us by virtue of our very nature as human beings—not because some doctrine says so or some institution grants them.

Therefore, although our Constitution is obviously written for the benefit of Americans, we cannot be true to our identity as Americans if we violate those inalienable rights of others, because those others are human beings too. Sheer logical consistency then forces us to honor the rights of non-Americans in actions that we justify as protecting our own life, liberty and pursuit of happiness. To do otherwise would be to deny our very own Declaration of Independence.

Therefore, it is worth taking a moment to consider directly the huge problem of violent intervention abroad. Just Google "American military interventions" to see the extraordinary extent to which our nation does this around the world.

I approach the politics of life-and-death questions, which include all questions concerning military intervention abroad, with a thought experiment: I imagine looking in the eyes of the mother of a person who would die if the intervention be carried through, but who would live if an opposing course of action were carried through. I imagine trying to justify to that mother why her son should die for the greater good that I believe justifies the intervention.

This approach sets a very high bar for justification of not only the good that will be done and the bad that will be prevented by a particular policy, but also the trustworthiness and accuracy of the knowledge on which one's analysis of a situation is based.

In other words, it gets one out of one's paradigm. At the very least, it puts life or, if you prefer, humanity, above our own inevitably imperfect understandings of complex situations.

Imagining speaking with the mother of a boy caught by the debris produced by an American cruise missile attack in a foreign country, I discover that I'd have to leave her house in shame if I could not confidently tell her that her son's death would be saving myriad lives, and explain convincingly the reason for my complete trust (or or at least conviction beyond reasonable doubt) in the knowledge on which I based my claim.

Logically, we can support violent intervention with no more certainty than our certainty in the accuracy, integrity and lack of bias of the sources of the information on which its justification is based, and of the people who would communicate that information to us. If past evidence leaves us in any doubt with respect to any one of those things, then a minimum moral requirement is to demand a clear explanation as to why, this time, the information, the people and their motivations, are better and more trustworthy than they have been before.

Given the myriad cases of violence perpetrated (by both the USA and other entities), to be worthy of our support, politicians who would blow up anything or anyone in foreign lands must share their evidence of the guilt of guilty parties with us. As a reference point, that evidence must be many times stronger than the evidence we had for Saddam's weapons of mass destruction and mobile anthrax labs—which turned out to be, as presented, false. Until that can be done, those with their hands on the buttons that unleash physical conflict must rebuild our trust in both their decision-making and the sources of their information. They must rebuild our trust in their personal integrity so that only the most paranoid American could suspect the manipulation of information for political purposes. They must do so even more convincingly to the extent that credible counter-narratives exist in each case, such as that described by the memo, publicized by American General and former NATO Commander, Wesley Clark, that revealed a decision made years ago to take down the governments of Iraq (check), Libya (check), Iran (cyber-war and economic war already initiated), Somalia, Sudan and Syria (ongoing attempt).[29]

They must also provide clear worst-case and best-case assessments of the upside and downside of intervention. The latter must take into account the fact that most of the consequences of unleashing violence are unpredictable in their specifics, mostly uncontrollable, and full of uncertainties that are almost entirely iatrogenic (harmful outcomes of attempts to solve a problem).

Does any American even know enough about the state next to the one he resides in—a peaceful, wealthy and lawful democracy—to say with any certainty how to solve its greatest problem? Of course not: so how can we possibly lend our moral weight to a solution to a complex moral, usually historically rooted problem in an entirely alien culture—about which most of us know nothing—when the one thing we do know about the solution is that it involves aggression and outcomes that we cannot determine? And do we really believe our Representatives know any better?

We should ask for a clear exposition of the causal thread by which military intervention will save lives.

And if that is not the goal, such as when action is intended "to fire a shot across the bow", as Obama said concerning the intervention he wanted to make in Syria in 2014, then how must we address the issue that empty threats are always the most dangerous—because such a shot across a bow is only purposeful if we are actually prepared (to run with the metaphor) to torpedo

---

[29] http://www.youtube.com/watch?v=lGAOJDtkzJU

the ship to sink it—with all the chaos that that doing so would unleash. Furthermore, what kind of "red line" (the term by which Obama described the use of chemical weapons by the Syrian regime when he was arguing for intervention) results in just a shot across the bows when crossed? Perhaps the red line is really pink—or no line at all. What should we make of such inconsistency from our leaders?

What kind of punishment do military actions really deal out to evil regimes if their chief operators are not within debris-flying distance of one of the cruise missiles that we fling? Why do we think dictators even care what we do when our actions are prespecified as limited? Saddam's tragic miscalculation was to believe that U.S. action in his country would be more limited than it turned out to be. What makes us so confident when we support one side of a conflict that we won't be tipping an unseen balance in favor of equally awful thugs, or worse? In that relation, consider our actions in Iraq, which have empowered Iran and favored the rise of ISIS. And what's the interventionists' comeback to the fact that Western interference in the affairs of Arab nations always carries a price in increased resentment and resistance—or the fact that bringing violence to bear on any country tends to unite it against the bringers of that violence, regardless of their intentions, as per the study of Robert Pape, described above.

Since I have mentioned Obama's hoped-for intervention into Syria 2014, let me apply my thought experiment there: the Syrian mother would surely ask for evidence that interventions such as the one proposed have had the desired effect in the past. Do we know enough about the intended rules of engagement in this intervention even to begin to answer that? Indeed, what about the most obvious policy question that was not (as far as I know) asked anywhere: surely the very fact that Assad used chemical weapons against his people (Obama's main justification for intervention) was evidence that all our previous attempts to punish tyrants who've overstepped the line hadn't worked—because if they had, Assad wouldn't have used those weapons, would he? So why would this punitive attack make any difference to the next dictator when our earlier ones made none to Assad? Are we sure we're not just doing all this to make ourselves feel better—either more moral or more capable than the outcomes will eventually reveal us to be?

Also, we must be able to answer the mother's inevitable demand for our own moral consistency: she'd ask us why we were acting in Syria, but not in other places where even greater evil has been done—and sometimes using the same class of weapons? Specifically, why don't we take down North Korea, where chemical weapons—and worse—are used in concentration camps daily to kill political prisoners?[30] Is our answer that North Korea has more powerful allies, or a greater ability to hit back? In other words, do we only hit bullies when they're weak enough to hit? That response might be defensible, but a supporter of a strike against Syria could only claim a moral basis if he had at least asked that question and answered it satisfactorily.

And if our motivation for intervention in a crisis is truly humanitarian, is there really no other way of responding except by action that is both unilateral and violent (the worst of all worlds)? With respect to Syria, for example, were we seriously being asked to believe that, assuming the evidence of guilt of the Syrian government was beyond reasonable doubt (was it?), the USA is the only nation on earth to care enough to do anything about it and that the only effective response involves blowing up things and people? In other words, can we tell the mother in our thought experiment that there really was no alternative to the death of her son, caught in the debris of our missile?

At first blush, the retort that "people will also die if we do

---

[30] http://www.youtube.com/watch?v=iBYDE6yWl0I

nothing", usually offered to imply that moral and informational standards for action should be lower than those imposed in a court, is appealing, but it misses almost all of the above points. People are dying all over the world as a consequence of myriad actions that we do nothing about. How many die when we do nothing in a particular crisis like that in Syria? How, exactly, will our intervention stop them from dying? How do we know that the number saved will exceed the deaths we might cause if and when we have to deal with the spiraling unintended consequences of our intervention? And what about all those other people who are dying in other countries every day because we do nothing: if our foreign policy is essentially humanitarian, why are we not intervening in them too?

On the other hand, if our motivation is not humanitarian, but rather a matter of American national interest, then which interest, exactly, is being served by this intervention and is it really greater than any other we could apply our military to today?

The truth is our politicians too often approach all of these questions with an astoundingly unjustified—and therefore quite arrogant—belief in their knowledge and analytical capabilities. That's not a theoretical claim: history stands witness.

Let us, for a moment, imagine a situation that hardly ever arises: there is overwhelming evidence for the guilt of some foreign regime; somehow we know that we can save many lives by acting and that our actions won't have unintended negative consequences that cancel out the good outcomes many times over. If all that could be true, and our interventionist politicians were right, then it would indeed be their duty to convince us of the same and bring us with them. It is the most terrible responsibility of our leaders and it is theirs because they chose to lead. But the proper fulfillment of that duty depends on the trust of the People.

But most of us don't trust our leaders, do we?

We don't trust them because, as a body, they say so many things that they contradict by their actions; because they put party before principle; because they swear an oath to uphold a Constitution that they vote to undermine (such as by passing the NDAA and Patriot Act); because they make one rule for themselves and one for others (such as by exempting themselves from elements of Obamacare); because they take money from corporations in whose interests they legislate; because, in the worst case, they lie (such as to gain public support for a war of choice) or, only marginally better, they are so credulous as to go along with the lies they are fed without demanding evidence proportionate to the consequences of acting on them.

In other words, our political class has form, and it's not very good. And just because the failings of our leaders should not prevent us as a nation from acting aggressively when it is morally right to do so, it should also not prevent us from demanding, before any such action, standards of insight, trustworthiness, statesmanship and consistency, that the political class has failed to display for far too long.

If our political class were true humanitarians, prepared to risk American lives and treasure for the good of non-Americans—something they should approach us very, very humbly to request—then they would every day treat their unique position in our society with a reverence and seriousness equal to the unlimited trust that they ask us to place in them in those moments when they seek to exercise the most awesome powers of this country in such a way.

Enough of what we do to others: let's return to what we do to ourselves.

Civil Rights Aren't Always Simple Rights

In April of 2014, Rachel Maddow, presenter of The Rachel Maddow show on MSNBC revisited an interview conducted with Rand Paul, junior Senator for Kentucky, in 2010. The motivation for doing so was Rand's recent visit to Howard University, during which he answered a question from a student with the sentence: "I do question some of the ramifications and extensions, and I have never come out in opposition to the Civil Rights Act … I have never questioned the Civil Rights Act".

The reference was to the *Civil Rights Act of 1964*, arguably America's most famous piece of civil rights legislation in modern times, which outlawed discrimination based on race, color, religion, sex, or national origin. It ended unequal application of voter registration requirements and racial segregation in schools, at the workplace and by facilities that served the general public (which it called "public accommodations").

In her show, Maddow showed a clip of Rand's giving that answer and then repeated his line, "I have never questioned the Civil Rights Act", but her repetition was without the context of the response—and that context was important, because it included the Senator's explicit qualification that he was concerned about the ramifications of the act beyond race.

Nevertheless, Maddow accused Rand of "flat-out lying" [31], and to prove her point, ran another interview that Rand had given in 2010 with the Louisville Courier Journal News paper, which went as follows.

> *LCJ: Would you have voted for the Civil Rights of 1964?*
> *RP: I like the Civil Rights Act in the sense that it ended discrimination in all public domains. I am all in favor of that.*
> *LCJ: But?*
> *RP: [Laughs] You had to ask me the "but". I don't like the idea of telling private business owners—I abhor racism; I think it's a bad business decision to*

[31] http://www.youtube.com/watch?v=9-IIOYDeiwg

> *ever exclude anybody from your restaurant—but at the same time I do believe in private ownership.*

The show cuts back to Maddow in her studio, who presents her slam-dunk: "That is Rand Paul, questioning the Civil Rights Act".

She went on to accuse Rand of having a sketchy record on racial discrimination and civil rights law, and of being condescending in thinking he can get away with his lie. She even displayed this headline in the New Yorker: "Rand Paul, at Howard University, Pretends He Favored the Civil Rights Act", to reinforce visually the idea that Rand is a) dishonest and b) disfavors the Civil Rights Act.

As someone who likes Maddow (and even has a signed copy of her book on my shelf), I am disappointed that she took this approach to what Rand was clearly trying to convey, for in her interview with Rand from 2010, Rand had been clear:

> *There are ten different titles to the Civil Rights Act and nine out of ten deal with public institutions and I am absolutely in favor of [them]. One deals with private institutions, and had I been around, I would have tried to modify that. But the other thing about legislation—and this is why it is a little hard to say where you are sometimes—is that when you support nine out of ten things in a good piece of legislation, do you vote for it or against it?*

To someone without an axe to grind in the matter, and I believe that includes myself, these are not the words of a man who is trying to hide his views about this hugely important piece of legislation. Rather, they are the words of a man who favors nine tenths of it and, because of his concern for civil rights, is worried about the gutting of one principle critical to everyone's enjoyment of liberty—private property—to help extend the reach of another (anti-discrimination).

...which brings me to a recent event in England that puts both Rand's interview and his views in an altogether more telling light.

A year or so ago in the U.K[32], an elderly Christian couple, Mr and Mrs Bull, who used to run a guesthouse, refused to offer rooms to unmarried couples—whether gay or straight. Some time ago, a gay couple, who fell afoul of their "no unwed couples" policy, sued them for discrimination. Britain's Supreme Court agreed with the offended party and fined the hoteliers thousands of pounds, which, along with the legal fees, and the elimination of their right to rent their rooms to whomever they wish, caused them to sell their business.

As a non-religionist, I completely disagree with the guesthouse-owners view of sexuality and, dare I say, love. But I am very disturbed by the use of law to punish them for following their conscience with their own property in a way that neither did, nor intended to do, active harm to anyone.

This incident raises a complicated moral and societal question about which well-meaning and intelligent people can disagree. To find answers to such questions, I often ask simply, "What would Love do?". And I have to say that if I were denied entry to this business (as I would be if I were with a partner as I am not married), I would probably pity this couple for their views, and I might even tell them so, but Love would require me to respect where they are on their spiritual journey, and know that they were not seeking to hurt me. I wouldn't feel that I had a right to use the force of the state against them, nor would I want to.

As I read about this sad tale, Rand's interview with Rachel

---

32 http://www.lifesitenews.com/news/christian-bb-owners-lose-supreme-court-appeal-forced-to-sell-business-after

Maddow came immediately to mind. For what happened to Mr and Mrs Bull is the very consequence of the concession of the principle of private property that Rand was so concerned about.

Just as Mr and Mrs. Bull had a right to discriminate (but a moral obligation not to do so), any group of aggrieved customers—such as gay people or unmarried persons who are sexually active—have all the right in the world to publicize this couple's views in a bid to persuade others not to frequent their establishment (easier today than it has ever been). In this way, no one has to act out of force or violate the one right that exists almost exclusively to facilitate the exercise of all other fundamental (natural) rights to life, liberty and the pursuit of happiness—which is the right to earn and deploy property to your benefit as long as doing so harms no one else.

In the case of Mr and Mrs Bull, the force of a British law that is equivalent to the one tenth of the Civil Rights Act about which Rand Paul is rightfully concerned, was used to deprive someone of something as punishment for an act that was not intended to harm, was in line with sincerely held religious belief, and materially deprived no one of anything.

Logically, Mr and Mrs Bull can only have committed a crime if the couple they turned away had an actual right to be served by them. Yet, the Bulls are not compelled to offer their service to anyone. So how can it be that party A's (the Bulls) making a free choice to transact with party B (a married couple) creates a new right for party C (unmarried couple)? What kind of right would that be? It is not a simple question.

Interestingly, to get to its answer, Rachel had pressed Rand on this altogether more concrete question.

> *Do you believe that private business people should be able to decide whether they want to serve black people, gays or any other minority group?*

The most important thing about this question is that it is utterly different from the following one.

> *Do you believe that private business people should serve black people, gays or any other minority group?*

...which she did not ask.

Those two questions are very different indeed; they rest on very different moral and even metaphysical principles and both consistently can, and perhaps, should, be answered with a "yes".

It is far from obvious, for example, that we should use law to punish a person who follows his conscience and does not harm another individual (such as Mr. Bull), but not a person who goes against his conscience and betrays another, such as by telling a lie to cover adultery. Typically, we make the leap from "an action is wrong" to "an action should be punishable by law" only in the very rare cases that an individual is in fact harmed or put at great risk of harm (murder, robbery, intention to do either, reckless driving, etc.).

In contrast, anti-discrimination laws in the private sphere almost uniquely work by the threat of harm (or in Mr and Mrs Bull's case, doing actual harm) against individuals who have neither done, nor intended to do, active harm against anyone else. This is extremely serious because it is exactly by prohibiting the state from harming those who have not done harm to others that discrimination against any group in the public sphere is prevented. In other words, anti-discriminatory laws in the private sphere are always in danger of undermining the very principle they purport to defend. Typically, that doesn't matter practically in the short-run, but it can do huge harm in the long-term.

What, after all, was the evil of slavery, from which modern discrimination in large part follows so darkly? It was not the evil of slavers' refusing to let their slaves buy services, analogous to the refusal of Mr and Mrs Bull to offer a room for their unmarried but sexually active clients. Rather, it was the legally sanctioned, complete abuse of the property rights of the slaves by the slavers—the refusal to let them earn property in exchange for their labor, the refusal to let them keep property with which they could have bought themselves out of their slavery, the refusal to allow them to decide what to do with anything they did in any loose sense own, and even, (by the definition of property favored by many who understand its importance to providing all individuals the means of defending their liberty against any impingement,) the denial of the slaves' exclusive property in their own beings and bodies.

This is extremely important. Property rights matter because property is the only secure means by which people can exercise their liberty over time and defend it when it is under attack.

Understanding why the two questions above can both be answered affirmatively is critical not only to understanding Freedom, but also to our ability as a nation to preserve it. We might even go a step further and say that it is the difference between those two questions that defines Freedom.

The story of Mr and Mrs Bull does not in itself prove that either Rand or Rachel is right on that one tenth of the Civil Rights Act that deals with private institutions, but it does (as sure as slavery is evil) prove that intelligent people can disagree about it—like so much in politics. And it proves beyond doubt that impugning the intent of a politician or any fellow American who has sufficient integrity and, frankly, courage, to grapple so publicly with the fundamental principles of liberty is not only unfair to him, but also a disservice to us all.

CHAPTER 4

A Land of Opportunity?

The "Land of Opportunity", where we can supposedly have our "American Dream", is strongly bound up with the idea of "American-style capitalism" or the "American free-market economy".

People may disagree about the rights or wrongs of this American system. Some of us may believe it is the best way of advancing our nation, providing opportunity for our poor masses and expanding our freedom. Some believe it is a greed-saturated system that hurts the masses through the very selfishness on which it depends. Nevertheless, all Americans immediately recognize what is being referred to when we hear or read an expression that involves some combination of some of the words, "American", "free", "market" and "capitalism". We recognize it as the economic system in which we live. It defines our lives' opportunities and limitations, and by affecting the resources available to us and our means of transacting with them, sets boundaries on how we act on our political choices.

Our unquestioning acceptance of the vocabulary of the American capitalism system is supported by the knowledge that we can go to a store to buy the things we want; that we can start businesses; that our money allows us to choose how to enjoy the fruits of our labor; and whether to enjoy them now, or store them for later gratification. We also know that it's only because the American people are innovative and have been extremely good at commercializing their ideas in a way that earns a profit by providing others things they need, that the USA has become the greatest economic power in the world. We experience this as no mere mathematical abstraction. It is enjoyed by everyone in the USA, whose poorest 10% are on average richer than the average human being on earth.

Despite the fact that every week we see examples of an uneven economic playing field; that large corporations appear not always to have to play by the same rules as small businesses or individuals; and that almost all actions of government, by definition, are not part of a free market (defined as the sum of voluntary choices of individuals concerning what to do with their wealth), most of us accept that most of the time, we are playing the game of life on a free-market board. At least, we live our lives as if we believe that.

If the game board is the free-market, then the tokens in this game are called "dollars". They have value—ostensibly the same value for whoever holds them. We may not be quite sure where they come from, but they represent a claim on real stuff. Individuals cannot make them out of thin air, which is just as well, or else the game wouldn't be very fair at all. But in this game, there are two privileged actors—banks and government—which do make money out of thin air all the time.

In this American game of life, the players are individuals, or companies and corporations that have broadly all of the economic rights of individuals. The force with which these entities can act is proportional to the amount of capital they can concentrate. Put another way, the wealthiest entities can have the largest effects on our world. Many of us believe that the free market is at fault when the effects of corporate actions are negative, since it is the free market, we reason, that "allows" these bad corporations to concentrate wealth and then deploy it harmfully. If that is correct, then it would follow that the only way to restrain such bad actors is to make the market less free. Indeed, we often use the words "untamed", or "unfettered" to refer to "the market" when it behaves destructively. These words conjure the image of a wild animal loose from its bonds.

Such an understanding places the blame for allowing destructive behavior, or at the very least, failure to protect people from destructive behavior, squarely on our capitalist system with which we identify as American. But that rests on two crucial assumptions: a) that we have a free market and b) that the concept of "free" includes giving companies and people the freedom to act destructively.

But what if those assumptions really describe a paradigm more than they describe reality—and then distort the reality that we think we see in a way that reinforces our error, just as in the Perceptions of Incongruity experiment, already discussed?

In other words, what if our market is not free at all? What if the rules of the game are not capitalist rules, but rules written with a very different intent from that of allowing people to make free economic choices on a level playing field. In other words, what if the prevailing economic system of the USA is not free-market capitalism, but something that is loaded with certain biases toward particular outcomes? Could it be that these biases in the market, rather than the freedom of the market, dominate our lives in unseen ways? Perhaps, to return to the game analogy, different players have different dice, some of them loaded.

Relatedly, we should ask whether the system causes economic problems, or allows them? And if the former, are capitalism and economic freedom the cause of all the trouble—or is something else? The answer to this question would go to the core of what America is, and shed light on the everyday experiences of Americans.

In short, could what we "know" about our country prevent

us from seeing how it really works, and be doing us harm as a result?

The "American system", the "American free-market system", or "American capitalism" is the context in which the "American Dream" makes sense. All of these terms refer to a set of principles, actions and liberties. For the average American, these phrases are associated with freedom of opportunity, entrepreneurism, and the fact that, at least in principle, anyone can strive for the basic American dream of, say, owning a house, being free of debt and enjoying financial security. Whatever else may be true about our economic life, that at least is right, right? If not, what are we even doing here? And does the fact that this American dream is admittedly difficult to achieve in practice mean that the theory is wrong or the goal is illusory?

To answer those questions, let us first clearly determine whether there is a single principle at the core of our economic life that explains, or better yet, inevitably leads to, the increased prosperity of individuals and our society as a whole, on which the American dream depends. Is there something in our "economic system" or just the way we operate, on which all technological advance and wealth creation depends? If so, we must hold on to it, and we must look very skeptically at anything that claims to be it but is not it. And if it exists, what should it most accurately be called? Are we really talking about this core principle when we lazily use words like "the economy", "the free market", "free enterprise", "capitalism" etc. or are we referring to something else—or perhaps even to nothing at all that we can even describe?

Clearly, there is something about our culture and economic life that has made America a land of opportunity for so many; that has made the USA the richest country in the world, and has, more or less, enriched other countries to the approximate extent to which their people interact economically and in business in a manner similar to Americans.

There is indeed a very simple principle that ties our

economic life to our delivery from the stone age to the 21st century of landing probes on comets, putting iPhones in your hand, and connecting you instantaneously with almost any information you could want more quickly than you can even ask the question you want answered.

It is the "secret" of all earthly progress that involves interactions among people. It is a "secret" thought that hides in plain sight, because it is so fundamental, and so much a part of our nature, that we don't even notice it. Like liberty itself, like freedom of thought (to which it is inextricably related), we usually are not consciously aware that we are acting on it, because it's just the nature of our being, and to acknowledge its reality and importance requires you to believe basically nothing about anything else. Without it, no transaction is ever freely made.

It is the Principle of Subjective Value, which is the simple statement that different people assign a different value to a particular thing or service. The principle makes no claim about why they do so, or whether the judgments of value are in any way "correct" or "reasonable". It just makes the observation—and observation that is verified every single time anyone buys anything from anyone else without coercion.

Subjective Value is why people trade. It is why, when you go to the supermarket, you would rather have the groceries than the money you spend to get them, and why the supermarket (or its owners) would rather have your money than the groceries. It is why when you go the corner shop and pay for your newspaper and candy, or go to the car dealer and pay for your vehicle, or say goodbye to the painters of your house and pay them for their time, you say "thank you" to them and they say "thank you" to you: both parties have benefitted.

This is the reason why people collectively get richer and happier over time through making individual choices for their own benefit.

Truly free transactions, which collectively can be called the "free market", are characterized by benefiting both parties involved as determined by those parties themselves, and by not imposing any harm (called an "externality") on any third party that was not involved in the trade.

The most natural and accurate definition of "free market" is, then, simply the sum of such free transactions in a population. It is also obvious that over time a population that enables private citizens to engage in such mutually beneficial activities by mutual consent will only get richer and happier—as who would voluntarily seek to engage in transactions that made them poorer or less happy?

For this reason, I don't much care for Adam Smith's "invisible hand" metaphor for the free market, because it implies there is some other, single thing, separate from other things (decisions by free people), that actually exists but is hidden. That is not the case. The collective improvement in wellbeing of a society follows from individual choices made freely for mutual benefit if no one else is harmed in the process, just as "four" follows from "two plus two". One is a logical consequence of the other—not a different, invisible thing.

It should also be clear that people who transact freely in this way have some incentive to innovate: a man who can develop a product or service that people want a lot and knows that he can freely dispose of that product or service to those people for something he wants more (almost always money), has the prospect of even greater happiness—to an extent that is, rather wonderfully, in approximate proportion to the extent to which he is bettering the lives of his "customers".

The farmer in Idaho doesn't have to care personally about the New Yorker who will be eating his potatoes as French fries with his burger, but he succeeds economically only inasmuch as he can provide a benefit to that New Yorker—and thousands others like him. The truly free market of subjective values turns self-interest into mutual benefit.

Those of us who want to preserve this truly free market—because human happiness depends on it—should be clear that that is what we are preserving, and we should be ruthless about not letting vested interests—either political or corporate—claim that whatever they are doing is essential to a free market if some poor American who is not party to their transactions is getting harmed by them.

The operation of a such a free market as an ongoing buzz of transactions among people for their betterment—happens naturally unless force, fraud or deceit is used to prevent it. It has done so since the Stone Age.

So why are so many Americans hurting today? There seem to be genuine victims of an economic crisis that the victims were not responsible for. Since free transactions based on subjective value for mutual benefit can't hurt anyone, what has caused the economic pain that so many of us are recovering from, following the housing and mortgage crisis of six years ago—and indeed, caused pain to millions of other citizens following crises throughout the country's history?

The answer lies in an entirely man-made problem built into our economic system—and specifically with the tokens we use to play our American game of life—our money. It turns out that the very nature of our money subverts the solid, commonsense idea of fair and voluntary exchange between individuals who seek to maximize their own well-being. That idea of free exchange and the right to maximize one's well-being—to pursue happiness in the words of the Constitution—is not just a Constitutional tenet. It also happens to be a fundamental idea, if not the fundamental idea, of classical liberalism, which we discussed in the preceding chapter.

The tokens with which we play are colloquially called "dollars". Before 1971, those dollars were called "silver certificates", redeemable for a metal commodity as a store of actual value. It said so right there on the top of the dollar bill.

In 1971, Nixon "closed the gold window" because the US government had printed up so much money to be able to finance the war in Vietnam, among other things, that when the French got concerned that there were too many dollars around for them all to be redeemable in gold and silver, and so asked for American gold in exchange for all the real dollars (silver certificates) they had, Nixon realized that the French were right: America didn't have enough metal to settle their claims. Nixon was therefore forced to declare that the dollar would no longer be redeemable for gold and silver. On that day, everything changed: the currency went from a real asset in the form of a claim on a specific amount of a specific asset (silver, gold) to Federal Reserve notes, which it also says, right there on the top of today's dollar bills.

The currency thus became a "fiat" currency, which the government won't give you any real stuff for (like silver)—except the means to stay out of prison by using it to pay your tax obligations.

This change is not just academic. It has profound consequences.

Now, some of the biggest and most important monetary transactions no longer satisfy the above definition of "free market". Why? Because these Federal Reserve tokens are created in such a way as almost to guarantee, in aggregate, that all real assets eventually flow to a small group of legal entities, quite independently of all those consensual transactions for mutual benefit, based on subjective evaluations of goods and services.

A Schematic History of Money

What follows is a story about money—about what it is and where it came from. It is a story that is largely favored by something called the "Austrian school" of economics, which saw most advancement in the late nineteenth and first half of the twentieth century. While this school of economic understanding lost influence throughout the second half of the twentieth century, it is now enjoying a resurgence as many of its adherents predicted our current economic turmoil, while others are offering some of the most convincing explanations after the fact.

This story will provide a huge insight into the workings of our monetary system—but it is not the whole story. We'll also consider a new school of monetary thought, equally important to understanding some of the most counter-intuitive aspects of today's economy, called modern monetary theory or MMT.

Austrian economists and MMTers don't see eye to eye on much. They don't tend to meet at the water cooler. Austrian economics and MMT are very different traditions. Their proponents expound their views of the world in separate groups and, usually, separate places, so presenting them here next to each other is a little radical—but it has a specific purpose. The story favored by Austrians is a kind of schematic history of money, which will help us better understand our "common-sense" intuitions about money, and how and why they are now entirely wrong. After we benefit from realizing that everything we believe about money is wrong, we will be better placed to accept and understand the nature of today's money (how it is created and what it is), which is importantly described by MMT.

Funny Money

When we think of old money—really old money, like that of the Roman Empire—we think of coins. Coins are bits of something valuable. Coins in their original form did not just represent value—according to a number that was stamped on them—they were in fact valuable per se. They were made of something like gold or silver, which has value in its own right, completely independently from the image or numbers that might stamped on it.

According to a "schematic history" of money favored by the Austrian school of economics, and indeed, consistent with the conception of money taught out of textbooks to many economics students, [33]centuries ago, in many towns would be one man, typically a goldsmith, whose premises had sufficiently secure storage facilities, through the use of a safe, vault, or even guards, that wealthy individuals in the community would give him their

[33] This is not an accurate history of money, which has arisen in different ways at different times in different parts of the world. Moreover, most moneys have been simply ways of recording credits and debts, and clearing them against each other, rather than things of real value. But our intuition is that money is in some way inherently valuable. This schematic history of money is a way to help us bridge the gap between our intuitions of money and what it is today.

valuables, including coins, for safekeeping.

In return for the valuables, the goldsmith would hand the depositor a receipt. Later, the depositor could claim his money back from the goldsmith using this receipt. The depositor would pay the goldsmith for the service of secure storage.

After a time, numerous people in the community were using the goldsmith's secure storage service in this way. The service had a wonderful secondary benefit for the community: it made trading easier. The reason is as follows. If a man has ten silver pieces in the goldsmith's vault, and wants to buy two cows for that amount of money, he does not have to carry the coins and give them to the seller. Rather, he can give the seller of the cows the receipt from the goldsmith for the 10 silver pieces, so that the seller can redeem the buyer's silver from the goldsmith at his convenience. That way, no one has to carry around all those bits of heavy metal.

Now, since the goldsmith is likely to be one of the richest fellows in town in his own right, he might well be lending money to the merchants in the community at interest, to make a profit on it. At this stage, our honest goldsmith is only lending out his own money—not his depositors' money. After all, his depositors' money is redeemable on demand, and if he were to lend it out, and a depositor was to claim his money back with one of those receipts, the goldsmith would have to tell him that he can't have his money because he's given it to someone else. That would not be good for the goldsmith's money storage business, and could damage his other businesses (goldsmithing and lending) by damaging his reputation.

As we stated above, before 1971, American money—and that of most of the world—was receipts for bits of valuable stuff. The American dollar was a certificate that allowed its bearer to receive on demand a particular amount of silver or gold, like the one shown above. So in a simple sense, this pre-1971 U.S. dollar was essentially the same as the goldsmith's receipts: both had a real, practical, tangible value equal to the asset (silver, gold) that "backed" it. Following World War II, for example, $35 was set (in the Bretton Woods agreement) to be equivalent to one ounce of gold, and that equivalence defined the value of a dollar.

Any market that involves the exchange of goods using this kind of money can be truly free, because the value of the money in the transaction is fixed, so when person A trades with person B, both know exactly what they are getting, and a certain amount of something valuable (precious metal, albeit represented by a paper certificate) is being exchanged for some asset or thing.

Let's go back to our goldsmith. Over time, he can't help noticing that he has hundreds of bits of valuable metal in his vault that belong to all these people in his community, and these people—now they are exchanging those receipts, rather than the metallic chunks themselves—never come and demand all their money back at once. Sometimes, the goldsmith has to give back a few percent of the money in his vault, but never all of it… or even half of it.

So our goldsmith has an idea: rather than just making profit by loaning out his own money at interest, he starts making interest on all the money that does not belong to him but is sitting in his vault… by lending it out too.

The idea is simple. It is, conceptually at least, the foundation of all modern banking and all modern economics.

This idea is extremely important, so let's imagine a specific example.

In the 15th century, in a small city state in Italy, a goldsmith has 1000 gold coins in his vaults that are not his. He loans out 500 of them at 5% interest. If he does nothing else and gets paid back after a year, he will have made a profit of 25 coins. If in that year, no one mined any gold, it means the rest of the world has 25 fewer gold coins, and the goldsmith, of course, has 25 more.

Alternatively, someone somewhere may have mined 25 gold coins that eventually found their way into the hands of the borrower, who used them to pay back the goldsmith. In the latter case, it is easy to see how real value in the form of labor has moved from someone who does real work (the miner and/or borrower), to someone who acts as a bank, who did not have to do any work (the goldsmith). This phenomenon set the stage for everything that came after it.

Observe that our 15th century goldsmith has, perhaps for the first time ever, come up with a way to transfer real wealth to himself without doing anything for it.

As long as people know that the goldsmith operates in this way, this system is not essentially dishonest. He is lending out something that exists, and putting this wealth "to work" by putting it in the hands of merchants or entrepreneurs who can use it to create wealth and produce and deliver goods for the benefit of everyone. It sounds like the kind of thing we'd actually want in a free-market—if we make the following slight change to the goldsmith's business model: since the depositors' money is going to be lent out by the goldsmith, it will no longer be available to them—and they're not going to be happy to pay the goldsmith to store their money if the goldsmith turns around and makes money from their deposits! Instead, they want a piece of the action: they want the goldsmith to pay them interest on the deposit. Then, the goldsmith can make the difference between the interest he pays the deposit and the interest he charges a borrower. This is still an excellent setup for the goldsmith—as it allows him to maintain his extraordinary magic trick of transferring real wealth to himself without doing any productive labor.

When this first started happening in Europe, no one minded very much, and many were in fact quite glad to have such banking geniuses as our exemplary goldsmith in their midst, because through them, capital could be allocated where it was needed—moved from those who did not need to use their capital to those who could use it productively, supporting economic growth.

If the development of banking had stopped there, all may have been good with the world. But the goldsmith got greedy, and had an idea that was not so benign. It was to become the basis for the fractional reserve banking system on which our global economy is based, and it is the idea without which there could be no such thing as a system-wide failure of the banking system.

Don't Look at the Man behind the Printing Press

The idea was this: since no one knows how many gold coins are in the goldsmith's vault, he can just write up new receipts for money in his own vault and go to the market and trade with them. As long as they keep circulating in the local economy and no one comes back to redeem them and claim the non-existent coins they purport to represent, the goldsmith has found a way of acquiring valuable things by exchanging nothing of value whatsoever. This process is the original counterfeiting, but rather than copying money (which is what we usually conceive of as counterfeiting), the goldsmith is really creating it. Of course, as soon as he does this, the meaning of the word "money" is changed: whereas the receipts that were formerly backed by coins in the vault had real value, these new, fake receipts have none. People only think they have value because they know that these receipts always used to stand for real, valuable metal that was deposited with the goldsmith.

With this counterfeiting ploy, our goldsmith has made himself the first modern banker. He is willing to take the risk that while he has created, let's say, receipts for 2000 coins in his vault, even though all of his depositors have in total put only 1000 coins in there, no more than half of the receipts are going to be redeemed at once, and he'll never be found out. Meanwhile of course, he's just counterfeited his way to 1000 coins' worth of wealth, which he may have exchanged for a big house, beautiful clothes, or a new horse or three.

The goldsmith's operation is now recognizable as the operation of a modern bank, and his scheme now has a very legitimate-sounding name, "fractional reserve banking". "Fractional reserve" means merely that the capital in the vaults of the bank (the reserve) is only a fraction of the money the bank owes its depositors.

Read that last sentence carefully: the bank owes you the money you deposit with it, meaning that when you put money in your account at a bank, you loan that money to the bank, just as the bank loans that money to its borrowers.

It gets even better for our goldsmith-turned-fractional-reserve-banker. Now that he is creating "money" out of thin air, he can loan this created money out at interest. He is both creating money out of nothing, and then making a profit from the money that was created out of nothing.

If this practice had been outlawed centuries ago when it started, American economic life would be quite different from how it is, but when this practice was begun, much of this fake money began circulating in the economy before anyone realized it was there, and certainly before they realized that it could be a problem. When they did realize what was happening, stopping the practice would have resulted in many people's entering poverty, as all of their "fake" money would have to be removed from the economy. Instead, therefore, when it was revealed just how much of the circulating money was backed by nothing, this fake money was legalized, and its ongoing creation was regulated.

According to the standard history, the first country in the West to legalize the creation of money ex nihilo in this way and to make the system stick was Great Britain in 1694, when a law was passed to allow banks to create money out of nothing to lend to borrowers, as long as they created less than a specified amount. This maximum allowed amount of fake money was, in those days, double the amount of the real money in the bank's vaults. Therefore, the value of the real assets in the bank was one-third of the "face-value" of the money that was created.

As mentioned above, since 1971, money has been not been

backed by gold or any other commodity. Although some text books specify that the theoretical ratio for normal deposits in a bank is 1 (real value) : 9 (fake money), meaning that nine dollars can be created by a bank for every one dollar of real capital in the bank, this is not really the case. In reality, the amount of a bank's deposits never constrains the amount of money that a bank can create. No modern bank will turn away a customer to whom it wants to lend with the words, "we'd like to help you, but unfortunately we don't have enough deposits to be able to create your money today". Indeed, the actual ratio of the assets of many banks to the money they have created is many, many times that text-book ratio.

Modern banks create money to lend at a profit. Whenever someone wants a loan, if the bank supplies the created money, then, like our goldsmith, it earns interest on that created money. In other words, it makes money for nothing, and gets paid to do so—giving a whole new meaning to the Dire Straits hit.

Modern Money Creation

Let's examine a little more closely what happens at the moment of creation of money at your bank. Bear in mind that over 95% of all money in the American economy is created this way—as debt, by banks.

Let's say you wish to buy a house, and you want to borrow $100,000. The bank agrees to loan you the money at a modest interest rate of 5%. The bank creates the money simply by typing it into your account (which is the equivalent or writing those receipts that the goldsmith used to give out without the gold in his vault to back it). In return, you pledge your house—a real, tangible asset—to the bank in the event that you cannot reply the mortgage. In other words, here is a mechanism for the transfer of something real to a particular class of institutions, banks, (and their shareholders,) in return something that not only a) has no intrinsic value but b) does not really exist. This brings us to the first surprising unknown that fundamentally contradicts our commonly held view of the "American free market" system. Our system depends on the systematic transfer of real things to those who run particular institutions (banks) with special government-granted licenses.

Of course, most people do not end up handing over their homes to the banks. Rather, they repay their loan at interest. On a $100,000 loan at 5% interest, over 30 years, the interest will exceed $200,000—or twice the original amount of the loan. Where will the homeowner (mortgagor) get this $200,000 of interest to give to the bank? There is only one place—his labor, meaning that in some way, the home owner must be productive, delivering a service, producing a good etc., to make that money in time to hand his monthly installments back to the bank. Once again, the real value of actual, physical, time-consuming labor, is being transferred from the worker to an institution that gains that value purely by its government-licensed position.

To get to the very heart of the matter, we must take yet another step.

That $200,000 of interest, like the original $100,000 for which the homeowner pledged his house, does not exist until it is borrowed, by someone, somewhere, into existence! Put another way, there must always be more money owed to the creators of money than there is money in existence. This must be the case, because money is created when it is borrowed, but the obligation of the borrower has interest added onto it, which is not created with the original loan! (Reread the last couple of paragraphs again if you have to. If it doesn't sound crazy and scary, you've probably not understood it.)

The implications of this situation are huge and bizarre. On any particular day, if all loans were called in, there'd not be enough money in the world to pay them back, and so some borrowers somewhere would necessarily be foreclosed upon or bankrupted.

It goes without saying: this is not what most people think of as a free market. This is more of an unstable system that exists by virtue of government's granting a special privilege to, and standing behind, the banking sector, which uniquely and inevitably aggregates wealth without producing anything.

Usually, people think of bubbles as unpredictable and unplanned events that can happen in one or other sector of the economy (tulips, technology stocks, houses). However, almost the opposite is true: the system itself is a kind of bubble, in that it only continues because debt, and therefore money, are being continually created fast enough to pay the outstanding interest on the previously made loans, the creation of which creates more interest obligations, and so on. As the bubble inflates, wealth is transferred from the producers of wealth to the banks. "Bubble" does not just describe a freak economic event. Rather, it is to a first approximation a fair description of our modern economic paradigm.

Don't take it from me. Listen to the people who are paid to know.

> *That is what our money system is. If there were no debts in our money system, there wouldn't be any money.*[34]

> *It's only the time lag between the borrowing of money and the paying it back with interest that stops millions from going bankrupt and the economy collapsing. Another consequence of all of this, is if there were no debt, there would be no money. Take*

[34] Marriner S Eccles, Chairman and Governor of the Federal Reserve Board

> *it from someone who is paid to know: I am afraid that the ordinary citizen will not like to be told that the banks can and do create money ... And they who control the credit of the nation direct the policy of government and hold in the hollow of their hands the destiny of the people.*[35]

If your head hurts, you're in good company:

> *The process by which banks create money is so simple that the mind is repelled.*[36]

A Keen Understanding

I have made a few broad generalizations in the foregoing. In fact, the system is not necessarily unstable: one of the greatest economists of our time, Steve Keen, of whom more later, has shown that this system of debt-money creation by banks would be stable under two special conditions.

- All the money created by debt in this process goes to entrepreneurs who use it to create wealth, which is used to pay workers, who spend it on the increasing range of goods and services in the economy that those entrepreneurs are producing.
- The principal lent by the banks to the entrepreneurs is never required to be repaid.

But these conditions are generally not met.

---

[35] Reginald McKenna, past Chairman of the Board, Midlands Bank of England

[36] Economist John Kenneth Galbraith

With respect to the first unmet condition, banks make a profit, regardless of the reason for which a borrower borrows, and as a matter of fact, the overwhelming majority of all money created as debt by banks is loaned for non-wealth-creating purposes. Most bank-created debt-money goes to non-producers who borrow it just to exchange assets (like houses) among themselves at ever-increasing prices (which rise precisely because of the increase in the amount of money created). That is exactly what happened in the run up to the housing crash.

With respect to the second condition, whenever someone defaults on their loan, the principal is demanded—a situation with which too many Americans became all too familiar in this last decade or so. In other words, the bank as creditor takes ownership of the collateral for the debt.

Given that the above two conditions don't apply, here's a good way to look at the problem built into our monetary system, in which most of our money is created by banks as interest-bearing debt.

P = amount of debt principal owed by people to banks today
I = amount of interest owed by people to banks today
P' = amount of debt principal owed by people to banks sometime in the future

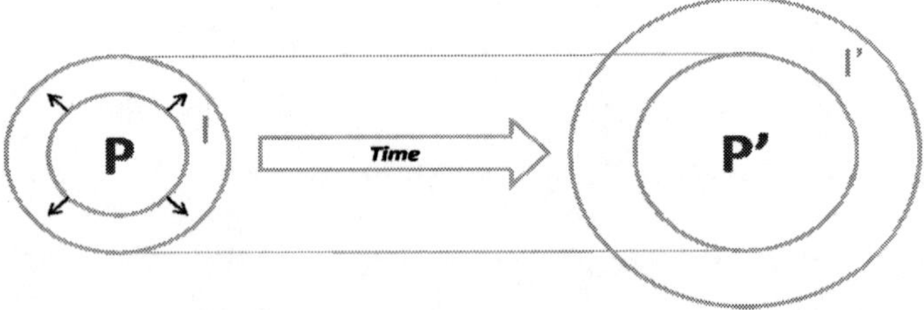

Over time, more and more debt must be created to create all the money to pay all the interest on the debt that was created in the past. The economy is a bubble that must keep expanding or else it bursts.

And it did burst in 2007/8. Invariably, in this system, the amount of private debt-money periodically increases to such heady heights that it can increase no further. At some point, banks no longer believe their customers can take on (or provide collateral for) any more debt and be reasonably expected to pay it back. Alternatively, the bank's would-be customers no longer believe they can afford to take on any more debt. At that point, the rate of debt/money creation falls.

This has two devastating effects. First, as the rate of injection of funds into the economy falls, reducing demand—the demand for both assets and workers falls. So the assets lose nominal value and works are laid off. Second, as things get really bad, not enough money is getting made to pay the pre-existing interest obligations and we get a huge bust—and the massive and actual transfer of assets from people to the banks, who created all that money and debt with the stroke of a finger on a keyboard.[37]

Without this money-as-debt and economy-as-bubble system, the dot-com boom and bust of the early 2000s could not have happened, and nor could the housing boom and bust of 2007 onward.[38]

---

[37] It is true that the banks didn't "make out like bandits" with all of our money in the recession, even though they did behave like bandits. But the losses born by the banks resulted from the collapse in prices of the assets (American homes) on which most private loans were secured, and bad bets they made in other markets (such as the derivatives market). None of this changes the fact that during a bust, real wealth is transferred from individuals to the banks who created the debt-money in the first place.

[38] This is not to claim that a non-bubble economy cannot experience booms and busts. It can – because people are prone to overvalue and undervalue certain things at certain times, such as tulips in the Netherlands in the 17th century. However, if money isn't created out of nothing as described here, then there is a limit to the amount of money that can chase any particular goods,

Most of the media and the political class acted as if the financial and housing crises of 2007/8 came entirely out of the blue—that it was neither predicted nor predictable. However, that was not the case.

A few people had noticed the staggering amount of debt-money creation by banks in the run up to those years, and that all that created money was not going into new businesses and the creation of products and services that really constitute physical wealth and value—but rather into bidding up the prices of houses—which creates nothing of value. Those people saw the bust of 2007 coming.

One of the men who predicted the recent bust, and deeply understands the dynamics and effects of the creation of debt money by the banking sector better than (perhaps) anyone is the aforementioned Steve Keen. That he does not buy into the disproved assumptions and consequent nonsense of conventional economics is captured nicely by the title of his book, "Debunking Economics".

On 15 December 2005—a couple of years before America's massive financial crisis, he was an expert witness for a case concerning predatory lending in the mortgage market in his then home country of Australia. In developing his testimony, he analyzed data on the rate of rise of private debt (loans made by the financial sector) relative to gross domestic product (GDP, a standard measure of the size of a nation's economy), and found that the growth of that ratio was almost exactly exponential—rising at an ever increasing rate. At 2 a.m. that morning, shocked by his own findings, he downloaded the relevant data for the USA, and calculated the same ratio, which he found to be also very close

---

constraining our animal spirits, and preventing governments and banks from manipulating the money supply so as to prolong such events. In other words, fake money greatly increases the number of booms and busts and enables them to be prolonged.

to exponential. He saw immediately this trend could not continue: it was impossible for people to want to go into debt to banks indefinitely at an ever-increasing rate, and since the level of private debt (as a percentage of GDP) was at its highest point in the post-war period, he predicted that when the rise stopped and the inevitable crisis hit, it would be the biggest since 1945. He called it.

He was right.

This specific prediction of the crash of 2007/8 is actually a corollary of a much more general and important result concerning debt-creation by banks that Keen has demonstrated:

> *The change in the level of debt is the main driver of change in the level of economic activity and if you have a rising level of debt, compared to GDP, then the change in debt is becoming a bigger and bigger component of the total demand in the economy, and if you get to the stage where it is obvious that that rate of growth of debt can't be sustained, at some point, the rate of debt will turn from positive to negative. And long before it turns negative—simply when it starts to close down—you'll have a crisis.*[39]

In other words, decisions made in our banking system, which is the source of nearly all money in the economy, drive asset bubbles and crises.

> *The level and rate of change of private debt are...key indicators.*

---

[39] http://www.bluerepublican.org/2015/01/26/debt-drives-employment-asset-bubbles/

This is not an axiomatic or ideological claim, but one based on hard, historical data.

Keen found an (R^2) (a measure of the strength of correlation) between the annual change in debt as a proportion of GDP and the change in employment of -.84 (from 1990), which is an unbelievably strong correlation. A layman might describe this as saying that 84% of the drop in employment is explained by a change in the amount of bank lending. And the strength of this correlation increases with the amount of debt in the economy.

In other words, the economic experiences of millions of Americans are dominated by the practices of banks—rather than the free transactions of individuals for their mutual benefit. And that has never been more true than now, when we are living in the biggest private debt bubble in the history of the United States.

Interestingly, Keen has shown that if banks did not collect borrowers' assets upon default, then we'd not be vulnerable to the financial busts that appear throughout our modern economic history.

That is worth thinking about. If you borrow my watch and don't give it back, then you've stolen it—and that is partially because I had to exchange something of real value to get the watch in the first place; it therefore represents physical wealth that I had to earn. As we have seen, a bank creates money at no cost to itself, and no one forces it to make a loan. So the question is raised: is failing to repay a loan that was created at zero cost and had no intrinsic value—such that a failure to repay represents no loss to the lending institution—the same as not repaying a loan to an individual or non-banking company, which would result in a very real loss to that individual or company, reasonably called theft?

Even though all people should keep their word and their contracts, not repaying a bank that created money from nothing doesn't seem naturally to be the moral or legal equivalent to not repaying your friend, who can't create his wealth but had to earn it.

We have discovered two hugely important things. First, our economy is not true free market capitalism, and second, the crises that hurt people most arise not from that element of our economy that is a free market—but from that part which is anything but. In other words, not only is capitalism not our culprit: it is a weird monetarism involving banks with special privileges provided by the State, that is responsible for the economic injustices—in the conventional and technical senses of that word—that are so frequently, and wrongly, attributed to capitalism. The transactions we make with banks are not any part of the free market, as it was defined above, and yet they dominate our economy (according to Keen's correlations) and therefore the lives of so many of us.

When the crisis first hit, the Fed asked for the right to inject 700 billion dollars into the banking sector to stop the bubble from bursting completely. President Bush said "I've abandoned free market principles to save the free market system". How little he knew: the system he saved never was the free market system.

He didn't abandon free market principles: he just abandoned his own consistency.

The Other Creator of Money—the State

When a bank creates money as debt for a private customer, the money is created with an equal liability (the debt to the bank), such that at that moment, no net financial asset is created in the private sector. If all money were created with liabilities that cancel them out (i.e. if all money were created by banks in the private sector), then the net financial assets in the economy would be zero.

Similarly, in all transactions among private citizens no new financial wealth is created. If you buy someone's car, the ownership of the car is transferred and when the seller deposits your check, your account is debited and his account is credited. No money is created in the system.

This is true even though people can own assets that go up in value. For example, imagine buying a stock for $100 from person A and it goes up in value and you sell it to person B for $200, no net wealth is created. Overall, B has $200 less, A has $100 more and you have $100 more. Zero net effect on the total amount of money or total dollar-valued wealth.

But the net financial assets in the economy are not zero. So at some point, some money was created without an offsetting asset. Where did that money without liability come from?

Unsurprisingly, it came from the government. Most economists have not yet fully come to grips with the full implications of America's (and hence the world's) coming off the gold standard in 1971, when Nixon "closed the gold window". Since then, the US dollar has been an entirely fiat currency, backed by no commodity, and issued by one monopoly issuer—the U.S. government.

The rules of money for a currency issuer (government) differ entirely from those for currency users (the rest of us). The school of economics that most closely examines exactly how this is so is called Modern Monetary Theory (MMT).

The fundamental difference is that users can only spend money they have, and must therefore acquire it by earning or borrowing before they can spend it. An issuer (the government) does not need to borrow or save because they can create money at the time they need it.

And that is precisely what the government does. Contrary to popular belief, the government does not raise money through taxation and borrowing in order to spend. Taxation and government borrowing have entirely different purposes, as we shall see later.

Rather, the government-treasury-federal reserve complex (I am using government here to refer loosely to the sovereign entity that issues currency and whatever institutions are involved in its issuance) creates money by spending it.

When the government purchases a service or product from the private sector, the bank account of the individual or company from which the purchase is made is credited. Before the purchase, that money does not exist in the private sector. The government's ability to credit the private account is not determined by how much money the government has in its own bank account. It may have no money at all: it can still make the payment.

The government is not revenue-constrained, just as a speaker is not word-constrained: he does not need to acquire words to give them away: he just makes (speaks) them whenever he needs to say something.

An immediate question arises: if the government does not need to collect money before it can spend it, why bother collecting any revenue at all? Why bother with taxation? And why bother with borrowing?

MMT provides fascinating answers to these questions. And it is in these answers that MMT most differs from Austrian—and all other—schools of economic thought.

MMT says that the purpose of taxation is twofold. First, it ensures that there is demand for the currency the government issues. By requiring taxes to be paid in a currency, the government (on pain of imprisonment) forces actors in the economy to acquire the money to meet their tax obligations. This causes the money to circulate in the first place. Second, taxation drains money out of the private economy. This is to ensure that the money government spends (and thus creates) into the private sector does not increase so fast that prices rise, creating inflation. In other words, by draining out of the economy by taxation most of the money that the government spends into the economy, the system remains stable (notwithstanding the instability that is periodically caused by the banks' running up private debt, as we discussed above).

What happens when you pay tax to the IRS? Simply, your private account is debited; but the money does not go anywhere—into some special government account or vault. It simply disappears. Your $8000 balance at Bank of America, for example, becomes a $6000 balance when you pay your $2000 of tax. It is a computer operation with no corresponding operation in a big government bank account.[40] Similarly, if you go to a tax office and pay the IRS in cash, they do not Fedex the dollar bills to a bank for deposit. Rather, the bills are simply destroyed. The money has been eliminated from the private sector, and the purpose of the tax is thus fully served.

Another question begs to be answered: why does the government ever borrow money? It certainly does not need to as again it never has a "shortfall". The answer to this question points to a massive failing of our media in explaining the economic situation of the USA, especially today. In this error, though, they can be excused, as many economists are similarly ignorant of the mechanisms of government financing, treasuries and bonds etc. The people who shouldn't be excused are the politicians that make huge decisions that involve this monetary system without having a clue about how it works.

Many Americans are today concerned that China is a huge creditor to the USA. They think that the American government borrows from China because it needs the money and that China has some political power over the USA for this reason. This is a perfectly reasonable, common-sense understanding that is consistent with our experience of individuals as users of currency,

---

[40] Although as a technical matter, a government account is usually credited at the time the tax is paid, the balances are not monitored to ensure that the government has a certain amount of money "in the bank". Rather, the money is eliminated later in a computer operation. The point is that the financial workings of the monetary system does not require that your debit is credited to and retained by the government to allow it subsequently to spend.

and it would be true if the American government, like individual citizens, were only a user of currency rather than its issuer. But it is not.

In fact, the USA does not borrow from China because it needs to. Rather, China lends to the USA because it can. Think about those dollars that China is lending to the US government: where did they come from? Of course, they were created by the US government by spending them into existence, or by a bank authorized by the US government to create them as debt-money. China can lend them back to the USA because the American government spent them or an American bank created them. The American government does not need to borrow them before it can spend them! Rather, China can only lend them because it has them since the American government spent them into existence. The common understanding is therefore the exact opposite of the (admittedly counter-intuitive) reality.

How did China get these dollars? A Chinese company sold something to an American company (or perhaps the American government), which sent dollars for payment. But what does "sent dollars as payment" mean? It means that the American company's bank account was debited, and the Chinese company's American dollar bank account—which also forms part of the American dollar economy—is credited. It may be, of course, that the dollars are sent to China and exchanged for the Chinese currency, renminbi (or yuan ¥), but in that case, the dollars have still been debited from the American purchaser's account and are in some other dollar account, controlled by a Chinese person or entity.

Here's the process step by step:

- American govt. creates dollars by spending
- American importer has some of those dollars
- American importer makes purchase from Chinese exporter, sends dollars to Chinese company. These

dollars still reside in US banking system but under Chinese control.

- Chinese exporter can't use dollars: it has to pay taxes in renminbi
- Chinese exporter accepts renmimbi created by Chinese govt in exchange for dollars at some exchange rate, mediated by commercial banks
- Chinese govt, now has US dollars in its account in the US banking system (and ultimately, therefore, the Federal Reserve).
- These dollars are not earning any interest for the Chinese: better for them to buy US Treasuries and earn interest. These treasuries owned by China are called "US debt to China".
- Buying these US treasuries debt is a simple computer operation at the Fed: the Chinese government's cash balance is reduced and the balance in its interest bearing Treasury account is increased by the same amount.
- The US government can "repay its debt" to China by simply making another computer entry—reducing China's Treasury account at the Fed and increasing China's cash account by the same amount.

The reason why the Chinese would prefer to have their money in US government Treasuries (debt) rather than cash is obvious. They can earn interest on the Treasuries, but they don't on a cash balance. Why does the US government allow those who hold its cash to buy its Treasuries? Why provide the option at all since it doesn't actually need the money from China, nor does it really acquire any by this process? The answer is that when China buys US debt, or lends the US money, the number of dollars in existence decreases by that amount for a set period (the duration of the note): selling Treasuries allows the US government to drain dollars from the economy, which enables it better to control the price of those dollars in the private market.

Government Debt is Private Savings

Since all the money that exists in the non-government sector (private economy) was originally created by the government, there is one equation that underlies all of economics.

When we talk about government deficits, we are referring to that amount of money that government has spent beyond what it has taken in as revenue. For the purposes of this section, government debt can be thought of as the sum of all government deficits over time.

But as we've seen, this government deficit is the amount of money spent into the private sector, or in other words, the increase in monetary wealth of the private sector (as measured in dollars). Therefore, another term for "government deficit" would be "increase in monetary wealth of the private sector". Similarly, the government can only run a surplus (take in more revenue that it spends) by draining that money (monetary wealth) from the private sector.

In other words, a government surplus is identically a private sector deficit, and a government deficit is a private sector surplus.

While that is a profound understanding in itself, it can be made more useful by realizing that the private sector comprises a domestic private sector—all Americans who use US dollars and are liable for taxes in dollars, and foreigners who collect dollars when Americans buy things (or foreign currency) from them.

Many non-Americans also trade in dollars, and by some estimates more than half of all US dollars are held and/or used outside the USA.

MMTers then consider three sectors—the government sector; the domestic private sector, and the foreign private sector. This leads us nicely to the most important equation in understanding today's economic system.

Government sector deficit (-G) = Domestic private sector surplus (D) + Foreign private sector surplus (F)

Or simply G+D+F =0

Therefore, if American citizens (the domestic private sector) want to save money, as they typically do during, and in the immediate aftermath of, a recession, then D is positive. Either the government must run a deficit (G is negative) to supply these saved dollars or, if it does not do so (G=0), these saved dollars must come from foreign private holders of dollars, and so F is negative, meaning that exports must exceed imports.

Media Failure in the Economic Crisis

The above is unknown to many Americans, as it does not fit our commonly held economic paradigm. But perhaps the most important thing to know about our financial system is that some people like Steve Keen and others, understand it deeply. If you get all of your economic knowledge from pundits on cable TV, you're likely to think that are as many "reasonable" opinions about economic causes, effects and events as there are economists—or maybe more, in the spirit of that one-liner, "If you laid all economists end to end, they still wouldn't reach a conclusion", or better yet, "If you laid all economists end to end, that would be a very good idea".

The media-supported impression of the American economy, then, is that not only is it not understood, but also that it cannot be understood. But that is an error. Just like the boom and bust of the early 2000s, the current housing crisis was predicted by those that understood the true nature of money, outlined above. In fact, the recent boom and bust were predicted in detail, and with accurate explanations that can be easily followed by anyone who will take the time. That it was predicted means that it was predictable. That it was logically explained means that it is explainable.

The above facts about money are both fundamental and consequential. When some people were trying to get us to understand, as early as 2005, that we were driving ourselves off of an economic cliff, why were the media being so indiscriminate and perhaps uninterested in finding them and doing the real work of evaluating their claims—rather than just finding someone else with yet another point of view?

Here's part of an interview with one of those more knowledgeable people on CNBC's Kudlow and Company from August 2006.[41]

> ***Interviewer:*** *Why do you think a recession is coming and just how bad is it going to be?*
> ***Peter Schiff:*** *I think it's going to be pretty bad, and whether it starts in '07 or '08 I think is immaterial; and I also think it is going to last not just for quarters but for years. You see, the basic problem with the U.S. economy is we have too much*

[41] This is not to endorse Schiff's understanding of money. Schiff is a good Austrian and therefore is well ahead of most conventional economists who rely on ridiculous assumptions about people's rational behaviors, which have been theoretically and empirically falsified time and time again. But Keen would point out, I expect, gaps in Schiff's knowledge that would explain some problems with some of Schiff's very "Austrian" preferred solutions to our problems. However, I am also quite sure that Keen would agree with the statements of Schiff quoted here.

> *consumption and borrowing, and not enough production and savings, and what's going to happen is that the American consumer is going to stop spending and start rebuilding his savings, especially when he sees his home equity evaporate. And when you have the economy 70% consumption, you can't address those imbalances without a recession. You know, rather than the recession being resisted, it should really be embraced because the disease is all this debt-financed consumption. The cure is that we stop consuming and start producing and saving again—and that's a recession. And sometimes, you know, medicine tastes bad, but you've got to swallow it.*

And then in response to a fervent disagreement from Arthur Laffer, who disagreed with him by pointing out by just how much wealth had increased in America in the preceding years, Peter Schiff continued…

> *It's not wealth that's increased in the last few years. We haven't increased our productive capacity. All that's increased is the paper values of our stocks and real estate; but that's not real wealth… When you see the stock market come down and the real estate bubble burst, all that phony wealth is going to evaporate, and all that's going to be left is all that debt that we've accumulated to foreigners.*

Peter Schiff, again, on Fox News on 31st Dec 2006:

> *Today's home prices are completely unsustainable. They were bid up to these artificial heights by a combination of temporarily low adjustable rate*

> *mortgage payments, by a complete absence of any lending standards, and by speculative buying, and what's going to happen in 2007 is that you'll see a lot of these artificially low ARM payments are going to be reset upward. You're going to start to see both the government and the lenders re-imposing lending standards and tightening up on credit and a lot of these speculative buyers turn into sellers, and these sky high real estate prices are going to come crashing back to earth.*
>
> *Most of the profits that people have in real estate are going to vanish—just like the profits in the dotcoms in 1999/2000. It's a fantasy. People can't sell their house. Inventories are exploding all over the country. Houses are on the market for six months or a year; there are no bidders. The prices are going to fall through the floor. You're deluding yourself if you think otherwise.*

The media, with very little exception, make no effort to find or even give extra time to those people who have a track record of accurate prediction. (Recall the section in the first chapter on the media's having a bad track record of identifying bad track records.) This is a huge problem for our understanding of important events that belie the foundations of our political economy and, for Americans especially, our identity. The kindest explanation we can offer is that of course most of the people who can speak about a subject will do so from the prevailing paradigm (which fact is almost the definition of "prevailing paradigm"). Based on sheer numbers alone, a random selection of experts will, by definition, reflect that paradigm.

But this is not a sufficient explanation of the dearth of useful coverage by the media. In fact, there are more important biases that cause the media to present to us the opinions of those who simply don't know. The first is that those who are most responsible for a (bad) situation are (again, by definition) those with the most power over it. Such men and women tend to have important positions and perceived authority. They are the natural go-to people even when they have proved themselves unable to understand the situation: if they could understand it, of course, they would likely have averted it before it had occurred! (Moreover, if they did understand it, would they be well disposed to admit it and take the blame?) We've already discussed the second bias, which is that for the media, finding the people who do understand how a complex system like our political economy works but whose views are held by a minority of commentators and experts, is to step out of the mainstream, and therefore to risk their reputation and market share.

The Price Is Right

The intuitive capitalist principle that is violated by our rigged monetary system is that reward should follow productivity, effort, and/or economic risk taken. Our current monetary system violates this principle by building into the nature of money the transfer of wealth to banks without any of these outlays.

The system prevents all members of society from simultaneously enjoying economic freedom by putting us into a form of collective debt slavery. Indeed, if one private citizen has money without debt, then someone else somewhere must have at least as much debt as the first citizen has debt-free money. This is not what most people think about when they say, "America-style free-market capitalism".

The principle that reward comes from risk and productivity means necessarily that reward requires the taking of responsibility. Both production and the management of risk require taking responsibility for actions and/or decisions. Those people who are unproductive, who make bad bets or who are irresponsible with their resources (or their customers) should be less likely to succeed. We intuitively know that the possibility of failure, as well as the desire for success, is critical to disciplining the businessman, trader, entrepreneur or independent contractor.

Unfortunately, not only has our money been corrupted in a manner inconsistent with this basic free-market principle: so has the nature of the corporation.

The subversion of the idea of the original conception of the company as an entity to conduct business in a free market rests on the combination of the rise of limited liability and the decoupling of corporate responsibility from ownership.

In a real free market, and in the market in which many small businesses all over America must survive today, competition keeps down margins and motivates innovation, including the development of more cost-effective ways of providing a product or service, or of new products or services that allow businesses to make a profit where there was none before. This mechanism is simple. All things being equal, customers will always prefer to spend as little as possible for anything they buy, and so if the profit margins enjoyed by a company are large, another person or company will have an incentive to sell the product more cheaply to take away the business from the more expensive producer, and enjoy the profits. Another company may compete by producing the same product at the same cost, but charging less for it, and so making smaller profits, or by producing the same product more cheaply.

The innovation that this process drives increases quality and reduces prices in the long-run, if left to play out without interference. It works for the benefit of everyone as long as companies are prevented from imposing costs (called externalities) on others without penalty, such as it may do when, for example, it pumps pollutants into the atmosphere or environment, imposing a clean—up cost on people of the community in which the company is situated.

Broadly speaking, we can see this process play out every day in competitive industries such as home appliances, handtools, electronics, computers—all of whose products get cheaper and better from year to year. In industries where competition is inhibited by government, such as in health insurance, or where government protects the profits of particular companies in a manner that eliminates their need to take risks commensurate with those profits, such as in student loans, prices tend to rise and/or service worsens.

In the case of health insurance, for example, before the Affordable Care Act, high prices were an artificial product of the fact that in most states, literally one or two companies had almost all of the health insurance market, because federal law prevents competition over state lines. Moreover, since most consumers of health services have no incentive at the point of use of those services to shop for better value—since their employers (most likely) have already paid the premiums and the insurance company will cover the service regardless of the price on the invoice—the fundamental driver of the market, which is price, is completely eliminated, and the outrageous costs of health care reflect that.

And when I call "price" the "fundamental driver" of the market, I am referring to that principle of subjective value again: it is customers' desire to get more for less that makes it profitable for producers and suppliers to supply those goods and services, in the field of health like all others, at lower prices. Having a non-competitive, third-party-involving system that removes price from the customer's consideration when obtaining a system will destroy the basic benefits afforded by the marketplace.

In the case of student loans, government allows private companies to provide loans but guarantees those loans, such that the lenders are essentially taking no risk in lending to students, and so are happy to lend as much as they are asked for, even without collateral. Obviously, then, universities and colleges raise their tuitions fees since they know that students have access to essentially unlimited sums of money. This is why inflation in post-secondary education is so huge: if government stopped guaranteeing student loans, private providers of those loans would limit loan amounts in a manner that takes into account the possibility that the student will not be able to repay the loan. Alternatively, they would charge much higher interest rates on those loans that reflect the true risk they are taking. Students would then borrow less. In either case, schools would have to set prices at an affordable level, based on the lower amounts of money that are available to students to purchase their educational "product". (As someone who receives dozens of applications from students with GPAs of the order of 3.9 who wish to join one my organizations, but don't know how to use apostrophes, I know that prices need to come down a long way to begin to reflect the quality of education that is provided by most of the U.S.'s institutions of higher learning.)

Property Rights Are Civil Rights

The happiest and richest countries are those with the strongest property rights, regardless of whether they may be largely socially democratic (such as Scandinavia) or more (in spirit, at least) capitalistic (such as the USA). In protecting property rights, we protect the inalienable right to pursue happiness, as we enable people to store the value of their labor and production, and deploy it however and whenever they choose. As people like Hernando de Soto have so convincingly documented[42], the economic and social disenfranchisement of the poor in the developing world depends largely on the fact that they do not have property in (legal title to) the things they own. For example,

---

[42] See the excellent book, "The Mystery of Capital: Why Capitalism Triumphs in the West and Fails Everywhere Else"

a family who lives in a South American city may have lived for fifty years in the same building that their grandfather built over months with his own hands long ago when the location was at the periphery of a growing city. That house may now stand on valuable land close to the center of the city, but, since the country does not have a system of property rights (including a land registry, contract enforcement etc), the family has no legal title to the land or the building. This lack of title prevents the family from using the equity in that property to start a business or meet emergency expenses, for example, which people in developed capitalist countries can do easily. The lack of legal property also enables governments to confiscate or destroy the homes of the poor, even relocating them without compensation. In many countries, such suffering is commonplace. Although we have eminent domain laws in the U.S., by which government can take property for the public good with supposedly just compensation, the practice makes us uncomfortable as a severe compromise of the right of an American to be secure in his property. We saw a good example of this in 2005 when a 5-4 decision by the Supreme Court favored the City of New London in their transfer of privately owned property to a developer solely for the purpose of increasing municipal revenues, resulting in a public outcry and the enacting by several states of legislation to restrict the power of eminent domain, and thereby to some extent restore and protect private property rights.

The existence of private property benefits society because when you own something, you care for it. That owners maintain what they own is so obvious as to be almost tautological. Accordingly, property allies rights with responsibilities. If I own a house, I have the right to live in it and do in it what I please. However, I can only enjoy that right if I take responsibility for its maintenance. This is a commonsense free-market principle, and a basic classical liberal understanding.

It is for this reason that property-based solutions can be so successful in solving the tragedy of the commons, which is the name that is given to the problem that arises when various individuals have simultaneously the right to consume and deplete a good that nobody owns. The text book example of this problem is the group of farmers who have access to grazing land for their cattle. Each has an incentive to put as many of his own cows as possible on that land to benefit from the free grazing. The inevitable outcome is that the land becomes useless through overgrazing. Arguably, the largest-scale tragedy of the commons that is evident today is in the fishing sector. Until fish are caught, they are not owned. All fishermen have an interest in fishing as much as possible. Over years, this results in overfishing—and nothing for anyone. The most successful schemes that have been implemented to solve this problem are those that make the right to fish a particular area a property. As property, it has a market value. The owner of this right has an interest in ensuring that he does not overfish (nor lets anyone else overfish) the area in which he has the fishing property, just as the investor-owner of a house has an interest in maintaining it so that he can enjoy the rental income that can then flow from it. The establishment of a property-rights solution more-or-less guarantees the preservation of the property (the fish in this example), and thereby eliminates the need for any government to pass regulations to protect the resource against abuse and then spend money to enforce those regulations.

If competition is the dynamic process on which true capitalism or a free market is based, then property, and the associated link between rights and responsibility, is the material from which the market is made. Competition and property are to economics what forces and atoms are to physics.

Bad Company

In the light of these two pillars of a true free market, let us turn at last to that ubiquitous part of American life—the corporation.[43]

Just like money, the nature of the corporation, also defined by fiat, has been historically altered in two fundamental ways that institutionalize non-free market characteristics. These are of particular interest because although these changes were made in relatively recent history, no one alive today has any experience of what companies used to be.

Although corporations were not mentioned once in the Constitution or the Bill of Rights, Thomas Jefferson famously noted that representative government's purpose was "to curb the excesses of the monied interests." On the face of it, that may not seem like a very pro-free-market sentiment, but it seems from other writings of Jefferson that he had a sense that unfair political and legal advantages would, if the country were not careful, accrue to those with an abundance of money.

The primary purpose of a company is to concentrate capital by making profit, but an American company today has an extraordinary characteristic: it has the legal status of a person.

This was not true in the time of the Founders. In the 18th century, for example, companies would tend to be incorporated for specific purposes, to execute well-defined projects, and would then be dissolved. Like a project, then, the life of a company had a beginning and an end. In 1886, however, corporations emerged from the Supreme Court case of Santa Clara v. Southern Pacific Railroad as "persons" under the law and thus could use the 14th Amendment to protect their equal rights. This meant that corporations were now entitled to free speech, protection from

[43] See the work of Lee Drutman, e.g. History of the Corporation, on which I drew in this section

searches and seizures, and could not be discriminated against. They were, in effect, artificial persons. The problem with this lies in the fact that they do not have—and cannot have—the same limitations as real people. Two differences are particularly important. First, corporations are immortal, and second, they cannot be punished in the same way as real people for illegal actions. Companies can be fined, but not incarcerated: what would even be the equivalent of incarceration for a company? It would probably be undesirable, if not impossible, to force a company to stop trading for a few years for committing some bad act. If we really believed that companies should have the moral rights of a person, then we would also believe that to own them would be a form of slavery—which is nonsense on its face. The problem does not lie in the idea of property—but in the giving of personal "rights" to non-persons, which, while fundamental to the way our market operates today in practice, is not required by the principles of true capitalism, and was not true in the original American free market capitalism.

In the time of Jefferson, companies could not make any political contributions, and could not own stock in other companies. Their owners were responsible for criminal acts committed by the corporation and the doctrine of limited liability (shielding investors from financial responsibility for harm and loss caused by the corporation) did not yet exist. The doctrine of limited liability began to appear in state corporate laws in the early to mid 19th century, when government policy shifted from keeping a close watch on corporations to encouraging their growth. In the ten years preceding 1871, for example, the railroads received nearly $100 million in financial aid, and 200 million acres of land, in one of the earliest corporate subsidies.

This doctrine of limited liability served a good purpose, by encouraging the concentration of capital in enterprises that could deploy that capital productively and profitably. But like all distortions of the risk-reward calculation, it is dangerous, because it allows company owners to enjoy the opportunity of great financial upside without full exposure to the corresponding downside risk. Companies cannot be punished like people, but nevertheless enjoy all the freedoms of people. Therefore, the only real means of enforcement against criminal action by companies is financial. Consequently, limited liability indirectly incentivizes risky or even legally grey behavior if the management and/or ownership of the company is sufficiently diffuse that legal responsibility for wrongdoing would be difficult to assign to any real person or small group of people.

The companies with the most diffuse ownership and management are large and publicly traded. These companies have the most impact on us because they are the largest in resources, geographical reach, and the number and importance of their products. To give a sense of the extent to which this is the case, 139 of the world's 500 largest corporations (by revenue) are American. Even the smallest of them, Whirlpool, with a revenue of $17 billion, is larger than 81 countries. The largest of them, Walmart, with a revenue of $408 billion is larger than all but 21 countries. It is, for example, larger than Sweden, Austria and Taiwan.

In 1925, Coolidge proclaimed, "The business of America is business." At that time, corporations were growing, and significant numbers of ordinary people were beginning to own stock. Accordingly, owners became an increasingly diffuse network of individual investors who did not direct the corporation. Rather, managers ran the company with no immediate and direct accountability to the owners.

In the time of the robber barons, J.P. Morgan, Cornelius Vanderbilt and similar magnates, ran the companies they owned with some pride. Their benevolent leadership, they insisted, benefited the public. But as ownership became increasingly divorced from management, owners had less interest in how their company was being run, and managers were able to mismanage with few consequences. When, eventually, even corporations were allowed to own stock in other corporations, the ultimate human owners were even more distant from the companies that they owned through companies.

Stockholders in major public companies do not manage, fund, or accept (civil or criminal) liability for "their" corporations, even though they are owners. In other words, the function of ownership has shrunk to the extraction of wealth. Huge numbers of shares are available in large public companies. This fact, combined with the limited liability provision, has enabled majority ownership by financial corporations who have no interest in, or liability concerning, the physical properties or purpose of the company. In these respects, the evolution of the company has strained—rather than manifested—free market principles. Even though share offerings (such as IPOs) enable a formerly private company to acquire more capital to invest in its own growth, trading in those shares after they have been issued is really only betting among traders, investors or speculators, because none of the money that changes hands goes to, or directly affects, the corporation.

As Schumpeter (1942), an early 20th century Austrian economist, famous for coining the phrase "creative destruction", noted:

> *The capitalist process, by substituting a mere parcel of shares for the walls of and machines in a factory, takes the life out of the idea of property. It loosens the grip that once was so strong—the grip in the sense of the legal right and the actual ability to do as one pleases with one's own; the grip also in the sense that the holder of the title loses the will to fight, economically, physically, politically, for "his" factory and his control over it, to die if necessary on its steps... Dematerialized, defunctionalized and*

> *absentee ownership does not impress and call forth moral allegiance as the vital forms of property did. Eventually there will be nobody left who really cares to stand for it—nobody within and nobody without the precincts of the big concerns.*

Notice, here, what Schumpeter is complaining about. It is not capitalism in its correct sense of protected property and the freedom of the individual to dispose of it as one sees fit. Rather, he is warning of a kind of ghost ownership of large companies through shares that decouple ownership from responsibilities, as described above. Exactly how complete is this decoupling? It is certainly related to the amount of money that can be created from nothing, and then sees its way into the markets, affecting the market values of the companies, and the profits and losses to be made from trading their stock—all in a manner that is technically independent of the company whose stock is being traded. When the value of a company's shares is dominated by such external monetary factors as the amount of credit/debt and created money in the economy, the tradable value of the company reflects less and less the quality of its operations, and those who are responsible for those operations have less real control. The overarching economic paradigm has a greater effect, and the actions of the company a lesser one.

So what if stockholders are "owners" of major public companies but do not manage, fund, or accept liability for them? All companies are run for the extraction or generation of wealth, and their valuation on a given day is at least theoretically determined by their capacity to generate wealth for the shareholders in the future. Since employees are compensated, and all agreements are transparent, no one seems to be exploited.

Perhaps. But let us do a thought experiment. Imagine a situation in which a landowner pays a tenant to farm some land, and the tenant builds a house there. Who owns the house? The landowner or the tenant?

In feudal England, it was the landowner. But in 1829, American courts rejected this particular understanding of property in the case Van Ness v. Pacard. The presiding justice, Justice Story wrote, "what tenant could afford to erect fixtures of much expense or value, if he was to lose his whole interest therein by the very act of erection?" In the American capitalist system, then, the house belongs to the person who built it and the governing rule became that "the value of improvements should be left with the person who made them and new wealth flows to those who create it. In this tradition, employees who "build" atop a corporation (creating new products or new efficiencies) would have a legal right to the value of their improvements. But in corporate law, they do not. The distinction does not alone prove one way is better than another, but it should give us pause: it is possible that the current American system of public corporations may not be the only way—let alone the best way—of realizing true capitalist, free-market principles.

The next big step in the separation of shareholders as owners from the companies that they owned came with the invention of mutual funds in the 1970s. Another very socially positive development in many respects, they allowed private citizens with relatively little money to invest by owning a diverse range of companies. Effectively, these small-time investors buy a share a fund, whose manager (which these days may just be a computer) selects the companies whose shares will be bought by, and held in, the fund.

Often, the small investors who provide capital for the purchase of shares in the companies held by the mutual fund do not even know what companies they are investing in! This change represents the ultimate dilution of the rights and responsibilities of ownership, making share ownership today, at least for most people, a financial investment that is completely free of any other kind of responsibility. Before the 1970s, small investors who owned shares in particular companies would often observe its management and strategy, and then show up at annual general meetings to put forward resolutions to ensure that the company succeeded, based on some knowledge of not only what the company is—but even how it operates. An investor-owner through a mutual fund who would do that today is about as common as a working American who wants to pay more tax for bankers' bonuses.

Ownership through funds raises another important issue: mutual fund managers tend to be compensated for generating short-term profits. After all, these are what drive those big banker bonuses. In some cases, financiers who actually own a large fraction of a public company can force decisions by the management that will result in making large profits in the short-run (such as by de-investment from projects with long-term payoffs, or even by forcing the selling off of assets) at the expense of the longer-term stream of profits that more traditional owners would gain more benefit from. We have thus come to an interesting point in economic history where the ownership of the largest corporations involves incentives that run counter to that singular reason why capitalism has been so successful—which is that it forces the owner to act in the interest of owned entity to optimize gains. This is the mechanism by which real capitalism supports real stewardship.

The fundamental point is, again, a paradigmatic one. As was demonstrated in microcosm by the "Perceptions of Incongruity" experiment with the playing cards, which we described in Chapter 1, sometimes we are looking at one thing (corporate ownership and trading, for example) and we think we are looking at something else (American free-market capitalism). When we're dealing with playing cards, that doesn't matter much. But when it comes to our own national identity, and to solving the fundamental problems that affect the lives of all Americans, it matters very much. We can develop our understanding by making explicit distinctions between things that our prevailing paradigms are too crude to distinguish—for example, corporatism and capitalism.

In so doing, we are likely to identify new conceptual ground to which our political Left and Right have no predetermined or standard reactions—and that can only be good for potentially uniting and improving our country.

You Can Take That to the Bank

Let's take another look at banks—not this time at the money they create, but at their nature as corporations.[44]

As economies have collapsed around the world in the last few years, the banking sector has benefitted from trillions of dollars from the same people for whom it creates inflation and from whom assets are transferred to them. The American taxpayer—it should now be obvious to everyone—provides a kind of free insurance for the banking sector. Banks "need" this insurance because they make bets—in the form of both loans and trades—without the capital to cover them.

Support packages ($ Trillions)	UK	US	Euro
Central Bank			
- "Money creation"	0.32	3.76	0.98
- Collateral swaps	0.30	0.20	0.00
Government			
- Guarantees	0.64	2.08	>1.68
- Insurance	0.33	3.74	0.00
- Capital	0.12	0.70	0.31
Total (% GDP)	74%	73%	18%

[44] This section draws on the work of Andrew Haldane, Exec. Director for Financial Stability, Bank of England.

Since the start of the 20th century, capital ratios (which measure the ability of a bank to cover its liabilities over the long-term) have fallen by a factor of around five. Liquidity ratios (which measure the ability of a bank to cover its liabilities over the short-term) have fallen by roughly the same factor in half of that time. Together, these trends have massively increased risk in the banking system and thereby in the likelihood of tax-payer bailouts.

Deposit insurance was first introduced in the U.S. in 1934 to protect retail depositors who had been burnt by the experience of the Great Depression. Deposit insurance is just a promise by the government to pay back depositors in the event that a bank cannot cover. This non-free-market device eliminates the incentive for customers of banks to assess the health of banks before making a deposit with them. Even more dangerously, it eliminates the need for banks to ring-fence or protect the capital they would need to repay the depositors were many of them to request their money at one time. Since the depositors don't care what the banks do to their deposits, but they will get them back anyway, there is not even any democratic pressure on regulators to ensure the true health of banks. Not that regulation is the answer, of course: if banks were not exclusively allowed to perform counterfeiting in the first place, and then to make highly leveraged bets using other people's money, limited only by those large fractional reserve ratios (which in fact are infinite for some types of bet), then there would be many fewer transgressions to regulate. Indeed, the same laws that govern the financial actions of other companies could then apply to banks. There's a thought.

Gains to the shareholders of a bank when it is profitable are potentially unlimited—since profits are distributed exclusively among its shareholders. But limited liability limits the losses to shareholders to about zero. Losses that must be covered in the event of bank failure by you and me, the American tax-payer.

Banks are taking advantage of this asymmetry of profit and loss when they "leverage" capital, meaning that they are making bets that could only be covered by many times the capital that they have. This is why a bank can lose all of its capital by making just one or two bad bets—beyond which point, their extra losses are socialized. Before the bets go bad, though, all of the profits are privatized, accruing to the shareholders.

Socialized losses are doubly bad for society. Not only do they raise taxes on average over time, but also these tax rises tend to happen most when they will be most painful to taxpayers—during or in the aftermath of a crisis, such as now.

On This Common Ground We Can All Stand

Many conservatives see private corporations and instinctively want to protect them from regulatory burden and government intrusion, rightly believing that these generally cause more problems than they solve and in the long-run, reduce the prosperity of the nation. Many liberals see the economic injustice produced by our current funny-money-as-debt system, not knowing where they come from, and rightly want to do something about it. In so doing, they lock heads with the conservatives.

The economy writ-large is a huge part of all of politics. Indeed, we usually say "politics" when in the past, people would have more accurately used the term "the political economy".

For that reason, I've gone into some detail to explicate the true nature of our economic life and contrast what is really going on with most people's assumptions and intuitions of what is going on.

Just as in the Perceptions of Incongruity experiment, we need to be able to see what is really there—instead of what we already (wrongly) "know"—to avoid the stress we are putting upon ourselves, physiologically in the case of the experiment, but financially and politically in the case of our nation and its economy.

Just as one of the subjects in the Perceptions experiment might be shown a black queen of hearts but "see" a red queen of hearts, a liberal who knows little about the fundamentals of American economic life an monetary system, might see the economic injustices that result from the system and instinctively rush to treat the symptoms by redistribution, regulation or other means, that do nothing to fix the problem—and likely exacerbate it, by instituting rules that only the really big, well connected banks can afford to comply with, making their privilege even more entrenched.

Just as one of the subjects in that experiment might be shown a black queen of hearts but "see" a regular queen of spades, a conservative who knows little about the fundamentals of American economic life an monetary system, might see banks like any other corporations and instinctively rush to protect them from the burdens of regulation and over-reaction by the state, doing nothing to fix the problem—but likely exacerbating it by protecting privileged entities from the very free market the conservative rightly supports.

When subjects in the Perceptions experiment eventually realized that the paradigm they brought to the table (the "normal pack of playing cards" paradigm) was wrong, they were able to see what was really going on, and they all started making the right calls.

Similarly, when we Americans get out of our paradigms—and the instinctive political reactions that they underlie—we will be better able to see things as they are, and treat the causes of our disease. When liberals see the economy as it truly is, they may see that there is no harm in free-market capitalism, but in the axis between the state and financial corporations, and in the giving of special privileges to non-human entities. Then, they will be want to treat the cause, rather than just the symptoms. And with that, conservatives should be delighted. Because similarly, conservatives who see the economy as it truly is, may finally see that state-privileged banking corporations do not practice, but subvert, the economic freedoms that are so important to our prosperity, and that protecting a free market is one thing, but giving certain entities privileges that individuals don't have is quite another.

A recurring theme in this book is that seeing only what we know keeps us divided from those who see only what they know but know differently from us! Finding common ground across tired political differences, so essential to the People's uniting for liberty and justice for all, requires the exercise of that core freedom—the freedom to think—but that freedom only "works" when it is applied to information about the world as it really is.

We face a circular challenge: nothing helps more to break down a paradigm than to see the world as it truly is, so we can see where the paradigm doesn't fit the world. But we cannot see the way the world is because we are stuck with our paradigms. This circle is for most people, most of the time, a trap, which can be exploited. We the People are suffering that exploitation today through a loss of liberty and prosperity that is unnecessary and not chosen with informed consent.

Fortunately, a simple act of will—of putting finding the Truth above enjoying the feeling of being right; of putting our nation's well-being first—can turn this trap into a virtuous circle.

Neither liberals nor conservatives have a philosophical reason to protect what is harmful to liberty and justice in our current monetary and economic system once that system is correctly understood. Both liberals and conservatives have every reason to protect the truly free market against cronyism, financialism and corporatism that claim the title of capitalism while offending its core principles.

In Summary, Real Capitalism is Progressive and Financial Corporatism Isn't

We have centuries of evidence for the power of economic liberty, and the recent memory of an economic crisis that, as we have seen, was nothing to do with the principles of capitalism and everything to do with the one part of the economy that is the least capitalist of all—big banking—acting, no less, within decidedly anti-capitalist parameters set by the state.

When a free-market supporter hears a left-leaning commentator talk about the banking sector, he may well be quick enough to point out that the bank bailouts were not free-market actions, but the opposite. The claim is generally heard defensively in response to some criticism of capitalism. Similarly, when free-traders are accused of supporting a system that exacerbates economic inequality, the free-market supporter points out, defensively, that it's not the free trade that is ultimately responsible for inequality but a financial system that concentrates wealth in a banking sector that enjoys special privileges. Or he might point out the anti-competitive nature of a system where large corporations can influence the writing of regulations by legislators whose campaign they fund and who exercise too much power in the first place. The effect, they rightly say, is to enable them to price smaller competitors out of the marketplace. Nothing capitalist about any of that at all.

Popular support for the free-market as the best way back to prosperity, conventionally important to the Right, and economic justice, conventionally important to the Left, depends on its supporters' making a passionate, positive, and systematic case for true free-market capitalism based on voluntary transactions and the principle of subjective value. We are missing, it seems, an easily understandable, even populist version of economic liberty that is as coherent and complete as the palpably false case against it —"palpably false" because it depends on a definition of capitalism that is not only incorrect: it often defines capitalism as the very opposite of what it is—such as when it refers to the trading of derivatives, which do not represent any asset, in an environment in which losses are socialized by the state—as in some way the epitome of a capitalist system, when it is closer to being a mockery of it.

The type of banking that brought us to the private debt crisis that triggered the current collapse is not capitalist. If anything, it is anti-capitalist because it violates at least two fundamental principles of free economic activity. First, capitalism requires informed, voluntary transactions between two parties that benefit both parties involved (the principle of subjective value), and do no harm to a third party (protection of individual rights and property). Second, capitalism requires that, down to the lower bound of bankruptcy, those who take economic risks bear the full consequences of those risks. We might also add that having people store their wealth in an instrument that is actually someone else's debt arguably violates both principles, especially when a cadre of market-making private corporations (treated in law as immortal people—nothing capitalist about that) have state-given privileges to do things with money that others may not do (nothing capitalist about that, either).

Rapidly rising economic inequality in favor of an elite is the deeper, moral issue that rightly feeds the fires of much of the Left and must be addressed. Supporters of the free-market should be embracing the issue—raising it more loudly, robustly and systemically than any of the Left who would seek to use it against capitalism.

Economic justice through the free-market is the ground of the solid ground of classical liberalism. Let all liberals declare their commitment to the free market precisely because they want more economic justice, not less, and precisely because they want to promote equality in a way that adds more value across society than it destroys. Let conservatives declare their love of the freedom to act economically, and see increased economic justice as a happy consequence. Meanwhile, the classical liberals can enjoy the increased prosperity and liberty that are bound to follow as the Left and Right discover what they knew along.

The Occupy movement talks about the 99%. They have the right point—but they have the wrong number. Most of the top 1% have much more in common with 99% than with the top 0.1%. Strip out that top 0.1% and inequality falls dramatically. The distribution of income in the USA, for example, is an L-shape—and most of its disproportionate concentration of wealth (disproportionate to real value that its holders have created for others, that is) depends on the aforementioned financial sector that operates, in many respects, in the least capitalist way of any sector of our economy.

Supporters of free markets let the Left get away with way too much when they do not challenge its claim that in a capitalist system, economic progress depends on inequality. It doesn't. Rather, it depends on the freedom of people to try to make themselves unequal—in whatever way they choose, including economically. (Is that a definition of liberty?) A "free market", defined as nothing more than the sum-total of people's voluntary transactions made for mutual benefit, is both "free" and a "market" with any income distribution. In a capitalist system, (rather than state-sponsored financial corporatism), economic success comprises entirely in giving people something they want. As we learned above, consumers make purchases only when the thing bought is more valuable to the purchaser than is the money they spend for it (the principle of subjective value). The capitalist, on the other side of the transactions, values the money more than the goods or services he has created. This indeed concentrates wealth—but only to an extent that is counterbalanced by the distribution of value among those who transacted with the capitalist. These capitalists are not the people who crashed our economy. So it is not capitalism that is our culprit.

Let us turn to Schumpeter again, for his beautiful summation of this truly progressive character of capitalism.

> *The capitalist engine is first and last an engine of mass production which unavoidably also means production for the masses… It is the cheap cloth, the cheap cotton and rayon fabric, boots, motorcars and so on that are the typical achievements of capitalist production, and not as a rule improvements that would mean much to the rich man. Queen Elizabeth owned silk stockings. The capitalist achievement does not typically consist in providing more silk stockings for queens but in bringing them within reach of factory girls.*

Clearly, the only parts of our political economy that do not work this way are the state (which concentrates wealth through taxation without a corrective mechanism when the transaction destroys value), much of the financial sector, and fraudulently operated business (and in a capitalist system, fraud is a crime).

Schumpeter's quote also tells us why simple measures of the distribution of financial wealth, so often quoted in the mainstream media, can be misleading. The Gini coefficient of inequality, for example, is a useful metric for some comparative purposes, but if financial wealth concentrates upward over time but does so more slowly than innovation makes better goods available to those with less wealth, then an increasing number of people get to enjoy goods that were previously only available to the super-rich. In such a case, the distribution of real wealth or value through the society may become more equal even as the financial wealth distribution becomes less equal. In short, it's not the money that matters as much as what you can do with the money you have.

By failing to explain clearly what the free market is (and isn't), including how it provides a way out of the economic turmoil felt by so many families, classical liberals continue to let the big-"L" Liberals equate "the free market" with things that are nothing to do with it. In so doing, we risk not only losing the political argument, but, more importantly, adding to the very social and economic injustices that we would all like to see overcome.

For example, the principles of capitalism do not require that corporations are treated as immortal people in law.

Capitalism does not require—indeed it does not permit—that corporations go unpunished when they harm people they do not transact with. Capitalism is not even opposed to organized labor. Rather, it champions the best kind of organized labor—labor that organizes voluntarily. Voluntary membership of unions is important to ensure that union leaders do not become exploitative masters in place of unscrupulous employers. It also ensures that their organizations have to earn their membership fees by providing a service of value to their members without causing (usually financial) harm to those who would not join.

Capitalism doesn't keep people in slums in the third world; rather, it gets them out. Why? Simply because capitalism depends on the establishment and securing of personal property rights. Hernando de Soto, mentioned above as the one economist that has earned the right to call himself progressive in the very best sense of the term, is motivated not by a philosophical commitment to an economic system, but to a human commitment to the poor of his continent as he urges leaders to realize that formerly destitute South Americans are being lifted out of the gutter into true economic opportunity by the most uniquely capitalist action of all: the formal recognition and registration of their property in the land and shacks that they have inhabited for years without any formal recognition. This, he has demonstrated, is making millions of the poorest people solvent, turning the products of their labor into actual financial wealth and collateral that can be used to raise credit.

Then there's China, which has seen the fastest reduction of poverty in history by allowing individuals to transact with each other freely over the last generation. And what most threatens its success? Their artificially massive, highly state-corrupted banking sector, and a property asset bubble pumped up by the State's financial controls that prevent privately saved money's being invested freely…once again, we see the gains that were provided by capitalism endangered by anti-capitalist practices in finance and regulation. And of course, if it all comes crashing down, they'll call it capitalism's fault, as so many have done in the West.

I've obviously not mentioned hundreds of issues that bear on economic injustice in our modern world, and I've not even claimed that a purely capitalist society (whatever that would be) is the best possible society. Nevertheless, the evident economic and social injustices that are being suffered today are much less caused by capitalism than they are mitigated by it. Moreover, those parts of our political economy that most need reforming for the truly progressive ends of improving the lives of the poor, working people, and the middle class, are the least capitalistic of all.

When it comes to big ideas, offense is often the best form of defense. And when it comes to political change, a big, clear, positive message beats a negative or reactionary one almost every time.

Most of the damage that has recently been done to economic and social justice in the Western world is evidence for proper capitalism—not evidence against it. We need actively to excite people about what proper capitalism is. It is not financial state-sponsored crony corporatism.

Classical liberals should stop conceding the initiative by defending capitalism in spite of its impact on social and economic justice; they should be seizing it by actively promoting capitalism because of its unparalleled positive impact on social and economic justice.

Why bother? Because in providing a mainstream account of

what capitalism really is and explicitly setting ourselves against those who have stretched its definition beyond breaking point, we who would promote liberty, can set ourselves squarely with all of the People.

And it is almost always "with the people" that liberty is won.

CHAPTER 5

We the People: Culture Precedes Politics

From Monarchy to Monarchy

THE TITLE OF THIS book, "If You Can Keep It" is, of course, taken from the famous words of Benjamin Franklin as he exited the Conventional Hall where he and the other founders had spent 116 days writing the nation's Constitution. A lady asked him, "What have you given us, sir—a Republic or a Monarchy?". Franklin replied, "*A Republic—if you can keep it*".

The first couple of chapters of this book were about, one might say, why we've been bad at keeping it. The third and fourth chapters were about, one might also say, a few of the ways in which we've most pervasively failed to keep it.

But those sections would be of only academic interest if we didn't still have a chance of keeping it—or perhaps more accurately, at this point, getting it back. That's what the rest of the book will be about. And if I didn't believe it was possible that the People could take back (or if you are less upset about the current state of things than I am, read "better enjoy",) their natural rights to life, liberty and the pursuit of happiness, I would simply not have bothered to have written a book at all.

This is a book about paradigms. The last two chapters

considered our self-identifying as the Land of the Free and A Land of Opportunity, and the systematic ways in which those American paradigms don't match American reality. Another huge part of what we understand about our nation is our founding myth—what we tell ourselves about where we come from. This is important, because what we believe about ourselves is inextricably bound up in where we believe we came from.

Franklin's quote is a perfect jumping off point for a brief consideration of the American historical paradigm, if you will, with a view to further unlearning "what we know that ain't so" so that we can better do what we need to do to get back a Republic that was Constituted to protect life, liberty and happiness.

Ernest Renan, a nineteenth-century French philosopher, noted, "Getting its history wrong is part of being a nation."

This truth has profound implications, chief among them is that the cultural and political trajectory of a nation is determined not only by its past, but also—and to a greater extent—by the stories it tells itself about its past.

The United States' founding myth rests on the idea that suppressed Americans fought for liberty against some tyrannical and foreign "other", and that to a first approximation, the nation was born as a liberty-protecting Republic in opposition to a tyrannical monarchy.

Since we "know" that not only are we not a monarchy Constitutionally, but also our very existence is owed to the very denial of monarchy as a morally decadent institution, we cannot possibly see the extent to which America has become, for practical purposes, a monarchy. It is yet another example of our paradigm's determining what we know and, therefore, (following Goethe and the Perceptions experiment,) what we see.

Monarchy has a simple meaning—the "rule of one". As Alexander Hamilton correctly said, "'monarch' is an indefinite term. It marks not either the degree or duration of power". The fact that our king is elected for four years, then, does not change his status as a monarch—not an absolute one, for sure, but a monarch nonetheless inasmuch as power is massively concentrated in his one person, and his one office.

In America today, the president can sign executive orders such as E.O. 13603[45], on "National Defense Resources Preparedness", in which he claims the right to revoke all contracts and nationalize all aspects of American life even outside a state of emergency. (Bill Clinton had signed a similar order, but with applicability limited to a state of emergency only, however that may be defined. Power only ever drives in one direction.) The Executive has also claimed the authority to strike militarily countries that do not threaten our own, without a supporting vote in the House, and even to kill American citizens without any independent legal process. It also works with its agents, again without the express approval of the people's representatives or, certainly, the knowledge of the people themselves, to receive by covert means the most private details of our lives, as we considered in the chapter "Land of the Free?". Furthermore, the Executive branch controls the actions of agents in myriad agencies, who can make, implement and enforce rules against the people with the force of law, but without a vote by our representatives.

Even in the late 18th century, George III, America's oft-caricatured tyrannical nemesis, could not and did not write or implement law by fiat. There was no such thing as an executive order written by that Head of State. He did not have the means to surveil the nation en masse. And certainly, neither was the decision to impose minimal taxes on the colonies to cover some of the costs of protecting them nor the decision to fight to keep them within the British Empire made in one monarchical mind.

---

45 https://www.federalregister.gov/articles/2012/03/22/2012-7019/national-defense-resources-preparedness

In fact, the last English monarch to sign an executive order was James II, who in 1687 issued the Declaration of Indulgence, in which he used his "legal dispensing power" to negate the effect of laws that punished Catholics and Protestant dissenters, which on the face of it, seems like a rather liberal purpose, except that it came with various concentrations of executive power to his office.

And what were the outcomes of this little piece of executive over-reach by James II?

Many of the forward-looking men of the time could see that James's executive order reflected of a much more wide-ranging, and therefore more dangerous, attitude to power. For this reason (and others), members of the polity, with popular support, overthrew him in what is known the Glorious Revolution. The British effectively ended the reign of the Stuarts (the royal House of which James was a part) by inviting William, Prince of Orange (in what is now the Netherlands), to take over the English monarchy. This "Glorious Revolution" of 1688 was called "Glorious" because hardly a shot was fired: but it was called a "Revolution" not only because the people had effectively chosen their monarch but, more importantly (and this is something American Constitutionalists should appreciate), because the representatives immediately and successfully limited that office by passing in the following year the (original) Bill of Rights.

The purpose of that Bill of Rights was to codify the ancient rights and liberties of the nation, limiting the monarch. Specifically, the Bill asserted,

The pretended power of...the execution of laws...without the consent of parliament is illegal.

The pretended power of dispensing with the laws, or the execution of law by regal authority, as it hath been assumed and exercised of late, is illegal.

In other words, the executive order and the signing statement—and most of what else of import the American president does unilaterally—were strictly illegal 100 years before

America's founding. America's 21st century presidency concentrates more power in one man than existed in the hands of the monarch of the very country against whom we supposedly rebelled for liberty in the 18th century.

What is even more shocking is in the old motherland, which retains its Monarch (capitalized as the position is official and almost entirely ceremonial) and is run politically by a prime minister, the former has no power to act politically[46], and, unlike an American President, the latter has no power to act unilaterally. Indeed, if 1776 is our starting point, the political settlement of the "tyrannical motherland" has perhaps continued broadly in the direction of individual liberty while that of the liberty-loving rebels has slid back an entire century to some pre-1688 concentration of power.

Without doubt, at the birth of our nation, Americans fought less of a monarchy than we now tolerate in the United States. More shamefully for us, even those English against whom (as we like to tell ourselves) we fought for higher ideals of liberty, had shed more blood over the centuries to rid themselves of a less monarchical government than exists in our country today.

If we are serious about our national identity as the Land of the Free, but we let stand what stands in America today, then we are surely kidding ourselves, blustering like a boorish adolescent who believes he is owed credit for the massive inheritance his father left him, despite the fact he's blown the lot.

Seeing history rhyme in this way, and with such consequence is sobering enough, but seeing the rhyme predicted is even more shocking ...

---

[46] Technically, bills must be signed by the monarch, who therefore has a right of veto. That has not been exercised since Queen Anne, who withheld her consent to the Scottish Militia Bill of 1708. More than 300 years a later, the idea of exercise of this theoretical "power" is unthinkable.

...I just mentioned William III, Prince of Orange, who was the figurehead of the Glorious Revolution against the last English monarch to issue an executive order. Fifty years after his death, the Prince of Orange was another William—William V—who watched, with deep engagement, the birth of the USA thousands of miles away. In a letter to John Adams, he wrote simply:

> *Sir, you have given yourselves a king under the title of president.*

How very right he was.

And perhaps the rest of this book is small contribution to the Glorious Revolution that will be required to make him wrong.

It's OK. We've Been Here Before

If the preceding chapters are anything to go by, things are looking pretty bad: our heredity as the Land of the Free and a Land of Opportunity is being greatly denied to us; our brains are wired to see the world in a way that keeps us stuck in biases, errors and political oppositions that cause us to stand by why things get worse around us; and the media, meanwhile, is systematically ineffective in getting themselves or the People out of those self-reinforcing paradigms.

An American could be forgiven for feeling quite helpless: when it comes to liberty and prosperity, she might note we are on a downward trend and the People are unable to stop what is being done to them by a Big Government and Big Money interests.

But it isn't hopeless at all—and always, history has a clue as to why.

It was Mark Twain who said, "History does not repeat itself, but it does rhyme". And it was Winston Churchill who said (and if anyone should know, it was he), "Study history, study history. In history lies all the secrets of statecraft."

And it turns out that what is happening today in the USA is rhyming more closely with what was going on about three and a half centuries ago than you could possibly imagine.

The United States is not the first Republic to have been set up by the People in a revolt against a tyrannical British monarch that was trampling on their natural rights. It is the second.

In 1649, the British did something even more dramatic than the Americans would do in 1776 in response to a tyrannical monarch: they killed him, and passed an Act of Parliament that abolished the office of king on grounds that it was "unnecessary, burdensome and dangerous to the liberty, safety and public interest of the people".

Britain became kingless for 11 years—and in that time, history gave us a little a lesson about Presidential monarchy and erosion of rights that 21st century America could benefit from revisiting.

Abolishing the (official) Monarchy is not the same as abolishing a monarchy (rule of one)—and during the eleven years of the British Republic, Britain saw perhaps the greatest concentration of power in one man that it had seen since 1066, when William the Conqueror successfully invaded England for the last time in its history. During the 11 years of the first of the Anglosphere's Republics, Oliver Cromwell, the "Lord Protector" as he was called, ruled as a Commander in Chief. He ruled without any of the customary constraints under which all monarchs had been forced, with various degrees of success, to rule, codified firstly in The Charter of Ethelred in 1014, famously in the Magna Carta in 1215, and most recently (at the time), the Petition of Right in 1628.

This is not the place to go into the massive elimination of liberties for which Cromwell was responsible. Suffice to say that under him, Parliament did not exist in its proper form and Cromwell was able to collapse the roles of legislature and executive, including Commander of the Armed Forces, into his single self. Under his rule, England saw a massive curtailing of individual liberties—especially those pertaining to lifestyle and religion—and they saw political power dispensed through the barrel of a musket.

Kings were limited by "customs", as they were called—universally recognized standards of behavior and political and cultural norms. One particular "custom"—that had existed in Britain for as long as the nation had kings—was that the king could not levy taxes without the consent of the representatives of the people. When Cromwell ignored that stricture and started imposing taxes under his own authority, even his hand-picked parliamentarians became so concerned that in 1657, they drew up a document called the "Humble Petition and Advice" to reduce his near-absolute power by asking him to do something that, at first blush, made absolutely no sense at all: they asked him to become the actual Monarch, an office they sought to re-establish.

What on earth were these representatives thinking? Why would officially making Cromwell a Monarch (big M) limit his power as a monarch (small m)?

There was a genius in it, based on the recognition of a critical point that I want to make in this chapter: culture precedes politics, and liberties are protected by the People who enjoy them, not political theories or documents.

Specifically, the English People had a history of kings, and they knew monarchs were not to be trusted; they also knew they had to work to force kings to honor their "customs", as defined above, developed as political and societal norms through centuries of development of the nation. These customs were indeed written down at various times in Constitutional documents to limit the king's power, and to enshrine in political institutions the expectations, rights, and demands of the people. But it was the insistence of the people that supported and produced those political settlements—not the other way around.

The point is that the People knew that kings, as ultimate

concentrations of political power, were dangerous and so they had to participate actively in protecting their own rights against that power. The People had won rights against the monarchy over hundreds of years and with gallons of blood. They knew they could only be maintained with vigilance, and they would not let go of something that they had fought so hard for. Making Cromwell king, then, would activate the self-protective and skeptical political instincts of the people against power, and the office and expectations of it would put Cromwell into a "box" that he was not then in.

Whereas monarchy (small m) as the rule of (any)one, in this case the rule of the Lord Protector, was unlimited because it was new, defined in the present by the actions of the one who was ruling, Monarchy (large M, referring to the institution) was profoundly limited by a culture and a historical tradition—including all the fights that the People had fought throughout the history of the nation—to win Constitutional constraints that had to be jealously guarded. In short, the powers of kings were known and limited: King Oliver, the parliamentarians thought, would have much less power than Lord Protector Cromwell!

The lesson for us, of course, is that no right or liberty, written on any piece of paper, or protected by any institution, is worth anything if the people don't actively insist on it. The attempt to make Cromwell king was an attempt to reengage the People in the protection of their own rights. Constitutional documents are just pieces of paper, otherwise.

This book is a tool, I hope, for the American People's re-engagement in the protection of their own rights in the early 21st century.

Oliver Cromwell and whoever-is-the-current-President of the United States have at least two crucial things in common: first, they are national leaders whose title and position are owed explicitly and directly to the insistence on not having a Monarch and second, they are national leaders each of whom, unconstrained by custom, rules as a monarch more powerful than any British Monarch since the seventeenth century.

Culture Is the Dog. Politics Is the Tail. The Dog Wags the Tail

The astonishing story about the attempt to make Cromwell regent to limit his power by custom both *reflects and arises from* a fact largely unappreciated by liberty activists in the USA today: *customs, or more broadly culture, precede politics*. Put another way, throughout history, customs—cultural norms or at least the limits on what the masses will tolerate—drive changes in political institutions, policy and law, in the direction of liberty.

Let us broadly define "culture" as the sum of actions of the citizens of a country, the attitudes that drive their responses to events, their expectations of what they may do and the memories of what they, and perhaps their ancestors, have always done. These prevailing attitudes and norms strongly determine people's responses to their personal, social, and political experiences. Culture overlaps morality, attitudes to outsiders, family, institutions, traditions, humor, philosophical assumptions and many other areas of life. In a sense, "customs" refer to a subset of culture, being those attitudes, expectations and habits that pertain to individual rights and responsibilities that prevail in society and the political institutions that interact with them.

The invitation to Cromwell to become regent is just one of many historical data points in evidence of this claim. In fact, in the Anglo tradition, the political elite has explicitly recognized that the feelings and expectations of the people are the ultimate limits on its power, and has conceded as much when it has had to negotiate with the people that it governed. The Magna Carta, various coronation declarations going back even as far as a millennium, the Petition of Right etc., all refer explicitly to these "customs" of the people—those freedoms that the people have a right to expect simply because they are commonly asserted and have been enjoyed for so long. These customs, existing in the minds of the people, define, albeit fluidly, the boundaries in which (earlier) kings and (now) politicians must confine themselves if they are not to risk a popular backlash that makes governing impossible.

In all of these major historical documentary references to customs, what were being honored were, in effect, those rights and responsibilities that the people take for granted. They could be said to be imperfect corollaries of those big three natural rights that the Declaration of Independence would later call self-evident—life, liberty and the pursuit of happiness. They refer collectively to the freedoms that are exercised and assumed largely because they are widely established in the minds of the people over whom government exercises its power, and they are entrenched in the prevailing attitudes of the citizenry.

Morally, the notion of "customs" acknowledges the fact that Power is being exercised against people, rather than for them, when it removes from them those freedoms that they already enjoy. Pragmatically, it acknowledges that governing will over time become extremely difficult if the people are caused to defend what they perceive is already theirs but is being taken from them by the abusive or self-interested exercise of power. Just as a people will fight harder to defend their homeland—land they already occupy—than to win new land that they know is not theirs, so, throughout history and rooted in the very same human nature, people fight for rights they believe they already have with greater clarity and ferocity (and therefore success) than they ever do to have things they have not had before or to do things they have never done before.

And so, at any given time in history, "the customs" provide the reference point in a collective memory of, or collective attitude toward, rights and responsibilities, which are the reference point by which the polity or political institutions can be judged to have gone "too far" in the practice of power against people, rather than with their consent.

Of course, that has to be the case. Inasmuch as any infringement of liberty by power affects a significant number of people; inasmuch as a significant number of people care about those effects, and inasmuch as people offended by those effects, complain about them, share ideas about them, make an issue of them on which they spend any time or energy, and eventually even organize to do something about them—inasmuch as all those things are true, it is in the Culture that the People's unease is first felt, and their actions against tyranny begin, and it is therefore in the Culture than any response to a trampling of rights must firstly arise.

The founding of the United States is just one example of this process. In 1776 (American Independence), as in 1689 (the original Bill of Rights), 1628 (Petition of Right), 1215 (Magna Carta), and even 1014 (Anglo-Saxon Charter), freedoms *that citizens already believed they had were* codified and concretized to shape political institutions. And in each case, this shaping of political entities with the purpose of increasing or protecting the rights of free individuals that were already recognized in the culture was triggered by the over-reach of the country's governing elite (or, at least, part of it). The same case can be made for the English civil war, the American civil war, the Reform Acts in England in the nineteenth century, and the civil rights legislation in the United States in the last century.

This is important because Americans who are exercised by Liberty and wish to return our nation to it often think (by default) that their work is essentially political—that their pressure must be applied to the polity to have an effect on the polity. It's a reasonable thought because political change, in the form of legislation or an electoral landslide, for example, is the most visible proof of a shift toward liberty or any political or social goal. But it is a marker of the end (loosely speaking) of a successful shift that has already happened—in the Culture—where most of the real work must be done.

Politics is the tail that is wagged by the cultural dog. Political change follows change in the culture, which is, of course, no more than change in the minds of a critical mass of the People—rather than in the minds of those who occupy political office.

The Founders Were Liberal Conservatives, or Conservative Liberals

The Founders were not ideological revolutionaries in the common sense of that term. They were, every step of the way, acting in the Anglo tradition of liberty, a tradition that the British elite in that time was failing to respect, as our American elite fails to respect it now. Their "revolution" was therefore a culturally-rooted resistance to a violation of the customs of that very same culture, but its outcomes were, as intended and as always, profoundly political.

Seen in this light, the American Revolution was not so much an American Revolution as a British evolution—another turn in the ratchet of Anglo political liberty, driven by the kind of cultural conservatism—the preservation of the rights of the individual against Power—that all liberals should celebrate.

Or we could say that it truly was a "revolution" but only in the technical sense of the term: a "revolution" is a turn of 360 degrees—something returning to its starting point—not to a position that "opposes" the starting position.

I use "cultural conservatism" advisedly, but I'm referring to the conserving of a profoundly and increasingly liberal tradition, in the true sense of that word. The Bill of Rights is a beautifully liberal document written to conserve liberty.

So were its writers conservatives or liberals? And what does the answer to that question tell us about our own political arguments between Left and Right?

The original meaning of the word "Patriot" was not a commitment to a piece of land or independence per se. It was a commitment to the principles of individual liberty that would eventually inform America's foundation.

The Founders came out of the Anglo tradition, as did those British old-worlders whom they left behind. No wonder, then, that the strength of support for the American patriots in the motherland was similar to that in the colonies—and for the same reasons.

Indeed, in the year of the American founding, William Pitt the Elder, statesman and former British prime minister, spoke against the Stamp Act, "I rejoice that America has resisted. Three million people so dead to all feelings of liberty as voluntarily to submit to be slaves would have been fit instruments to make slaves of the rest [of us]."

For our purposes, Pitt's use of the word "feelings" is telling.

The notion of the liberty as something born and protected in the culture is implicit in it: feelings, after all, are not defined in law or carved over the doors of our most important state building. Rather, as Pitt was acknowledging, they are the sentiments, determined by the prevalent attitudes and expectations in society, that drive political change.

Those of us who care about our nation's falling short of its founding promise must take heed of this lesson: large-scale popular movements against power, like the one that founded our nation, are triggered not when enough people see that an abstract right has been taken from them—but when enough people feel the loss of something that they take for granted in their everyday lives.

Political Over-Reach into Culture Is the Trigger for the Defense of Liberty

Since 9/11, the rate at which our basic liberties have been eliminated in Law and policy has increased immeasurably. Between the Patriot Act and the National Defense Authorization Act alone, our rights to due process, privacy, and freedom of speech have been utterly trampled.

Libertarians, Constitutionalists and civil-rights-driven progressives have been trying to draw the nation's attention to the massive destruction of our rights that is implied by such legislation. The Patriot Act allows you to be held and your assets seized on the basis only of a warrant written by an agent who would execute that warrant, based on his own suspicions, bypassing due process. The right to due process was not just enshrined in the fifth amendment of the Bill of Rights. It was first enshrined in Clause 29 of the Magna Carta of 1215—a clause that is still statute in England. In other words, not only have our leaders passed rules that allow them to do things to us that they were not allowed to do even on the first day of this nation's founding: they are arrogantly overturning much more deeply engrained, and universally held, principles of common law. And should such a without-process warrant be served against you, it is illegal for you to talk about it to tell your loved ones. So much for the first amendment. Forget shouting "Fire" in a crowded theater: without due process, you may not even talk to your husband or wife about a violation of your rights that would utterly change your life. And under the NDAA, of course, the State is able to collect data about your life without any reasonable suspicion that you have committed—or intend to commit—any crime that such data would help to solve.

But as the Patriot Act was passed and renewed; as the NDAA was brought to bear on us, as Snowden revealed the extent of the abuse of our rights, almost no one marched in the streets. No significant events of civil disobedience were organized in defense of even our most basic civil rights, and certainly no one who (rightly) claims that his second amendment right was enshrined to enable the People to fight against a government that has abused the People's rights has fired a shot.

Why not? There are no more basic rights than indicated by the first, fourth and fifth amendments. Americans pride themselves on being a free people. Does the fact that they let the State violate their most basic rights prove Americans are lying to themselves, or just lazy?

Fortunately not. Americans are a freedom-loving people and their lack of reaction as these evil laws were being made is as much in the pattern of the Anglo-history of liberty as was the founding of the nation, itself.

I made the claim that the fight for political liberty always starts in the culture; in other words, it starts in the feelings and attitudes of the people and with their actions: those that prevail most broadly most characterize that culture.

It is unsurprising, therefore, that to understand when and how the fight-back begins, we need not just to look at the laws and policies of Power that infringe on our liberties, but to see how those infringements are felt by the People in the culture.

You don't react to the elimination of your right to due process because due process isn't something you need or use or otherwise experience from day to day. Until you need it, you don't feel it's gone. You don't react to the elimination of your privacy if you don't notice it and it causes no change in your everyday experience. And until someone puts you in a position where your speech is curtailed, you'll not have any direct experience of the violation of the principle of the freedom of speech.

The historical and psychological truth is that people—and the culture that comprises their attitudes and actions—react to protect or reclaim their liberties only when the abuse of power has become so great that it reaches beyond politics (in the form of Law and policy debates) into their everyday lives in directly experienced ways. At that point, the People feel a violation: the feeling that something that is already theirs is being taken from them, because they are no longer freely permitted to do today what they innocently did yesterday. This is the political equivalent to someone's breaking into your house and taking your stuff—rather than just telling you that you cannot buy something you want. Or to go with the analogy we used earlier, it is the political equivalent to an invasion of your homeland, rather than a fight to gain ground that isn't yet yours.

This dynamic is beginning to play out in our own time. Why else have both the Left and the Right in our time sat relatively silent as our rights to due process, privacy, and free speech have been removed by such legislation as the Patriot Act and the NDAA, and yet become very vociferous over our right to smoke weed (on the Left) or own guns without restriction (on the Right)? The answer, at least in part, is that smoking and/or guns are part of the sub-cultures of many Americans, so government overreach into those areas actually feels like a personal infringement, rather than just political abstraction. In contrast, removing your right to due process doesn't feel like anything until you need due process, and invading your privacy doesn't feel like anything if you don't know that it is even happening.

This simple cultural fact also explains why the Tea Party and Occupy formed as popular, apparently independent groups over economic issues while the civil rights issues remained largely untouched by the population for so long. One's economic state is perhaps the one factor in one's life that is felt all the time in all areas of one's life. When the irresponsible or self-interested use of Power (either the concentrated political power of the State or the concentrated economic (and therefore political) power of privileged economic actors, such as banks), causes economic hardship, the effects are felt very deeply in the culture and the resistance is likeliest to be the swiftest of all. The effects of economic hardship are some of the most immediately felt and most clearly and perceived.

Moreover, this hardship is clearly related to perceived economic injustice of "bailouts of the rich"—and a society-wide felt injustice motivates a cultural shift like nothing else can. Note how the bank bailouts have offended Tea partiers, Occupiers and the man in the street. One's political ideology might affect your favored remedy, but the taking of offense at the injustice of it all needs no political ideology at all.

These movements (Tea Party and Occupy) have had clear effects on the politics of various states, and the composition of the American House and Senate, while no such single issue movement focused on policy or political freedoms per se, has yet had such a large and immediate effect.

This all plays out in less visible ways, too.

In recent years, for example, people who smoke e-cigarettes, "vapers", have organically come together as an overwhelming political force (yes, really) and prevented the creation of a new tax on the content of their devices.[47] When e-cigarettes first came to market, in many states they did not satisfy the criteria to be legally taxed (beyond straight sales tax in the states that have a sales tax) so legislators around the country naturally pounced. Vapers saw that something they were used to having yesterday and today (an untaxed habit) would be lost tomorrow, and they resisted hard, forming grassroots groups in state after state. In almost every state where an attempt to tax vaping has been made in the legislature, vapers have successfully prevented the taxation of their habit. In contrast, neither they nor any other Americans fight with anything like as much passion (or success) to reduce any

---

47 http://robinkoerner.com/grover-norquist-and-harnessing-the-leave-us-alone-coalition/

of the other taxes that they are already used to paying—even though success in such efforts would leave more money in their pocket than their success against new vaping taxes.

I used the term "political freedom" just now deliberately. I use it to mean all the things government and the Law allow you to do without punishment. It refers, in other words, to the limits on your legal action. This is in contrast with "cultural freedom", which refers to that part of what you may do that you actually choose to do: it is the latter that you actually experience. For our purposes, one might say that cultural freedom in this definition is a subset of political freedom.

This perspective helps us understand why the exercise of freedom is critical to its preservation—because it determines when people begin to fight back against a loss of their liberties, regardless of how they politically identify.

As the state expands, regulating and criminalizing away behaviors of individuals that do no harm to others, impinging on the political rights of citizens, the initial loss of freedom is political: it is not immediately felt if the loss of rights is not evident in the everyday life of the typical person. The fact that the rights impinged upon may be the most fundamental that the government is instituted to protect is immaterial.

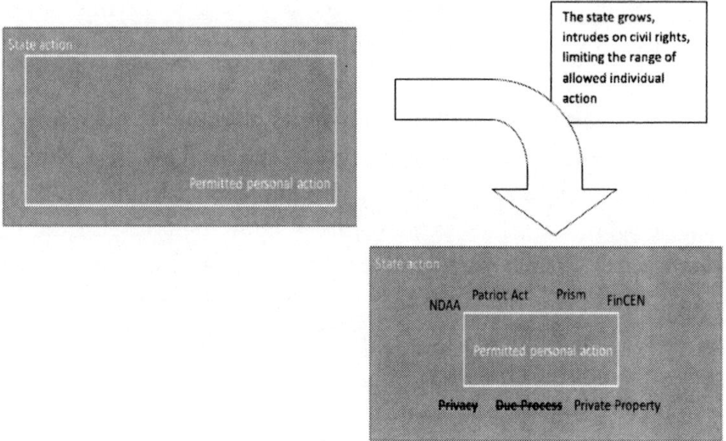

This loss of political freedom is, by our definition, the reduction of the people's freedom to act.

The state and other Power interests can go a long way in the direction of removing political liberty as long as they don't start affecting the everyday lives of individuals—as long, in other words, as they don't impinge on our cultural liberties.

The reaction against injustice, tyranny or deprivations of liberty invariably begins when Power over-reaches into the culture—when cultural freedoms, rather than just the abstract political freedoms—start to be affected.

This is when people feel that they are losing something that they already have, marked by a  in the diagram below!

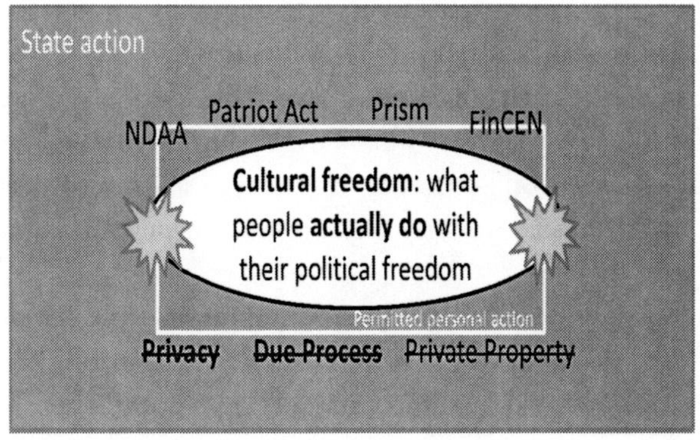

It is in this regard that Edward Snowden is a truly historic American.

Edward Snowden's revelations have altered American political discourse by changing the everyday American experience of sending an email or a making phone call from one of privately communicating with a loved to one of sharing one's life with the State. In reality, Mr. Snowden's revelations did not tell us much that was new in theory about the massively invasive power that government has assumed for itself since (at least) 2001. (There are myriad accessible articles about the Patriot Act, NDAA etc. and their implementation that anyone could have read any time in the last decade.) What he did was much more important: he has turned our government's violation of abstract or theoretical political liberties, which most of us know only as words on a document, into a felt violation of our experienced, cultural freedoms, which we can feel as we go about our lives.

How?

Because Americans now actually do feel that they are being surveilled. Making a private phone call doesn't feel like it did before. Having an intimate video chat online with a loved one doesn't feel like it did before. Many times a week, a typical American—especially a young one—is likely to second-guess—if only for a moment—what might be done with some information he has shared with another private individual.

I had a particularly powerful personal experience of this.

Not long ago, I was sending two T-shirts with the logo of my political organization—one that promotes the kind of pro-liberty paradigm promoted in this book—to a friend, Ismaine, who works with me.

A few days later he called me to tell me that the envelope had arrived but there were no T-shirts inside: just an old book, so I must have muddled up a couple of envelopes when sending, putting something I meant to send to someone else in the envelope I had sent to him, and vice versa.

But I had not sent anything to anyone else when I mailed those T-shirts to my friend. This made no sense.

So I had Ismaine photograph the envelope that arrived. Sure enough, it was the one I had sent him.

I had him photograph the contents that he had received—a tatty old book.

The T-shirts were gone. They had been removed and the envelope nicely resealed with colorless sticky tape.

I called Ismaine. My stomach was slightly affected. For a few minutes, all I could think of was "is someone trying to tell me something?". After all, I am a political activist. I speak and write against statist attacks on individual rights and the Bill of Rights. I know that the government now photographs every envelope that is handled by the US postal service, giving them an exact understanding of every family member, friend, company, etc. with whom any American communicates with by mail, along with their addresses (of course), the dates of communication, and even the handwriting of the sender. (Did you know that?)

If they were checking my mail, they were probably listening to my call to Ismaine about this extraordinary event, so, just in case the NSA was listening to the call, I spoke to them directly, with my tongue only half in my cheek, and told them where to go.

For what it is worth I took the matter to the post office from which I had posted the T-shirts to Ismaine. They were astonished. Two workers who had been there for decades explained that they had never seen anything like that—lost mail, yes, but not the removal of contents, the insertion of other contents, and then mailing to the originally intended recipient. It was sinister. It was also, by the way, a Federal crime.

Whoever and whatever were responsible for this event, we now live in a country where the experience of simple the everyday act of sending mail, performed by millions of Americans ever hour, has been affected by politics. I wasn't spooked because of what happened; I was spooked because, thanks to Snowden, the obvious explanation is a sinister one. Whereas yesterday, I took for granted that no one was going through my mail, today I do not. Snowden's revelations have given me, like millions of Americans, the visceral sense of being surveilled by our government without any probable cause—and that was what drove my experience of this bizarre incident.

For me, at least, when it comes to privacy and the fourth amendment, then, what was the take-down of an abstract liberty has now become something actually felt. Put another way, Power has over-reached into the culture, and I have finally felt the loss of my political freedom from search and seizure as the loss of my cultural freedom from search and seizure.

I'm not the only one. As I said, the People have hit  . And the resistance against the use of power against the People's rights is beginning in the culture, where these losses of liberty are being felt. 'Twas ever thus.

At Times of Tyranny, Democracy is Liberty's Friend

We have seen that, in the Anglo tradition at least, the re-establishment of liberty against a wayward State is not typically triggered by the most egregious denials of liberty, but by those most easily felt.

We have even more examples in America today. For instance, by most measures, the loss of a healthcare plan that you liked and its replacement with a similar one of a higher price (from which this writer has suffered) is less of an abuse against your liberty than is your loss of privacy, the elimination of right to due process or even the funneling of your taxes to connected corporations—but you feel the loss of your healthcare plan much more immediately in your life than you feel any of those other things.

Or perhaps your thing is gun rights. The fact that people who wish to purchase a gun must go through a few more checks than before is much less an abuse of your freedom than the fact that the government now believes it can assassinate you without a trial, but the prospect of those regulations generate much more upset, because one's enjoyment of one's firearms, or the sense of security they provide, is part of the cultural experience of many Americans—something that provides part of their identity, and perhaps many happy memories at the range with their sons.

When Power's abuses against Liberty remove from us not just the rights that we have (political), but the rights that we actively enjoy in our daily lives (cultural), we take them personally and respond to them more viscerally—more as human beings than as political beings. When the everyday expectations and experiences of enough people—rather than the ideas of a group of people with one political ideology or another—are challenged, political change that is not possible in normal times becomes possible. That change is, in the proper sense of the word, democratic (with a small "d").

The word "democracy" comes from δημοκρατία (dēmokratía), which combines demos (people) and kratos (power). In its full sense, it means much more than pressing a few buttons on a voting machine every couple of years.

According to our Declaration of Independence, the power of the American government is the power of the people—the kratos of the demos—delegated. In that respect, at least, our nation is a democracy, and that democracy is not only consistent with our Constitutional Republic, it constitutes it. And by that same Declaration, "whenever any Form of Government becomes destructive of these ends, it is the Right of the People to alter or to abolish it"—the ultimate democratic act.

Constitutionalists and libertarians are quick to point out that the USA is not a Democracy but, rather, a Constitutional Republic. Their point is that in a pure Democracy, a majority can remove the rights of the minority, including the smallest minority—the individual—and that so doing goes against America's very raison d'etre. They are not wrong—and, in fact, much of what ails us now has happened in just that way, albeit mediated by the poor decisions of our representatives.

But this is not the whole story—because success in the shrinking of the intrusions of the State into our lives and undoing its most outrageous offenses against Liberty (as we must) depend on an awareness that we are engaged in a deeply democratic process, just as were the Founders: only the kratos of the American demos can push back the kratos of the state far enough that it will result in substantial political change.

Whereas in normal times, individual liberty protects the citizen against the tyrannies of both Democracy and the State, when the State becomes sufficiently tyrannical, democracy fights on liberty's side.

And this point is made directly in our founding documents. From the Declaration of Independence:

> *That to secure these Rights, Governments are instituted among Men [demos], deriving their just powers [kratos] from the Consent of the Governed [demos], that whenever any Form of Government becomes destructive of these Ends, it is the Right of the People [demos] to alter or abolish it.*
>
> *But when a long train of Abuses and Usurpations evinces a Design, it is their [demos] Right, their Duty, to throw off such government.*

And from the Constitution itself, its three most famous words:

> *We the People [demos] ...*

In fact, it's no accident that "Republic" comes from the Latin, "res publica", meaning "affairs of the people [demos]". The meanings of the words, one Latin, one Greek, essentially overlap!

Paradoxical as it may appear at first glance, it was just such a democratic process that created this Constitutional Republic in 1776: enough people were moved by felt injustice (not some new political ideology) that they resisted their own political establishment (which is what the British state was at the time). The movement that became the American Revolution began among the People, and ended in a political change that altered their relationship with Power to the benefit of the liberty. The other Bill of Rights—the English Bill of Rights in 1689—came up in just the same way: the kratos of the demos crystallized in resistance to abuses of Power that were perceived in the lives of common men, and the political result (the Bill of Rights, itself) was the end of the process. Before that was the Grand Remonstrance of 1641, and before that was the Petition of Right of 1628, each crystallizing in the political realm popular disquiet in response to direct experiences of the abusive exercise of power—not ideological dissatisfaction. And yes, although the farther we go back the smaller is the demos with any power to exert against the state, the same argument can be made for the Magna Carta, too.

All of these political achievements—each one a roll-back of state Power in response to offense against liberty, felt in culture rather than seen in Law—were the end of processes that began among the People, whose power, aggregated, was set against the State, motivated by a sense of injustice mostly unmediated by any political ideology.

The founders knew that, too, and captured it in the most metaphysical sentence of the Declaration of Independence.

> *We hold these Truths to be* **self-evident**... *that all Men are endowed with certain unalienable Rights, that among these are Life, Liberty, and the Pursuit of Happiness.*

They wrote, "self-evident"—not "obvious if you think about it", nor "demonstrated by overwhelming evidence"—but "self-evident".

And that has a very particular meaning.

It means that those rights are known to all human beings by virtue of nothing more than their experience of themselves: communicating this truth alone suffices to convince the listener.

Offences against these rights are offences against human nature, not against any particular paradigm or political ideology or other cognitive or philosophical commitment. They are felt immediately and viscerally, as offences against our person, unmediated by political ideology. You feel them as people: not as political animals—not as conservatives, liberals or even, possibly, as Americans. No wonder, then, that at those times when politics overreaches into culture and limits those rights, that the democratic reaction begins.

We are at that point now: lovers of liberty and of the Founding principles of America need not teach our fellow Americans some particular political orthodoxy but, rather, must help them see what is being done to them, and let their humanity—including specifically their sense of justice and instinctive desire to keep what they already have—take care of the rest. Their reaction does not need to be managed.

To respect the importance of democracy is to respect history and to embrace the tool without which liberty has never been won back from the Power that would trample on it.

Such a democratic reaction, in the sense above, against Power in defense of liberty, has begun again in our time, as it has at various points in our thousand-year Anglo tradition.

Now we are ready to ask the question: How do we accelerate this reaction, and harness the kratos of the demos to get back the Republic, so much of which we have already failed to keep?

How do we free what we see and what we know from our old, tired political paradigms, allegiances and partisanship, which have taken America off its rails, so that we might unite in defense of what really matters—Life, Liberty and the Pursuit of Happiness—against political and economic interests that continue to want to erode them?

To this most important question we now turn.

CHAPTER 6

Liberty Is the Politics of Love

IT HAS NOT been the purpose of this book to expound on all the things that are wrong with America. These have been comprehensively tackled by excellent writers elsewhere.

I am rather taking it for granted that if you picked up this book, you don't need convincing just how far American politics has become removed from the original intent of the founders and the country. The chapters in which I did expound on some of the ways we have lost our freedoms concentrated on the losses that are both most pervasive and most poorly understood—in other words, the shortcomings of our operating paradigms as Americans that blind us the most, where it most matters.

The "You" in "*If You Can Keep It*" refers to the People—where ALL the power of this nation resides. And this book has been about what is wrong in Our thinking that has enabled us to be undone by those to whom we have delegated our demos-kratic power.

As we saw in the preceding chapter, the People are the source of power not only in theory, but also in practice. And history has shown time and time again that this is so, and moreover, why it is that the People sometimes say to those who govern, "enough is enough: we are taking back OUR power, now".

But the truth is that laying out what keeps the People blind to truth counts for little if we can't also find how to activate ourselves as a People united in reclaiming what is our fundamental birthright as Americans.

The last chapters may therefore be the most important. They are about the turning of political passion and activism, which is so often aimed by some of the people against some other people (Republican vs. Democratic, Conservative vs. Liberal etc., religious vs. secular) against any abuse of Power that removes the basic rights of all Americans, regardless of their political or other persuasion.

If you don't think that we need a new approach to politics, and, despite this book, you believe that the important battles really are the ones fought between partisans within our current establishment, then you don't need to read further. If you believe that we will solve America's biggest problems by empowering the Right even more against the Left or the Left even more against the Right, then please close the book here.

However, if you are one of many Americans who feel that the problems with our nation run deeper than just one party, and that, indeed, our current two-party, statist-corporatist, welfarist-warfarist establishment has brought us to this point, then this will be the most important chapter for you. If you are increasingly uncertain about the political loyalties you have carried for years, increasingly skeptical about the accounts of any of our political life that you hear or read in the media, or better yet, you actively identify as one of the largest growing political group of Americans—Independents (affiliated with no political party), then, read on.

The American people are not politically lazy. In fact, most of us have been in recent times as energetic as ever in opposing our political foes on our favorite political issues. The problem is that we have been so involved in the issues that have defined our old political identities, that we've largely missed how the fundamentals have been changed around us.

As we were all having our "I'm right, you're wrong" Democratic vs. Republican, liberal vs. conservative, secular vs. religious arguments, the Powers that Be have managed to make themselves more powerful, and while we the People have been arguing among ourselves, we have lost most of the rights that we weren't arguing about because we just took them for granted.

It is as if we have suddenly looked up from an argument at the kitchen table over which sofa we should buy for the living room, only to find out that the house has been foreclosed on and we're homeless. Sure, the issues we were arguing over were important—but they were not the most important, nor are they now the most urgent.

In the first two chapters, we saw how we the People are divided among ourselves and from others. We saw how our prevailing political paradigms cause us (and those who present us with critical information) to see things not as they are, but in a way that reflects those prevailing paradigms.

At first blush it seemed hopeless, but we have also seen how our humanity is much more fundamentally and powerfully uniting than our political tribes are divisive.

And our greatest hope lies right there—that our shared human nature is the key to uniting the People against the wrongs that are being done to us, and in our name, by a rotting political establishment.

And in that regard, the best news is that many apparently unbridgeable political divisions are not only bridgeable—they are not really even political.

Your Problem with Guns or Gays is Not Political

Last year, I did something I'd done only once before: I went to a range and shot some guns. Lots of guns... all shapes, ages and sizes. This is a very strange thing to do for a guy born British, as guns feature practically nowhere in present-day British culture.

Accordingly, I was unsurprised by the reaction of my mother when I called home and told her that I'd had a great time learning about firearms and discovering I wasn't a bad shot, even with a second-world-war Enfield. "That's the last thing I'd ever imagine you'd enjoy doing," she said to me. She wasn't being judgmental: it was an expression of genuine surprise.

I expected she'd say something like that and had an answer ready: "That's because you just can't imagine why nice or normal people would enjoy guns…because you don't know any…no Brits know any".

Mom thoughtfully agreed.

Many decent people who have no interest in guns simply can't imagine what it must be like to be someone who is passionate about something whose primary purpose is to kill people. Although the gun debate is waged using words, logic and fact (to different ends by both sides, of course), the arguments constructed using these three tools are not what brings people to their pro or anti-gun position. Rather, most people are emotionally or intuitively committed to a position first, and deploy these tools retroactively in defense of their position. Despite what we like to think, we form most, if not all, of our political views this way. Studies show, time and time again, that David Hume was right, when he claimed:

> *And as reasoning is not the source, whence either disputant derives his tenets; it is in vain to expect that any logic, which speaks not to the affections, will ever engage him to embrace sounder principles.*

What most anti-gun people are really feeling (rather than thinking) is that there has to be something strange about you if you like guns. I mean, why would you get turned on by something whose primary purpose is to kill people? If you do, you can't be like me. You are sufficiently different that I am suspicious or your worldview or your motives or both. You are culturally "other".

It is in this sense that all politics are the *politics of identity*.

Productive engagement, and the pervasive acceptance of individual rights, involves bridging such cultural gaps. With the gun-rights issue, as with all others, the best way to do so is the same way all forms of cultural segregation (because that is what we are really talking about) have been permanently broken down over time: to get to know, and spend personal time with, those on the other side of the gap.

It works both ways. People who favor more gun regulation are not actually motivated by taking away your liberty. And people who favor robust 2nd amendment protections do not have a lower threshold for the acceptance of violence or aggression. You'll know this when you have them as friends, and having such friends causes the all-or-nothing arguments that make such dramatic claims about the fundamental differences between you and the people on the other side of the issue to cease to be credible.

This mistaking of differences of cultural identity for political differences or, the erroneous idea that political differences drive different cultural identities, rather than the other way around, severely hobbles our ability to protect all of our liberties and empowers political partisans who have a vested interest in maintaining power by keeping us insolubly divided.

Just as gun-owners form a kind of (albeit highly porous) sub-culture, the LGBT community does so too. Some people who have been brought up in a socially conservative or religious sub-culture simply can't imagine being able to do (let alone actually doing) the things that those in another (LBGT) do as a matter of course. Again, if I can't even imagine your experience or desires, then we are deeply culturally separated. Just as gun-control advocates feel a twinge of disgust, or at least, condescension, toward the culture of gun-owners, some of our religious friends feel similarly about the LBGT sub-culture. "Disgust" is of course a very strong word, and most of us sublimate it deeply, but it captures the sense that the division among our "political" sub-cultures is more visceral than rational. Reason is applied later to justify in the conscious mind the position that the subconscious makes us emotionally comfortable with.

Now, I have a distinctly conservative streak when it comes to the raising of children, and I have an instinctive respect for any political position that is genuinely motivated by requiring adults to do the best by the children whom they create. I can understand, then, the real discomfort of those who sincerely believe that children benefit from having male and female role-models at home, and that society should be very wary of sanctioning anything that does not place the well-being of children above the proclivities of their parents.

However, two of my friends—and two of the kindest and most responsible people I know—happen to be gay partners who adopted a(n American-born) daughter. Phil and Michael are giving their adopted daughter a wonderful life. Their love for her is boundless. The security, values and richness of experience that they are providing her will set her up forever. And the gap between the life that Mia Joy has and that which she would otherwise have had makes the general question, "should gay couples be able to adopt?" sound something between silly and faintly insulting when applied to this particular, inspiring case.

I am blessed with close gay friends with whom I identify as much as I do with many of my straight friends. So for me, the question of gay marriage and adoption, for example, is not so much a political argument that needs logically "deciding"; rather, the very intuition of the existence of some gay "other" on which the very argument depends, has disappeared. As that cultural gap is bridged through actual human relationship, the separateness of that "other group", on which any suspicion I may have of their motivations depends, ceases to exist.

I've had many gay friends for many years. And now I am getting some gun-owning friends too. And because they are all good people (they'd not be my friends otherwise, would they?), I see both groups as doing essentially the same thing when they defend their rights—insisting on being allowed to be themselves, and defend the validity of the way they experience the world—as long as they harm no one else.

Of course, if you're reading this and you don't like guns, you're thinking, "That's wrong. Guns harm people." Not in the hands of my friends, they don't. And if you're reading this and you don't like gays, you're thinking, "That's wrong. Gay adoption is bad for the children." Not by my friends, it isn't.

If I were going to take a stand against gay adoption, I would have to imagine saying to Phil and Michael, "You should not be allowed to what you have done for Mia Joy, and I would use the force of law to stop you." Even if I could make an abstract political argument against gay adoption, I cannot say that to them in good conscience. And if I were going to take a stand against my open-carrying friend, Rob, I'd have to imagine saying to him, "You should not be allowed to own that to protect your family—or to protect your country against a tyrannical state, should it ever come to that, and I would use the force of law to stop you". Even if I could make an abstract political argument against private gun ownership, I could not say that to him in good conscience. By becoming friends with Phil and Michael, and with Rob, their respective sub-cultures cease to be alien to me.

The truth is that, because I know Rob as a grounded, kind man, I also know that the rest of us are better off when people like him have a few of the guns—rather than their all being in the hands of our political masters. And because I know Phil and Michael as being rather like Rob in those respects, I simply know that the rest of us are better off when people like them have a few of America's children.

And there's not a political argument in sight.

You'll appreciate my delight, then, when, during my day at the range with Rob, he told me that his local organization in defense of the second amendment accepted the open offer made by the organizers of his city's annual gay pride event to support them by marching with them. The two groups have now formed an ongoing alliance, reflecting the fact, of course, that they are really doing the same thing: protecting the right of people to do anything they want for people they love as long as they harm no one else.

That's when you know that you really care about liberty: the excitement of marching in support of someone who wants to protect and celebrate their freedom overcomes your "cultural discomfort" (should you have any) with what they want to do with it.

If we can challenge ourselves by focusing as much on nurturing our human connection with our political opponents by relating to them as people, we'd discover a wonderful paradox: we'd all feel, from our opposed initial positions, increased success in getting our opponents to see the world our way.

How is that possible?

It's possible because collapsing the sub-cultural divides in our society through actual human relationship does something bigger and better than resolving our political differences: it dissolves them. It dissolves them because it reveals that much of what we thought were differences of political principle are really rationalizations of the suspicion we feel toward those whose experiences and pleasures we simply cannot imagine sharing.

As in history, so in psychology: culture precedes politics.

Liberty Is Love Politicized

All very well, you might be thinking, but where does that really get us? Even if we look for relationship where we used to look for logical argument to bring those who disagree with us over to "our side", building relationships in the manner described above takes a long time, and in any case, even if I am a leftie who comes to have loads of gun-toting friends or a religious conservative who enjoys spending time with gay friends with offspring, we are still likely to disagree on quite a lot.

So where is the common ground? What exactly can we point to that has a unique power to unite us—and to unite us for *the right purpose*. Actually, almost every human being knows the answer. It stares us in the face; it is arguably the most powerful force in our world, but for some reason, we don't call on it in our politics.

And astonishingly, it is ready-made for use in a kind of politics that seeks to liberate people—that seeks to do what the Republic was established to do—which is to let people build the life they choose in a way that harms no one else. Just as a politics of liberty seeks for everyone that they seek for themselves, this missing ingredient always seeks for another what he seeks for himself.

I am writing about Love.

You know you love someone when you want for them what they want for themselves.

The three little words that really convey this sentiment are not, "I love you," which can mean all kinds of things to all kinds of people; rather they are, "As you wish." [48]

Love is kind, expansive, proactive, and fundamentally non-constraining. And although some of us may disagree on a positive definition of love, we can surely all agree about what it is not: restricting, compelling, imposing, or violating the right of another to pursue his own happiness and self-actualization. Those characteristics attach to something altogether incompatible with

---

[48] This powerful idea is taken from the work of Neale Donald Walsch

love—and that is Fear, which, as we have already seen has being driving our nation's politics for many years.

In a divided nation, as partisans work to use the political system and the institutions of power to impose their worldview on those who disagree with them, could we develop a politics not of Fear or imposition, but of Love? What would it look like? What system or philosophy could possibly be Love, politicized?

The answer is the politics of Liberty. Liberty, like Love, says to its recipients, "As You Wish" or "I want for you what you want for yourself." Liberty seeks to build a society in which people can express themselves most fully because they can express themselves most freely.

While this identity between Liberty and Love is for me the best argument for the former as a political philosophy, it poses serious challenges to those of us who are fighting for it.

As I discussed with the wonderful Jeffrey Tucker[49] on two episodes[50] of my Blue Republican Radio show, liberty that is not Loving is not true liberty.

If true Liberty ("as you wish") is the politics of Love ("as you wish"), then what does that tell those of us who seek to bring more of the former to our national politics? The power of this question follows from the fact that most human beings have a very deep and clear experiential understanding of Love.

Some of the specific qualities of love are so obviously those of Liberty that there is little that needs to be said about them. For example, both refuse to aggress against another. Neither seeks to constrain another, except in emergency situations, perhaps, when someone's life is in immediate danger, unperceived by the

---

49 http://www.bluerepublican.org/2014/09/03/against-libertarian-brutalism/

50 http://www.bluerepublican.org/2014/05/30/jeffrey-tucker-and-robin-koerner-blue-republican-radios-most-important-interview-to-date/

endangered party.

But Love is more multi-faceted than that and, therefore, so is Liberty.

First of all, Love is inherently *humble*. If you love someone, then you want to know what makes them happy, so Love shuts up for long enough to hear. Love listens. It listens to the beloved and acts on what it hears. Love acknowledges that different people experience and express Love in different ways. Even when it hears from the beloved something that seems misguided, wrong or even unloving, it doesn't assume its own superiority, acting in a way that rejects what it heard as valueless. That variation in experience and expression of Love among people is in no way inconsistent with Love as a universal—and perhaps the fundamental—human value.

Similarly, the politics of Liberty must understand that Liberty, itself—like Love—may mean different things to different people. And similarly, also, that variation in experience and expression of Liberty is in no way inconsistent with Liberty's being a universal—and perhaps the fundamental—political value.

Love is concerned with consequences, seeking to improve itself and adjust when the actions of the Lover are received badly by the Beloved. In other words, it is concerned and it is responsive. That makes it *empirical*. There is not, and there cannot be a dogma or orthodoxy of Love. No formula. It remains rooted in the human experience. And so Love is not measured theoretically by some abstract or impersonal metric: rather, it is measured in large part by the experience of those at whom the Love is directed. Like Love, Liberty should never forget that its primary purpose and measure is the happiness of people—and the facilitation of our own and others' self-realization.

Further, Love recognizes that it has *various manifestations, flavors and expressions*. It even allows that sometimes, in the hands of imperfect people, it can produce completely opposite results.

In our life, we may love different people differently, and we may love the same people differently as they change, or as we do. The lesson for those who pursue political liberty is the need for sensitivity to context: an appreciation that different societies, cultures and historical traditions may use liberty to build different institutions, emphasize different principles, evolve in one way or another. Libertarians benefit their cause by respecting what a culture has already built with it. Just at "Love" that is maintained against the will of the Beloved, and denies what the Beloved values, is not Love, so a form of "Liberty" that is rejected by the people for whom it is promoted, is not Liberty.

Love is *unifying*. Just as Lovers do not divide against each other because their Love brings them to opposing conclusions in a few areas of their lives, so libertarians should take care not to divide among themselves because various of their number experience Liberty in ways that lead them to opposite positions in certain specifics. If they do so, they lose the opportunity to build what otherwise they may have been able to build together.

Love is *respectful*. It allows people to follow their own path, even when the one who Loves can see the pain that the Beloved is about to choose. By definition, letting people follow their path is the essence of Liberty, too. Sometimes, sadly for the one who Loves, the Beloved is not ready to receive the Love that is offered to them. At such times, the person who Loves may have to wait patiently and calmly, remaining open to the Beloved but standing far enough back not to impose. Parents, for example, when they look at their children, have a particularly deep sense that the point of the human experience is the journey—not the finding of a "right destination" and sitting there. And when they see their kids follow a path that will result in pain or difficulty, they don't put down their children for their idiocy or lack of moral rectitude, but allow them to make their mistakes, as they did, being ready to support them when the request comes.

Said John Ruskin in 1870:

> *One evening when I was yet in my nurse's arm I wanted to touch the tea urn, which was boiling merrily. My nurse would have taken me away from the urn, but my mother said let him touch it. So I touched it. And that was my first lesson in liberty.*

And it was entirely consistent with his mother's love.

Love lets people follow their own path that not only for this metaphysical reason that life is a journey, but also for the practical reason that judging someone for a mistake that they cannot perceive and insisting that they comply with your judgment always backfires. It breeds resentment and alienation.

For most people, politics is the society-wide application of morality. These are the same people who, when they love their children or their husbands or their wives, don't just express that love by allowing them their freedom and doing them no harm: they do more than that—they actively care. Ultimately, Love cares. People who love make compromises. They go out of their way to ensure that their interactions with their beloved are fair, not just in their own sense of fairness, but in a way that is judged as fair by their beloved.

Similarly, those of us who seek to reclaim our political liberties might appreciate that some of our ideas, if implemented without consideration of the thoroughly illiberal circumstances of many of our countrymen whom they'd effect, could do immediate harm—not because the ideas are wrong, but because we would be disrupting an equilibrium, transitioning from one state of affairs to another, in a way that some people who did not chose the change with us, are not ready for. Many of those are people who have been disempowered by their dependence on the state. Think of the young adult who's been brought up in a house where he's never seen a parent work, but watched his one parent cash the welfare check to survive week after week. And others have been made promises by the state which—although they perhaps should not have been made—should not be broken without extremely good cause. Think of the old state worker who's paid his payroll tax for a lifetime and has expected for a lifetime the huge pension he is contracted to receive from his nearly bankrupt state.

If Liberty is the politics of Love, then caring for such people during a transition to what is Good and free is as much a duty of the civil or economic libertarian as the transition itself. It is the very society that we seek to change that, after all, put many of them in the positions they are in.

I am convinced that such a humble, respectful, empirical and actively caring posture of Love is the best way making the case for true individual liberty sufficiently congruent and compelling that it will change our nation. The Love = Liberty equation reminds us that to speak of Liberty is not to speak about a political system, but to speak about the state of the spirit, or the soul, or simply humanity, itself.

We generally don't use the word "Love" in political discussions. We should. It works. I've tried it.

No one has an ideological objection—political or otherwise—to Love. It is the ultimate concept for subverting paradigms and undermining the paradigmatic walls that people put up, consciously or unconsciously, to defend their position and their rightness. It is the ultimate indicator of shared human experience. Using the word "love" explicitly in a political conversation simultaneously disarms and invites people to come to the topic and to you as their highest selves: it tends to make both the person who says it and the person who hears it, take one psychological step back and observe their motivations. It moves the discussion from one of positions to one of people—who are, or at least should be, the ultimate end and only purpose of politics at all.

Love and Sales: The Thankless Art of Political Persuasion

We've seen the importance of culture over politics in more ways than one. We've seen the importance of Love. But if we care about liberty and we have something that we desperately want to share with our fellow Americans because we want to spread knowledge or even proselytize for a perspective that can help repair our country, then we still need to share ideas and persuade others.

If you wish to be an activist for the protection of life, liberty and the pursuit of happiness inasmuch as we still have them, and for retrieving them inasmuch as we've already lost them, then you must become a sales or marketing expert, with your ideas as your products.

We have already seen how no one arrives at his or her political preferences as a result of only, or even mostly, logical argument (despite fervently held feelings to the contrary). Rather, people find themselves most easily convinced by arguments that support political views to which they have become committed for often highly complex reasons that the their conscious mind may never even know.

Political allegiances and views are sticky: If you significantly change them, you are potentially changing your relationships with everyone with whom you have shared them—perhaps including your wife, husband, or kids etc.; you are potentially saying that you were wrong in hundreds of conversations when you insisted you were right; you may even have to stop doing things that you have been doing passionately—or start doing things that you'd rather not be bothered with.

When you're discussing politics, then, you're really not doing politics: You're doing psychology. And if you're a political activist, you are doing sales and marketing. Selling a new political perspective to someone is at least as hard as selling any other kind of product—but sales it definitely is.

No good salesman tries to change his customer. Rather, he finds out what matters to her, and then, using that uniquely human and humane quality called empathy, shows how his product satisfies her needs or desires or concerns.

Nevertheless, many of us advocate for our favored candidate and passionately held beliefs by trying to show our opponents that they are wrong. It never works—even when they are wrong—because being right is not the same thing as winning an argument. And even more importantly, winning an argument is not the same thing as winning a supporter.

Worse than the tendency to insist that one's opponents are wrong is the tendency to suspect that they must also (therefore) be bad. The logic usually runs something like this. "Person X claims to care about Y [insert value here, such as peace, liberty etc.], but he believes or does Z. Z is incompatible with Y. Therefore, X is a hypocrite [or deceitful or otherwise ill-intended]."

This is how to lose votes and alienate people.

It ensures that person X will never be persuaded by you in anything—and causes him to associate your views with people they don't respect because they don't respect him. You see, the sine qua non of persuasion is respect, and preferably even Trust—every salesman's best friend.

If you want to take someone on a journey—whether it is emotional, intellectual, political or even spiritual, you have to start by engaging them where they are—not where you are or where you think they should be. That means finding a position or principle or passion that you share. (There is always one.) Then, explain why that point or principle or passion leads you to your point of view. Be gentle. Remember that you are offering something, not forcing something down someone's throat. The spirit is, "This works for me. Maybe it could be useful for you?" You are going to lead by example—not force, because everyone resists force.

As in sales, so in all of life: Seek first to understand—and only then to be understood. This is an idiom that actually makes your life easier, because people will always tell you how they can be persuaded if only you listen for long enough to let them.

The fundamental, psychological truth here is quite simple: No one cares what you think; they only care what they think. But if they respect you—and only if they respect you—will they let your thinking affect theirs.

We all know it. Have you ever once been persuaded by a person you disrespect?

Exactly. So in fighting for your ideals, always show respect—in order to gain it. Do it however wrong your interlocutor may be, and however incredibly incoherent their views may seem.

If you are more concerned with improving your world than being right, then remember that from any given paradigm, you can find areas of disagreement—and oftentimes disagreement of principle—with everyone.

But if we activists, and I count myself among them, choose to get on our high horses about what we disagree about (and it is always a choice) rather than choose to see what good we can do together, we have no right to moan when we fail to make progress.

The very worst thing to do is to impute someone's intent or moral quality based on their views. Doing so is always divisive. That's what one does when one calls someone a hypocrite or a fool or a shill. From one's own paradigm, it may indeed be true that their saying or doing A may be entirely inconsistent with their saying or doing B—but why on earth put down a person whom you're trying to persuade to your way of thinking?

In short, *self-righteousness isn't effective—even when it's well-*

founded.[51]

Love—which is unifying, inclusive and kind—is ultimately your only way of getting people to come to your side. (Not only is Love right, as we saw above, it also just works best.) Criticizing a person (rather than his views) with whom you have any common ground achieves little or nothing—so why do it?

And (not But) always stay true to principles. Act from your own truth even when others disagree with you. Realize that doing so requires only stating your beliefs honestly and never acting against them. It does not mean refusing to work in some areas with those who you differ profoundly in others.

Winning arguments against people who are wrong is easy and, frankly, pointless. Spreading your values, by definition, requires communicating with people with whom you don't agree. That necessarily involves respecting those people enough to build trust and find those starting points of common ground. You can always do that without endorsing those views with which you disagree. But build the respect first: Leave the disagreements for another day.

John Knox, who was in the persuasion business 500 years ago, famously said, "it's impossible simultaneously to antagonize and persuade". By all accounts, Knox had a lot less love in him than I'm calling for, but his insight was true then, and always will be.

Blue Republican

On 11 July 2011, the following article appeared on the progressive news site, Huffington Post.

> *The world lost its goodwill toward the USA when Americans voted for George W. Bush the second time*

---

[51] Neale Donald Walsch, again!

around.

I don't endorse the idea that American politics should be dictated by foreign opinions but a reading of the foreign press over the last six years reveals that the first election of President Bush Jr. was largely excused around the world since no one could have known what this new president was going to do.

Moreover, America arguably didn't vote for him anyway in 2000.

However, the second election President Bush was not excused, because by 2004, the modus operandi *of the Bush administration was clear. He wanted to 1) conduct wars against countries that did not threaten us (e.g. Iraq), 2) oversee large financial benefits to companies with which those in his administration were close (e.g. Halliburton), 3) establish a legal framework for riding roughshod over the liberties of private individuals who are not suspected of crime (e.g. Patriot Act), and 4) establish a massive federal apparatus to carry out such intrusions on innocent Americans in what is becoming a police state (e.g. domestic wiretapping, TSA etc...)*

The more-or-less global delight upon Obama's election in 2008 followed largely from the hope that Americans had realized what a mistake they had made with Bush's second term and were therefore voting against the egregious actions of the then Republican establishment.

When most Americans voted for "Hope" and "Change," the above four objectives were at the top of their list of what they "hoped" would be "changed."

After two years, however, we now see that Obama 1) conducts wars against countries that do not threaten us (e.g. Libya, Yemen etc.), 2) oversees large financial benefits to companies with which those in his administration were close (e.g. Goldman Sachs), 3) supports the legal framework for riding roughshod over the liberties of private individuals who are not suspected of crime (e.g. Patriot Act), and 4) is growing a massive federal apparatus to carry out such intrusions on innocent Americans in what is becoming a police state (e.g. domestic wiretapping, TSA etc..)

Put another way, when it comes to such things as the killing of innocent people, taking from the common man to support cronies, and the elimination of the basic values that make our lives worth living, we had the hope, but we haven't had the change.

Just as in 2000, Bush hadn't shown his true colors, in 2008, Obama had not either. A vote for either in those years was fair enough. But in 2012, if you vote for the Democratic nominee for president, you better have a moral justification that is SO good that it is a) worth killing innocent people who don't threaten you, b) transferring wealth to the rich and well connected, and c) the complete suspension of your right to privacy and such basic rights as protecting your child from being touched by a government official with the full force of the law behind him as he just follows his orders.

Do I labor the point? Good.

I don't believe that such a justification exists. I'm having difficulty seeing how a Democrat who voted for Obama (whom I supported) for the right reasons in 2008 can in good conscience do so again given that there is another candidate who has been consistent in his opposition to all of these things—not just in words but in deeds.

If you've read my other pieces, you already know who he is. But if not, you should also know that Ron Paul has voted to let states make their own laws on abortion, gay marriage etc. and to let individuals follow their own social conscience—even when he disagrees with them (as I disagree with him on some of these issues). In other words, he is consistent in his beliefs in civil liberty.

If you are a Democrat, and you sit tight and vote Democrat again "because you've always been a Democrat" or because you think that some group with which you identity will benefit more from Democrat programs than a Republican one, then that is up to you, and I wish you well. But don't you dare pretend that you are motivated primarily by peace, civil rights or a government that treats people equally.

That Ron Paul, who has been standing up for these principles quietly for half a lifetime, happens to be a member of the Republican party is a lot less important than the principles that we should be voting on. The fact that he is not a party guy should be obvious from his extensive differences in policy from his party and the fact that many think, given his views, he should not run as a Republican at all.

As Dr. Paul often points out, however, we live in a country with a corrupt political party duopoly... and the system is stacked against anyone who would run outside the two party system. So he's doing what he has to do. And so should we as Americans who love peace and freedom. It really isn't complicated.

Now, I know that the Republican Party stinks to many Democrats and Independents who care about social justice and civil rights, but we all need to be smart and play the system to get the political outcomes we seek: you don't have to like a party or even identify with it to sign up as a Republican for a year to help make sure that the Republican primaries are won by the one representative who has always been for peace, has always voted against bailouts, and has always opposed the reach of government into your bedroom, your relationships and your person.

And if you are a Democrat or socially progressive Independent, you can't tell me you weren't hoping for all that from Obama.

Perhaps you see too much small-mindedness, or mean spirit or religious craziness in the Republican party. Sure you do. You can find all of them in spades. But since you can't change the Democrat ticket for 2012, why not act where you can make a positive change—by telling the Republican party where you really *want it to go... in the direction of peace and civil liberty (both of which, if you go back just a little way, can be found in the traditions of republicanism).*

Just in case you need to make it absolutely clear for your friends at work that you have not gone to the dark side, I offer you a special moniker to set yourselves apart and give yourself a way back once you've done what needs to be done—the "Blue Republican"*—to signify, of* course, *your liberal* *sensibilities and perhaps even your history as a Democratic voter. (Or why not just tell your friends that Bill Maher and Jon Stewart seem to have already gotten the message?)*

I am aware that the main objection to Ron Paul from the left concerns his belief that private charities and individuals are more effective in maintaining social welfare than the government. To this I ask one question. Do you believe so much in the effectiveness of our current centralized delivery of social welfare that it is worth the war making and the abrogation of civil rights supported by both Bush and Obama's administrations? Moreover, while Ron Paul would look to transition out of the huge federally run welfare programs in the long-run, that's not where he wants to start: his immediate fight would be to bring our forces back to the USA and to re-implement the Bill of Rights.

Ron Paul's electoral weakness is not a difficulty in winning a presidential election. It is in winning a primary in a party with a Conservative constituency that includes the religious right and neo-cons. An influx of peace and freedom-loving independents and Democrats would change the math on the Republican side and potentially the future of America by setting up a presidential contest with a pro peace, pro-civil rights candidate (who could outflank Obama on those issues, at least, from the left).

Again, this isn't an endorsement of the Republican Party or a claim that the Republican record is better than the Democrat on any of the issues discussed in this article. (It isn't.) It is not even a statement that Dr. Paul is some kind of

> *panacea of American politics. Rather, it is to recognize simply that the one potential Presidential candidate who wishes to stop killing innocent people in foreign wars and stop transferring the wealth of poor and working Americans to the corporate elites happens to be—this time around—a Republican.*
>
> *It is also to recognize that any other political choice is for a status quo in which all the issues that really matter (war and peace, civil rights) are settled for the military industrial complex and the interests of the State over the individual.*
>
> *So what'll it be—same old team allegiance or new, Blue Republicans?*

This article struck a chord with hundreds of thousands of Americans, and led, with the help of some extraordinary individuals[52], to Blue Republican's becoming something of a movement. As its writer, I had the pleasure of speaking to Doug Wead, a senior advisor on Ron Paul's campaign, soon after its publication, and then being interviewed many dozens of times about the position I was advocating.

I have it from the inside of Dr. Paul's campaign that Blue Republican was the largest coalition in support of Ron Paul's presidential candidacy. I believe it is a sign of a shifting zeitgeist that the largest coalition for an octogenarian white conservative Republican was born out of an article written for self-identified Liberals and Obama-supporters on one of the nation's largest progressive news outlets. I'm not just writing about this common ground stuff...I'm doing it.

The movement ended up outlasting Ron Paul's campaign and the Presidential election, and as the "original Blue Republican", I

---

[52] Most notably, Israel Anderson and Zak Carter, but plenty of others too.

have had the pleasure and privilege of becoming increasingly involved in the large and growing liberty movement of which it is just one of many parts.

Since the birth of this movement, I have had the privilege of presenting on, and advocating for, individual liberty to myriad audiences. Many of them include educated, well-meaning people who are "Liberal-by-default", which is a label that would have fitted me nicely for most of my life.

The "Blue Republican" group is set apart from other Liberty-oriented groups by being less interested in winning philosophical purity contests than with winning supporters for Liberty, on the understanding that the most valuable principles are those that make a practical difference. It is a vehicle for finding common ground with people who don't yet identify with the liberty movement, to develop a civil discourse that helps them see how some of the ideas, policies and politicians that they typically support frustrate their liberal principles, when those principles are properly and consistently understood. Blue Republican is not concerned with pushing a libertarian orthodoxy (which will be discussed in the following chapter), but with helping all people, and especially those who regard themselves as broadly Liberal, see how so many of our prevailing political assumptions are wrong. Hopefully, this book has done the same.

Blue Republican is entirely non-partisan. The Blue Republican seal says "Principle before Party". There's a big market for that sentiment nowadays. Millions of Americans are already primed to reject the idea that the Left or the Right is the problem and that the Right or the Left is the solution—but many of them haven't been exposed to an alternative account of our politics that promotes liberty without pushing an entire worldview that represents a paradigm shift too large for them to accept. Blue Republican fills that niche.

Based on all the knowledge in this book, and my talking to hundreds of Americans, some broadly liberty-driven, some Democratic, some Republican, some Green, some other, and some completely uninterested in politics, I have honed the Blue Republican message down to a few bullets. I offer them here for those who care about "Keeping It" to use in speaking to others.

They find common ground with the increasing number of disaffected Americans by reflecting back to them so much of what they feel but perhaps can't articulate. They point in a remedial direction but without demanding allegiance to any new political label or orthodoxy.

✔ Seek Common Ground with Others

Seeking common ground with people who don't yet identify with the liberty movement helps to develop a civil discourse that helps them see how some of the ideas, policies and politicians that they typically support frustrate their liberal principles, when those principles are properly and consistently understood. Do not push a libertarian orthodoxy (which has always failed), but helps all people, and especially those who regard themselves as broadly Liberal, see how so many of our prevailing political assumptions are wrong.

✔ See Through the Left vs. Right Paradigm

Millions of Americans are primed to reject the idea that the Left or the Right is the problem, and that the Right or the Left is the solution—but many of them haven't been exposed to an alternative account of our politics that promotes liberty without pushing an entire worldview that represents a paradigm shift too large for them to accept.

Left and Right have together brought the USA to where it is. More harm is done to America in the huge areas of tacit agreement between these two sides—against civil rights, for the growth of the State even when no positive results can be demonstrated, for militarism and for cronyism—than in any areas of disagreement.

✔ Value Principles over Party

Partisanship has brought us here. If you think that the problem is either the Left/Democrats or the Right/Republicans, then you're the problem. It's that political tribalism that has allowed both flavors of Power to undermine American liberty and justice—while we stood by as long as our side was winning. Parties only deserve loyalty to the extent that they promote, rather than undermine, those values.

✔ Love is Part of the Solution

Our political system should be based in Love. Love is accepting and kind, wanting for others what they want for themselves. Love tries to solve problems by increasing freedom, rather than reducing it, and by understanding others, rather than judging them. Love is not dogmatic, but celebrates differences. Do not put down the morality, motivation or intelligence of those with whom you disagree.

✔ Believe in Liberty

Liberty is the politics of Love. Love says to its object, "I want for you what you want for yourself". Our political system should say exactly the same thing to the people it serves, rather than being a vehicle to impose one world view or another on our fellow Americans.

✓ Pragmatism over Purism

Support anyone in any party, or none, in advancing liberty and justice. All dogmas are dangerous to liberty.

✓ The Constitution

There is no better outline for the values shared by us all than the Constitution, which is both a profoundly liberal and a profoundly conservative document. We all want freedom of speech and conscience, privacy, due process, a government prevented from intruding into our personal lives, a high bar for sending our men and women off to die abroad, and protection from cronyism. All of these have been undermined hugely in our lifetime.

✓ Culture Precedes Politics

Throughout history, major political change has started in the culture. By educating and opening minds, we make taking back our basic rights possible. Politicians can only do what the culture allows.

✓ Be Optimistic

"There is nothing wrong with America that cannot be healed by what is right with America."—Bill Clinton

If the above resonates with you, then I hope you'll join us. If it does not, that's fine too, because if your goal is to Keep It, we are already working together.

CHAPTER 7

Against Political Purism

THE DANISH PHILOSOPHER, Kierkegaard, said, "If you label me, you negate me". That rings true to me. Not least because, as we have seen, if your label differs from mine, then we are divided before we even start to talk. Given what we have learned about paradigms, and our identification with people like us (exhibiting cultural similarities, as described at the beginning of the preceding chapter), we might reasonably say that all practical politics are ultimately the politics of identity. Labels, then, limit our identification to our philosophical or cultural in-group.

So if you ask me how I label myself politically, I just quote Kierkegaard. If you press me further, I'll go with "classical liberal"—a term I've touched on throughout this book.

But in many respects, the closest prevalent political philosophy or "identity" in modern America today to the kind of philosophy that this book has been indirectly espousing, is called libertarianism.

When Ron Paul failed in his bid to become President, I personally interviewed Gary Johnson, the former Republican who was running for President on the Libertarian Party ticket. Of all the candidates running, he had just about the closest philosophy of any presidential candidate to Blue Republican's political philosophy of putting principle before party to achieve liberty, peace and defense of the Constitution. He also had an excellent track record as (a Republican) Governor of New Mexico.

Interviewing Johnson, I discovered that not only did I like his philosophy, I liked his approach to politics, reflected in the article that I wrote to endorse him following the interview, "Never Say Never: Gary Johnson, Humble Libertarian".[53]

One of the best examples of his approach was evident when he was on stage as a Republican Presidential candidate (before he switched to the Libertarian party). Both he and his fellow candidates on the stage were arguing for large cuts in both government spending and the government deficit. When the moderator asked the candidates if they would vote for a deficit reduction bill that would eliminate the deficit through 90% spending cuts and a 10% tax increase, his follow candidates said they would not, grand-standing on their love of spending cuts and hatred of tax increases, which the hardcore Republican audience loved, of course.

These are the same candidates (with the exception of Ron Paul, it's worth adding) who have supported their party for years as it has been increasing government spending and deficits that they pretend to be uncompromising in opposing. In other words, they say the right things but don't walk the talk.

Gary Johnson, in contrast, reasonably said that if the offer (of deficit reduction that of which one tenth is achieved by tax increases) was on the table, then of course he'd take it. I call that pragmatism over purism. I like it because it works much better than its opposite, and is invariably much less hypocritical.

But more to the important general point: many political activists mistake purism for standing on principle, and by making

---

[53] http://www.huffingtonpost.com/robin-koerner/never-say-never-gary-john_b_2072284.html

that mistake, ensure that their principles will never be realized. We have been watching this in politics for years. They say the right thing and then do the opposite.

In fact, the political principles worth having are the ones that you can bring to bear practically on the life of the nation. Margaret Thatcher, prime minster of the United Kingdom from 1979 to 1992, saved a nation from economic devastation and turned its politics away from old-style socialism. She said, "politics at its purest is philosophy in action". What she didn't say was, "politics at its purest is philosophy at its purest".

For many years, libertarians have been espousing the basic principles on which this nation was founded while the social-democratic big-government Republicans and Democrats were perpetrating many of the things we have discussed in this article. I am convinced that if the Founders and the Framers were here today and had to join a political party (most of them would have not liked that), they'd join the Libertarian Party rather than one of the "big two". Unsurprisingly, then, I'd like to see them be much more successful than they have been to date.

As we have seen in this book, we are in a period when Power has over-reached into the culture, removing the People's civil, social, cultural and economic freedoms, and the People are reacting in defense of the same. Libertarians were sounding the alarm before it was cool—before Snowden, the National Defense Authorization Act, the Patriot Act, the financial crisis, the Iraq war etc. etc.

That is why my work as a political writer and activist is so exciting. I am watching this happen in front of my eyes. It's like the tectonic cultural shifts of the 60s, but instead of espousing a progressive statist politics, it's espousing a politics of social tolerance and civil rights, allied with fiscal responsibility and personal responsibility.

The rise of Blue Republican has been concurrent with the recent remaking of the GOP from the inside by extremely enthusiastic liberty activists. This process is well underway and arguably the most exciting thing in American politics today. These (mostly young) activists are pro-peace, anti-corporatism, and pro-Love, and they don't get their ideas only from the media and professors who can't help but teach what they were taught in the big-state progressive era of the 60s and 70s. These new Republicans are, in other words, driven by many of the things that many Democrats believe have been far too absent from the Republican party for far too long, and are more absent from the Democratic party than they have been for a long time.

These new Republicans also include the GOP's recent intake of more libertarian politicians, such as Rand Paul and Justin Amash. The media apply the old paradigm when they say things like "Rand Paul is left of Obama on civil rights/foreign policy, but he's to the right of the GOP on regulation and taxation". Much more accurate would be to say that on the real axis of Liberty vs. Tyranny, both the established Left and Right are toward the latter end while Rand et al. are toward the former. Old paradigms are sticky, but they are becoming unstuck.

So this chapter is written for those who already identify with this rising liberty movement, which I effectively joined when the original Blue Republican article made such a splash.

This is our time. History is on our side; human psychology is on our side. Grateful to libertarians, whom I recognize as the cavalry in the current fight to reclaim our liberties, and in a spirit of talking to friends, then, I humbly offer this word of caution against the only people who could really cause us to fail—ourselves.

Robin Koerner

Principled Compromise is Not a Compromise of Principle

(Nothing that follows is written to endorse a candidate or a party, but I refer in it to one or two politicians as concrete examples to illustrate a general point. Please don't let your feelings for or about any of the people mentioned in this section get in the way of hearing my general point. If they do, please just replace their names with anyone else whom you would prefer to use as examples.)

Whereas to many outside the liberty movement, including the mainstream media, politicians like Rand Paul seem quite libertarian, many Americans who actually call themselves "libertarians" seem to despise Rand Paul for not being libertarian enough in various areas, and so they call him a "neo-con" or a "shill" or similar.

To other libertarians, Rand Paul is exciting not only because he's standing up for important pro-liberty and pro-Constitutional positions but also because he's getting significant parts of the libertarian message into the mainstream, and doing it in a way that isn't making everyone roll their eyes and marginalize him as some kind of a kook. The latter may be his most important work because culture drives politics, and cultural change is what makes political change stick.

Among the latter subset of liberty-lovers, there is some frustration in the perception that as a movement, we actively refuse to make the best of every opportunity (and goodness knows we have so few of them) to move the dials of the cultural and political mainstream toward liberty.

Like it or not, it is almost impossible to discuss political effectiveness without an understanding of the nature of compromise. Speaking as an insider of the liberty movement, I believe we have a particularly uncomfortable relationship with it, which we must examine if we are going to cease to be political outsiders.

A good way in to the topic is to consider the sentiment, felt by so many of us who realize that both sides of the political duopoly (or monopoly disguised as a duopoly) are responsible for the destruction of our liberty: "I'm sick of supporting the lesser of two evils."

What does that really mean? For a libertarian, liberty is the direction of the Good, and tyranny is the direction of evil. In a complex society of competing interests, and especially in politics, you almost never get to move directly toward where you want to go (your version of the Good). Imagine it on a diagram. Draw a line from where we are to where we want to be: we are moving in the right direction when we move not more than 90 degrees from the direction of that line.

On our political spectrum of evil (tyranny) to good (liberty) stand those who would actually make things worse than they now are. They want more Patriot Act, more state killing without due process, more NDAA, more curtailments of speech, more invasions of privacy, more welfarism—especially corporate, and more militarism. In 2012, Romney and Obama both fitted that description. In other words, they stood between where we are and the "evil" end of our spectrum. To support either was to move more than 90 degrees away from the line to the good that we are seeking to follow.

And indeed, if you thought one was less bad than the other, then you could accurately call him the "lesser of two evils".

I wonder if, though, in its passion, the liberty movement sometimes mistakes the lesser of two goods for an evil? For consider another situation. Consider two imperfect candidates (the word "imperfect" is redundant, of course: people are not perfect). One that stands between where we are as a nation and the Good (liberty) cannot be said to be "the lesser of two evils". At worst, he is the "lesser of two Goods"—since should he take office, we'd have moved in the direction we are seeking to go, even if not as far as we would wish, and even if not along that direct line to the Good.

Let's say you like the Libertarian Party's Gary Johnson on nearly everything; you like the Libertarian Party because it's unapologetically libertarian. And let's say you like Rand on civil rights and due process, but think he's as bad as Obama on everything else. (I don't think this is reasonable, but there are plenty of Libertarians who say this, so let's go with it for the sake of argument.)

If that's what you think, then don't call Rand the lesser of two evils. Call him the lesser of two Goods. If you don't actively support Rand because you have a more libertarian alternative, that is great, but take great care before standing against those who support him—for one simple reason. If he were running the country, in important respects, we'd have shifted closer to your ultimate destination...not just politically, but, more importantly, because one of the greatest media platforms in the land would be in the control of someone who promotes—and normalizes—many libertarian ideas, rather than in the hands of someone who promotes—and normalizes—statist ones.

"That's all very well", say some libertarians, "but even if I like him on some issues, look at how he's sold out on others, and on his endorsements". This is worth considering because someone's consistency speaks to their integrity and you can only really tell the value of someone's principles when you see the price he's prepared to pay to defend them.

To stick with Rand Paul as an example, when he endorsed Romney in 2012, I felt physically sick for most of the day. I campaigned against Romney fervently—as fervently as I campaigned against Obama, and as fervently as I had campaigned for Ron Paul. I did so out of principle. Which begs the question, does that mean that Rand's endorsement of Romney necessarily violated the principles on which my campaigning against Romney was based—or worse, was an act of selling out? Put simply, how could a person who campaigned against Romney on principle support a man on the same principle, who campaigned for Romney?

When Rand ran for Senate in Kentucky, he made a deal to gain the support of the Republican party, which he calculated he needed to be able to win the Senate seat, if and only if he supported the eventual presidential nominee of the party in 2012. So in 2012, Rand kept his word. What did he get for keeping his word and doing that (literally) nauseating thing of endorsing Romney? Simply, he got the platform that has enabled everything he has done since. Now we might say, "but he didn't have to: he could have won in KY without selling out". Perhaps. But that is a hypothetical and necessarily uncertain. Rand had to make an actual decision to maximize his capacity to achieve a specific purpose. What we know is that he made that decision for a reason and he got the result he played for.

So that endorsement, when seen in its full context, has moved the dial toward liberty inasmuch as Rand has, since making it, stood against the NSA, against drone killing of Americans without trial, against militarization of the police, against unconstitutional declaration of war, and all the other things Rand and his staff have stood for since he's been in the US Senate. Did the endorsement make me sick? Absolutely. Does that mean I stand in judgment against of it from a libertarian position? Based on the analysis above, of whether the net effect of his actions was to nudge the culture toward liberty or away from it, I cannot—because principles are made valuable when they are acted upon.

As the liberty movement comes of age, it will have to understand that, whereas some endorsements and other political moves are made purely out of principle, some are made—and must be made—strategically to better place a principled politician to act on his principles. Usually, those of us on the outside of the game cannot see, or even guess, the factors that a politician must consider in the strategic calculation at the time he must make it—

and we cannot see the outcome until much later.

When Rand endorsed McConnell a few months ago, what was the calculation then? More libertarians were sickened. McConnell is a partisan, after all—and a partisan man of a party that has undoubtedly promulgated anti-libertarian after anti-libertarian policy. Was Rand's endorsement of him a compromise of principle or a means to gain something that will enable him to get support for a practical change in the direction of some principle in the future?

A fair answer must consider this: is it better to make an unprincipled declaration to be able to make positive principled change—or better to make only principled declarations and thereby be excluded from being able to make that principled change?

Even more important is this question: is it better to go along with a bad state of affairs when you believe that your overt support cannot make it worse if it enables you subsequently to do good—or is it better to state one's opposition to that current state of affairs from the get-go but in so doing reduce your chance of being able to put your principles into practice and change it with great effect later?

Clearly, good and principled people can and do answer both of those questions differently. But the differences in answers are not necessarily themselves differences of principle: they are just as likely to follow from differences of beliefs about method or strategy.

All this means that a political act cannot be judged in isolation from the context in which it is made—both situational, and personal. When it comes to the horse-trading of politics, we, the public, are very far removed from the game. We have no idea, say, of what was given or taken for that endorsement of McConnell. Does the fact that McConnell's victory speech stakes out for the first time ever (?) a non-interventionist foreign policy indicate that Rand's strategic concessions are bringing concessions from the Republican party on philosophy? I don't know, but if so, great—because that's exactly how you want to make those trades: make concessions that make nothing worse, to win concessions that actually make things better. (Consider this the political equivalent of exchanging Federal Reserve Notes for gold.)

But we still haven't gotten to the most radical challenge of political compromise for principled citizens: we are often too quick to label as "compromises of principle" decisions that not only aren't compromises of principle at all, but are their very opposite—principled compromises. For example, if a statement or endorsement is not going to actually make a practical difference to anyone's liberty in the short-run, but has a significant chance of enabling the person who makes it to make a material difference to our liberty in the long-run, then at the level of principle, the statement or endorsement is not a compromise at all: it is actually principled act inasmuch as it is a step toward the practical manifestation of principle.

While the unapologetic statement of principles is a critical component of cultural and political change, principles that never become more than statements are worthless. Libertarians have been purely stating their principles for a long time—and look at where we are. Let's at least allow that playing to win is a reasonable approach for a libertarian and/or Constitutionalist politician who wants to be in a position where his principles can have a practical and long-lasting impact.

Winning means being in the game. It also means collecting enough good cards throughout the game to be able to play a strong hand for liberty when the opportunity to make actual change arises.

If you can't stomach that game, then don't play it. But if you are of the "no good can come of politics" mindset, please be careful about taking a position whose logical consequence is that all who fight for liberty within the political process are irredeemably compromised—for that position is denied by history time and time again. Throughout a thousand years of Anglo history, the established political process, with all its flaws, has been the arena in which hard-fought improvements in liberty, won by the People, moved first in the culture, have been secured for future generations. In times and places where it hasn't been, change has typically been violent (think of the Russian revolution, or the French revolution), and less successful in securing liberty at all.

Indeed, fighting for liberty "in the system" vs. "outside the system" is an entirely false dichotomy: history and common sense both say that when real society-wide change happens, it reflects attitudinal changes outside of politics that are eventually realized in the political establishment.

One of my favorite examples is that of Thomas Clarkson, a student of my alma mater, who in 1786 wrote a thesis on the "slavery and commerce of the human species". He spent two years travelling on a horse around England, interviewing people, collecting information, sharing information, talking about the issue of slavery, publishing engravings of instruments used on slave ships etc. He wrote another tract in 1788, "Essay on the Impolicy of the African Slave Trade". There were myriad currents and reasons that explain the shift in Britain against slavery, some to do with the economics of empire, others to do with the loss of the American colonies. But none of that marked the actual beginning of the end of the slave trade: that came because of a principled politician, but a politician nonetheless, called William Wilberforce, who directly incorporated Clarkson's work in a speech in Parliament in 1789 that resulted in the vote to end slavery. It may not have been done without Clarkson. But it certainly could not have been done without Wilberforce—or someone else playing the game of politics. Wilberforce and his supporters were committed to advance the one classically liberal (libertarian) issue the country was ready for, compromising as the situation required.

I campaigned against Romney for president, on principle. As I mentioned above, the organization with which I am associated campaigned against him fervently, supporting Gary Johnson, also on principle. But I don't get to sit in judgment of Rand on principle—because my context was not, and is not, his. Rand was operating in a world where such a compromise may enable him to do more for liberty than I can do. In other words, a compromise that for me would definitely have been one of principle, for him it may have been just methodology.

That the same principle can result in different decisions in different contexts has profound implications for political strategy. Once we admit that we never can fully know the context in which others operate, the humility gained should help us not divide our small libertarian house against itself.

I wonder if there are a few Libertarian Party supporters, or Independents, reading this and caring about liberty as I do, who couldn't imagine voting for Rand for president if Gary Johnson was also running. Just as I endorsed Johnson in 2012, I'd be delighted to see him run again in 2016. But remember this: If Johnson becomes the Libertarian nominee for president in 2016, and there is every sign that he shall, it will be because of the compromise he made to run and win as a Republican for Governor of New Mexico, in which capacity he did more for liberty—and especially economic liberty—in his state than any Libertarian or unaffiliated governor has ever done.

That's unfair because there hasn't been a Libertarian or unaffiliated Governor? Well, exactly.

It's not beyond the realm of possibility that soon, libertarians and Constitutionalists may have the opportunity in a Presidential election to choose between a very small chance of moving the country a long way toward liberty (say by a vote for a Libertarian Johnson for President) or a much larger chance of moving it toward liberty but less far (say by a vote for a Republican Rand for President). Good libertarians can make that call differently, but none can claim without arrogance that those who decide differently are choosing the lesser of two evils: in this case, they'll be deciding between two goods. That is a fundamentally different thing, especially when you consider that even the lesser of two goods on paper might become the greater of the two if it is better placed to do the Good it wants to do.

My purpose is emphatically not to endorse Rand Paul or Johnson or any other politician. Rather, it is a plea for libertarians who put more weight on moving the dial toward liberty at all and libertarians who put more weight on the need to turn the dial a long way, to recognize that you are not opponents of each other. It's the very fact that each group is using liberty as the primary metric for choosing whom to support—that, in other words, they are all seeking to move to the Good—that puts them on the same side.

Of course, there are those who just hate all parties and the electoral process, on principle. And that is a perfectly defensible position too. But the problem is the same, because the measure of Good is not just what you stand for; it's what you deliver. That is a truth that all libertarians see clearly when it comes to Republicans who talk about small government and individual rights and deliver none of it, or even its opposite. Consistency demands we apply it to ourselves.

I, too, am a purist by instinct. At Thomas Clarkson's university, I studied physics and the philosophy of science. For purists, I recommend these subjects heartily. But now I'm doing politics—and political purism, alas, is a contradiction in terms.

Humility, Tolerance and Civility: the Dispositions of Liberty

At its simplest, libertarianism is a philosophy that asserts the simple principle that we are all free to live our lives as we please inasmuch as we do not limit the freedom of others to do the same. It recognizes that we all have different backgrounds, desires and ambitions, and different metrics and systems for judging the behaviors and choices of ourselves and others.

Since it rests on the notion that one human being cannot know what is best for another—or at least cannot know it better than the other person, himself, it is an essentially humble philosophy in disposition and an essentially tolerant philosophy in prescription. Indeed, tolerance, manifest as lack of aggression, is just about its only hard-and-fast prescription.

Because libertarians put the moral burden of justification on those who would use coercion (reduce liberty) to do good, and the State is inherently coercive (it puts you in jail if you don't comply), they emphasize civil society as critical to delivering welfare to those less fortunate among us. Civil society includes non-state organizations, formed voluntarily, that act privately to better the lives of their members and, usually, their non-members. These organizations can be more nimble and effective than the state as the good they do does not involve the forced transfer of resources from some people to others, nor does it involve the use of such co-opted resources in ways that the people from whom they are taken would not approve. Moreover, civil society can often deliver much more targeted remedies of social and economic injustice than can the one-size-fits-all programs of government. A libertarian society, then, harnesses for social good the civility of the people who comprise it.

So there we have the three dispositions of a good libertarian: humility, tolerance of diversity, and civility.

There are those who insist that those who would pursue liberty within the political duopoly—usually by trying to change the Republican party from within—are naïve. On the other hand, there are those who believe that those who would try to go outside the duopoly to do so are naïve. Both groups include those who are so sure of their own rightness that they won't even celebrate the attempt of their fellows to pursue a different path to the same end, just in case their ability to predict the future might be imperfect and/or their shared goals might benefit from multiple approaches by people with different experiences and perspectives.

Such purists are the people who see any agreement to reduce an infringement of liberty as "selling out" if it does not eliminate that infringement altogether; these are the people who will dismiss all liberty-promoting actions of a politician just because that politician is actually willing to play politics and even make concessions to circumstance to stay in the game so that he can do any good at all; these are the people who see all compromise as proof of a lack of values—or of virtue; they see the choosing of battles as proof of a lack of commitment to the war rather than tactics for winning it; these are the people who won't listen to an idea—or even consider a quotation—from someone they have decided isn't a "real libertarian" even if that someone has special experience of the issue of which they speak; these are the people who will never admit a tension between libertarian means and libertarian ends. In short, these are people who insist that everyone should be free to think and do as they please—but will happily put you down should you disagree about how best to make everyone free to think and do as they please.

None of this is to say there is necessarily a problem with what these purists believe. In as much as these are better-than-normally informed lovers of liberty, there usually isn't. The problem, rather, concerns the way they believe it: it is epistemic. One can't identify a purist from the content of his beliefs; one can't even identify him by looking at how he regards contrary beliefs: rather, he is identified by how he treats fellow advocates for liberty who hold different beliefs.

Such political religionists, who broach no ecumenism, seem to lack the moral humility on which their purported political religion depends: they are entirely convinced, albeit subconsciously, that there can be no new idea, and no new piece of information about the world or their own perspective, or anything in the experience or thinking of those with whom they disagree, that could show their view of an issue to be incomplete, let alone wrong, in any way that really matters. To quote Bertrand Russell,

Subjective certainty is inversely proportional to objective certainty.

This sometimes leads them to impugn the character or capacity, rather than just the positions, of those who could be allies in the pursuit of liberty with whom they disagree. It allows them to dismiss their opponent, and the possibility that he might know something that they don't know—that he may have, in fact, read what they read, thought what they thought and even previously shared their position—before discovering something new, or unusual, that warranted a revision. In short, they disrespect the very use of the intellectual freedom that they purport to celebrate and protect. Russell again:

The degree of one's emotion varies inversely with one's knowledge of the facts—the less you know the hotter you get.

The premise of this book is that the exercise of freedom depends on freedom of thought—the freedom to explore the world, physically and intellectually, and then, based on what you find, to form ideas, to change those ideas, to grow and to evolve. To insist on a politics of liberty, and therefore of tolerance, without tolerating others' approaches to promoting just such a politics, is to falsify one's philosophy—and to justify the skepticism of all those who want nothing to do with a libertarianism that lacks the very civility in which it puts so much store.

Put another way, if you're promoting a particular form or manifestation of liberty, then it's probably not liberty per se that you're promoting.

Why am I picking on libertarians? Aren't political advocates of all stripes guilty of lack of humility, tolerance and civility? Aren't such purists found among conservatives, progressives, etc.?

Of course they are.

But for libertarians, things are a little different. Libertarians must hold themselves to a higher standard. They preach freedom, and its complement, tolerance, as the core of their worldview. They, then, are alone in making hypocrites of themselves when they aggress in their manners or words against those who have different ideas about how best, in practice, to make a freer society. Other political philosophies (socialism, religious conservatism etc.) make no claim that freedom of thought and action, and its compliment, tolerance, are at the core of the Good life.

My second reason for picking on libertarians is, as I have indicated, that they form the broad political family to which I belong. And while I am quite content to let the statists and religious right, for example, break themselves on their own arrogance or ignorance or both, I hope that we, who put liberty front and center, never do the same.

Liberty does not stand alone. It is not the be-all-and-end-all—for it pre-supposes Truth. First, a commitment to liberty, as to all political principles, assumes that true statements can be made (such as, "the Good life depends on liberty") and second, liberty only has value if people can seek and establish truths based on which they can make conscious choices in their own self-interest.

This commitment to truth both depends on and creates the intellectual humility to which I've already referred. This is most easily seen in the progress of science, which advances toward truth by recognizing that it has not yet found it. Science goes one step further—to seek actively to falsify itself and thereby to improve its current understanding of the world. That the search for truth is, in this way, always asymptotic, is perhaps the most important paradox of life: to move closer to Truth, one must be continuously aware of one's inability to know it completely.

In contrast, the attitude of the intellectual dogmatist, libertarian or otherwise, is more like, "I have found the truth that matters, and from this position of 'having arrived,' I can see that those who are not here are intellectually or morally flawed." This is the very opposite of the humble epistemology of robust libertarianism, and plenty of libertarians behave this way.

Most of us have probably experienced this unbecoming attitude among some of religion's least attractive adherents. For example, many of us know people who proclaim a Christian faith but use what is essentially a philosophy of Love to justify behavior toward others that is clearly unloving. What is particularly interesting—and relevant—is that they will often be able to explain with some coherence, depth, and clear sincerity, why their actions are loving, even though our human nature—our own direct experience of loving or being loved, for example,—tells us that there must be something wrong with their explanation, even if we cannot exactly articulate it.

It is as if their actions speak louder than their words. If such people were to design our political institutions and occupy our political offices, would it be their words or their behaviors that would determine what it felt like to live under them? Now replace "Christians" with "libertarians", and "love" with "humility, tolerance and civility", and ask the same question.

If I had to choose, I'd rather inhabit a world of civil, open-minded statists, with whom I profoundly disagree, than one of dogmatists of any stripe—even libertarian. Why? Because if the statists are open-minded, then they will be interested in the evidence of experience and, if they are civil, we will have a healthy exchange of ideas and be able to improve our shared community. Meanwhile, I will enjoy my humanity in relationships of mutual respect. Sharing space with the dogmatic libertarian, however, will be tolerable, if dull, until we disagree—which we will, because we are human. At that point, the lack of any compromise or, therefore, the prospect of being able to improve our community in a mutually satisfactory way, along with the being looked down upon for my erroneous understanding of liberty—even as I am politically "free" to act as I will—would make me quite miserable.

If a libertarian world is made happy by replacing political aggression and force with the actions of people who are civil and tolerant, then we cannot expect people to come to our side if we cannot even exhibit those qualities when we interact with allies who seek such a world, just because they seek it in ways whose effectiveness we question.

Surely, libertarians will have the best chance of turning our present "libertarian moment" into a sweeping libertarian movement if we pursue liberty with the humility, civility and tolerance of diversity with which we are seeking to replace the arrogance, corruption and authoritarianism that infect our politics today.

For liberty's sake, and because I want We the People to Keep It, I ask libertarians to be libertarian about their libertarianism.

If Liberty Is the Politics of Love, Then...

Part of loving liberty, and part of loving people—and those two things are the same thing—is to be respectful in the face of people's mistakes and ill-informed opinions. To succeed, we who love liberty must recognize that part of being human is at times not to behave consistently with one's values, or the facts on the ground. We must treat the mistaken with respect because only then will they be open to you and your ideas when they are ready to hear them. Although their live-and-let-live and don't-tread-on-anyone philosophy is undoubtedly the one that most perfectly manifests the Founders' intentions, they too are imperfect and have plenty to learn.

Love is not indifferent. Libertarians may be entirely right that civil society should take care of most of what the state does today. But if the rest of the country cannot see the movement care, they will rightly believe that libertarians—or just liberty-driven Americans—are more concerned with our philosophy than with people.

More concerned, in other words, with Liberty than Love.

And that would be a contradiction in terms.

Put Another Way, There is No Orthodoxy of Love

Should libertarians fall into their own orthodoxy, the cost will be the very principles for which all of us in the liberty movement claim to stand. Orthodoxy reflects a tacit assumption that one's own understanding of principles is as sacred as the principles, themselves. And it divides our house against itself.

Orthodoxy is not consensus. It is a state of mind: it is the idea that there is only one right set of views that liberty can support, when, in fact, the idea that there is only one right set of views is at odds with the notion of liberty, itself.

Until we win, liberty activists are political deviants. If I may be thoroughly unorthodox for one sentence, and quote Anton La Vey, "There is less room for deviance in deviance, than in any other human endeavor." Having been highly active in the movement for four years, my greatest hope is that this never becomes true of us. (We are already displaying the signs.)

If there is one group of people who are not entitled to make an orthodoxy out of their views, it is we who claim to fight for liberty. Why? Because "orthodoxy of liberty" is a contradiction in terms. The belief in freedom, including freedom of thought, should prevent us from judging others who are exercising that very freedom to think about freedom, itself.

That is the epistemic basis for a big-tent culture-moving critical mass for liberty

Orthodox libertarianism may currently be less dangerous than other orthodoxies, such as religious orthodoxies, just because it has much less power and reach, but it is fundamentally worse because it is self-contradictory and so makes liars out of its practitioners.

I love being a part of the American liberty movement. Never have I had so much meaning in my life, nor had so much to play for. But as someone who still remembers what it feels like to be politically situated elsewhere, may I suggest that when self-identified libertarians put others down for understanding their freedom in a way of which they do not approve, those others feel nothing of the expansiveness and the glory of the human spirit that the very idea of liberty, shared with Love, invariably brings.

Given our imperfections, the incompleteness of our knowledge, and our diverse life experiences, lovers of liberty will always holds some contradictory beliefs. If we set ourselves apart from others because they disagree with us on one of our litmus tests for liberty, then we elevate that test above the principle of, and commitment to, liberty, itself.

Tyranny cannot destroy liberty all the while the People are truly committed to using their final freedom—the freedom to think.

Ultimately, as 1984 so beautifully and terrifyingly showed, to destroy liberty, you need something else: you need a commitment to a political paradigm rather than to the People whom that paradigm exists to serve.

CHAPTER 8

First, Do No Harm

THERE IS SOMETHING fundamentally pro-American about all of the apparently anti-American content published in foreign newspapers around the world—even that published during the Bush years, when the USA was regarded by people everywhere else as more alien than it had ever been. In those years, most non-Americans regarded the idea of American exceptionalism as a statement of arrogance and, often, hypocrisy.

Strikingly, nearly all of the polemics about U.S. policy that have been translated by WatchingAmerica.com (a website, started in 2005, that translates foreign opinion and commentary about the USA in mainstream media outlets all over the world) do no more than hold the U.S. to standards that those same polemics admit, sometimes implicitly, are American. In criticizing America, foreigners often ram home their points by highlighting the gap between the universal ideals on which America was founded, on the one hand, and American action, on the other. In this way, most criticisms of America appeal to, and implicitly approve of, American ideals and standards.

This only makes sense in a world that agrees that the Truths stated in the most famous lines of the Declaration of Independence, which comprise the fundamental basis of American idealism, are indeed self-evident:

> *...that all Men are created equal, that they are endowed by their Creator with certain unalienable Rights, that among these are Life, Liberty and the pursuit of Happiness.*

This purpose of the nation of the United States is thus widely regarded as a good thing even if many Americans have forgotten what was really intended by those words. It is impossible to imagine America apart from this political axiom. It is almost impossible even to hear the words "pursuit of happiness" and not think of America.

As many commentators have explored, "America" is very unusual in that it is simultaneously a nation and an idea. The only other countries of which this can be said are those that are devoted to a religious idea (such as various Islamic Republics). America stands apart from all of these, though, because it is constitutionally devoted to the rights of individual, rather than the precedence of a philosophy or religion over the individual. As a matter of fact, this is exceptional, and is, of course, why "American freedom" is celebrated by people everywhere in the abstract even as the American government is removing those freedoms from its own citizens and others. It is also an observable, empirical fact that freedom can only be experienced and exercised in the mind, heart or soul of an individual person—the singular moral agent. That is why George W. Bush was right when he said that it is something desired deeply by people everywhere. After all, no article has ever criticized the U.S. because its actions have in fact brought liberty: The U.S. is criticized only when it does not do so. No one has criticized the American invasion of Iraq because the U.S. liberated that country, but because it failed to do so in any practical sense.

But if we all know, at some level, that liberty is attached to the individual, and that we would rather have it than not, then its statement in the Declaration is not that novel. No; the truly novel idea comes in the next line:

> *... That to secure [the above] rights, Governments are instituted among Men*

In other words, the "raison d'être" of government in America is to secure something that is always and critically in tension with the very idea, and certainly the practice, of government.

It is in that light that we should seek to understand *American exceptionalism*. Frequently in the global press, the idea that any country is exceptional per se is presented as mere arrogance or hubris. But, again as a matter of historical fact, this foundation of the American nation is exceptional.

To espouse Liberty and the pursuit of happiness as a natural right, rather than anything given by men or earthly institutions, is to say only that it is in the nature of a human being to express himself or herself in words and deeds. When unpacked in this way, it is clear that the assertion of the Declaration of Independence is indeed self-evident (which very few assertions are), as opposed to obvious (which very many assertions are): the assertion stands above any opinion or politics, and follows directly from the human experience, unmediated and uninterpreted.

It is critical though to understand why the statement that the principle of the right to individual liberty is an absolute is not akin to a religious doctrine. The difference exists in the fact that a religious absolute is either a factual statement about something that exists outside of oneself (God, the Prophet, an historical event etc.) or it is a prescription. The American absolute is truer than any religious statement, thus defined, can ever be, since it is neither of those things. The American absolute is merely a statement about the personal experience of anyone who experiences herself as an individual with her own preferences and a free will. It does not require you to posit anything at all, but only to experience yourself as an individual consciousness. As such, it also refuses to require anything of you. Precisely because you are a free entity, any limitation on your behavior can only be set by yourself, even if you believe that it is required by something or someone else, such as God.

In this remarkable sense, the American Declaration of Independence and Constitution are the "Cogito ergo sum (I think, therefore I am)" of American politics. One could paraphrase it as, "Sum ergo libero" (I am, therefore I am free).

Twice Blessed

The writing of the Constitution was surely a double blessing to the USA. The first blessing, as we've described, was to found our nation on a profound metaphysical truth concerning human nature. But it was not just the content of the Constitution and Declaration of Independence that set up the USA for success. It was the way in which those truths were stated—so concisely, simply and memorably—that have caused them to infect the American psyche. That's the second blessing—and it may not have been the case. The Framers could have confined their thoughts to dusty academic treatises full of opaque language or to no Constitution at all.

Because of the extraordinary clarity of the Declaration and the Constitution—one of those rare instances in history in which a document is simultaneously popularly accessible and insightful of philosophical truth, the basic ideas of the Framers continue to infect the American psyche, underlying the very identity of Americans, even though many of the freedoms and rights established in the Constitution have in practice been eliminated.

We might say that the substance of the Declaration and Constitution is what Americans must hold fundamental to ensure their freedoms, while their presentation makes those fundamentals easily understood and therefore easily claimed by anyone who identifies as American.

This enduring basis of American-ism provides an immovable reference point for evaluation by the electorate of the acceptability, or otherwise, of any practice or policy that may be imposed on the citizens of the country. It is commonplace abroad to patronizingly roll one's eyes at the lack of political awareness of the median American voter. To the rest of the developed world, an industrialized nation in which gay marriage, the place of the church in political life, the right to abortion etc., are still even issues, seems politically immature. However, as someone who has come from abroad to engage in the political life of this nation, I am impressed that in the United States, more so than in any other nation with which I am familiar, political debates are almost always about truly fundamental political principles, explicated in the founding documents, and that it is those principles—rather than policies of the day that have a more or less baneful effect on some constituency or other—that brings the people onto the street. Love or hate the Tea Party, at its core, it's a political movement concerned with a vision of the country, fundamental values, even an identity—not merely with the correction of a single injustice or the undoing of a single piece of legislation

All the above notwithstanding, one could easily argue that the Patriot Act has made the people of the USA no more free of its government than the people of many other Western democracies are free of theirs. Such an argument may have been correct before 1 Dec 2009, when 27 Western Democracies gave up their sovereignty and democracy under the Lisbon Treaty, which came into force as the new European Constitution against the will of Europe's people. On that day, the supra-national European government (whose legislators are unelected) ignored the negative results of referenda held in multiple countries throughout the continent to impose its will on 300 million people. With that huge step backward in Europe, the liberty-gap between the US and all those countries grew again hugely in favor of the

New World—even in the face of the elimination of habeas corpus in the US, the extensive regulation of many business sectors here (much more than in many Asian countries), the right of the federal government to know all of your communications of any kind without probable cause, and the fact that Americans can be detained without trial.

Since America is the one nation that has been blessed with a unique statement of the right to liberty and happiness, even in the face of its government's transgressions of the Constitution, there remains the unyielding possibility that it may yet save itself from the actions of its elites that may have compromised those rights. That the founding statement of those rights is seared into the popular psyche automatically makes any appeal to those rights a popular appeal rather than an intellectual or elitist one. As history shows, time after time, it is popular opinion, or mass opinion, that must be stirred to reverse the greatest abrogations of rights and liberty.

In this relation, consider the following. Greg Palast, a now celebrated liberal journalist and author who works for the BBC and the Guardian, having moved to the U.K. based on a belief that his (rather excellent) investigative work was not getting the air-time it deserved in the U.S., was asked in 2005 on a Californian radio station, whether he wanted to bring up his new children in England—the country where he had made a very successful career —or in the United States—the country of his birth and most of his life. He answered unhesitatingly that he wanted to bring them up in the U.S. Asked for a reason, he said that in the U.K. the average person knows a lot more than the average American about what is wrong with their political system and how their leaders and money-masters abuse them and their country, but they have an apathy and cynicism that prevent them from getting very exercised about it: they don't care because they expect to be screwed; they therefore are resigned to compromised rights and the incompetent, over-reaching or self-interested wielding of governmental authority. In the U.S., on the other hand, said Mr. Palast, people are much more ignorant of all these things, but were they to know, they'd be much more angry, and would therefore be likely to exercise their popular power to change things, since Americans do have ideals, and more importantly, believe not only in the possibility of those ideals' being realized in practice, but also in the requirement that they be realized. As a Brit who has lived in the USA, I get what he is talking about, and I suspect that what Palast says is true, because of the power of the legacy of the Founders. Palast concluded, then, that his choice was to bring his children up "informed but apathetic, or ignorant and angry", to use his words, and he would chose the latter over the former. So would I. That anger, suppressed only in proportion to the ability of those who would take our rights away from us to do so invisibly, originates in the sense that individual liberty is a birthright and an absolute. Only in America is it so defined; everywhere else, it seems, all rights are subject to discussion, and the compromise of all principles can be considered to the extent that the times seem to demand it.

A Very Practical Philosophy

The Constitution was not written to enable. It was written to limit. If every man has a birthright of all freedoms, which is the presupposition of the Constitution, then clearly, the document needs to do nothing to give those rights to the people that already have them. That would be utterly pointless. The only purpose of the document in the light of the pre-existence of liberty and natural rights is to ensure they are never reduced. Accordingly, the Constitution is confined to limiting the one entity that can wield the power to reduce those rights unchallenged—the government.

Thence, it is simply a matter of logic to note that any dilution of the Constitution can serve only to facilitate the restriction of individual freedom.

The burden must therefore rest on those who proclaim a "living Constitution" to explain what that means. Those who say it seem usually to mean that it must be modified or interpreted to reflect our times, or more specifically, the moral sensibilities of our times—but that is precisely what the Constitution is to protect us against. The claim of the Declaration and the Constitution is that what is worth protecting is the right of people not to be limited by any opinions or mores of the time, of any time; that the only thing it is concerned with—the right not to be subjected to any of these against one's will—is constant, and must be held above all restrictions that may be imposed by well-meaning people who may have a great idea that, if adopted by all people, would make the world a better place.

In other words, just as writing the Constitution was an act of liberal conservatives, conserving what is most liberal (in the proper, classical sense) about their tradition and national identity, it was written to help us who would come after to continue to do the same.

Restated, a true desire to improve everyone's lot is simply an insufficient justification for bending the absolute right of individual liberty, even when it seems entirely reasonable to do so. If bending that right never seemed reasonable, then there would be no need for a Constitution. Obviously, I don't need to be protected from the unreasonable, selfish individual who wishes to advance himself at my expense, because normal law, criminal, civil, contract, tort or whatever, is good enough to handle that. No, the need for the Constitution is the need to protect me—me alone in a nation of 330 million—not just from the majority who would affect my life for the "greater good" but even against the entire population. You all can do what you wish and it may be much better than any plans I may have for myself or the world, but in America, my right, my utmost right, the one right that accrues to me by virtue of my simple existence as a human being, is that you don't get to make me do anything. You can stop me doing things that hurt you, but you can't make me do anything. As Judge Napolitano says, the most general right of Americans is the "right to be left alone".

In a book that warns against "black vs. white", this is as close to something's being black and white as I'll advocate for. For the philosophically minded, it is the synthetic a priori of American politics. That means that while that is not a logical truth (with the force of 2+2=4), it is a truth without which none of the rest of what we do and experience makes any sense at all. It leaves no more room for interpretation than there is the possibility of being "a little bit pregnant". Of course, in the metaphysics of the Declaration of Independence, to argue against it is to argue that you are not, in fact, an individual human being.

This word "living" is, then, a dangerous one when used in the same sentence as the Constitution. This is a shame of course, because there is one sense in which the Constitution is very alive: it was written to enable all individuals to live in the least bounded way—to celebrate Life that can create, change and even run riot so long as its so doing does not suppress Life anywhere else.

And so the Constitution binds down political institutions, which are always inferior to the individuals that they are supposed to serve. In America, this, too, is not up for negotiation.

Off the Rails

It is hard to argue that since the writing of the Declaration and the Constitution, Americans haven't chosen, or been led to choose, to give up certain rights to improve security against attack from foreigners, poverty, or other perceived evils. Many Americans are now beginning to feel that too many such choices have been made. If that is so, then it is my hope that Americans will rally around their Americanism—their very identity (given by God, or the universe or nothing at all, depending on your spirituality or lack of it) as free persons.

Almost all of the important problems of America today follow from unwitting compromises of the fundamental Constitutional principle. While many questionable things may be done in the name of a good cause, fighting poverty, defense, or even the American flag, anything done that is truly consistent with the Founders' intent will be on solid ground, which was to hurt no one for the benefit of anyone else.

As this nation revisits its underlying political philosophy, as it seems now to be doing, a studied process of elimination of that which is incompatible with the original Declaration, and its underlying vision, may provide, if not a solution to all of America's ills, an almost-solution to most of them.

I've already bastardized Descartes. Let me do the same to Hippocrates: the fundamental principle of the Hippocratic oath is, "First, do no harm". The Declaration and Constitution are nothing more complicated than a political Hippocratic oath for those who would lead the citizens of a country, "First, do no harm". The only difference is that, for a doctor, "harm" is that which affects the wellbeing of a person as a physical and emotional being, whereas for a politician, "harm" is that which affects the wellbeing of a person as a moral agent with free will and human rights.

To my mind, this is a particularly useful analogy, because there are some ethical issues that are intuitively simple to resolve when applied to a person's body, but seem (wrongly) more complicated when applied to a person's life in general. Considering the former can clarify the latter.

A doctor could save, say, five people, by killing one and transplanting his liver, kidneys, heart and bone marrow into five others. Five saved for one killed. By cold calculation, and from a utilitarian perspective, that seems like a good deal. But we know it isn't because of the infringement of the rights of the one killed, even though it would be for a good cause. Our moral sense, however, is easily encoded in the Hippocratic oath: since the doctor must, "first, do no harm", he is forbidden from practicing such mad science, regardless of the good it would do for the five beneficiaries at that particular time.

Just as the Hippocratic oath is intended to protect the rights of the individual as a physical entity, the Constitution protects the rights of the individual as a political entity. It says not to the doctor, but to the politician, "you may not do what you think is good for anyone or even many persons, at the expense of a person who is unwilling to be a party to it." Isn't that a good standard to apply? It is the standard we expect from our doctors. And it is the standard of the Declaration of Independence and the Constitution.

The only difference between the mad doctor, doing harm in an attempt to do good, and the mad politician, also often doing harm in an attempt to do good, is that the politician is voted to his position and can then direct the governmental monopoly of force. Of course, this makes the politician all the more dangerous than the doctor, and the Constitution all the more important than the Hippocratic Oath. That we live in a Democracy makes the constraints imposed by the Constitution more important, not less so, for the obvious reason that, without protection of the individual, 51% could pass laws that disenfranchise 49% for their benefit. This has already happened in many areas. It happens socially, such as when government says on behalf of the majority that some people may not enjoy the rights enjoyed by others by virtue of their color (fifty years ago) or their sexual orientation (today). Even more pervasively, it happens economically, such as when the majority take money from the few, on pain of incarceration, to be redistributed among their own number. We may like some such practices and not others, and as reasonable people, we should debate them, but the greater gains are made by understanding how the proper application of the Constitution could eliminate many of the problems that we have already created.

In considering the route that America should take from here to realize its potential and claim its birthright, let's return for a moment to what the world doesn't understand of America.

I lived in the USA for about five years before I became a permanent resident, and for most of that time I would, like most non-Americans, roll my eyes at that rather banal old saw that "America is the greatest country in the world" or "the Shining City on the Hill". The obvious objection to such a claim is, "Even if that were true, how could Americans possibly know?"

I don't roll my eyes as much any more.

While the media of the rest of the world cherish the ideals of freedom that they associate with America, and therefore judge American action by those very ideals, there is something that they do not understand about American liberty.

Most foreign articles that broach freedom in relation to the USA, whether implicitly or explicitly, are written, understandably, with the idea that freedom in the USA is qualitatively the same thing as freedom in the writer's country, such as Germany, Britain, Spain etc. They assume that whereas the USA may be more explicit about ideas of freedom, and may even be a symbol of individual liberty, American liberty is not philosophically different from liberty anywhere else. Indeed, the idea may be quantitatively more prevalent, but it is qualitatively the same. How many meanings can "liberty" have, after all? This is a perfectly reasonable assumption for at least two reasons.

- Since we can only perceive the "other" through our own paradigms, our concepts determine what we can perceive in the other (an idea that has been reiterated throughout this book);
- American behavior on the world stage neither manifests nor explains the American idea of liberty. Often, it seems decidedly at odds with the notion.

But the American conception of liberty is qualitatively different from non-American conceptions. The difference may rest on an idea of government that is not at the core of political discourse elsewhere. Americans realize that government is an ontologically different entity from any other. They realize that government is inherently dangerous because it is the only social or cultural entity that has a monopoly of force. It is so obvious to Americans that it is not often said. To everyone else in the world, government only has the potential to become dangerous by virtue of what it does, but it is not dangerous by virtue simply of what it is. In other words, outside America, government may earn the people's trust or distrust, but it is not inherently untrustworthy, while in America, by contrast, the protection of individual freedoms must first and foremost be protection from government. Everywhere else, freedom is something that a society may have more or less of, but it is just another social good, which may be protected by government (rather than from government)—just like any other social good.

The American conception of liberty as preceding politics rather than being an issue or social good within the realm of politics, is then, exceptionally American. It also explains why I no longer roll my eyes at those one-liners that seem to claim American exceptionalism, if those one-liners are properly understood to celebrate that the American political settlement is the protector of something of philosophical and practical value, whose practical manifestation benefits the world.

The Constitution is arguably the greatest classical liberal document of all time, and as such, is as good a rallying point for those on either side of the illusory left-right divide. The Constitution protects the social liberties dear to the left as it does the economic liberties dear to the right. It prevents the monopoly of force from interfering with what I do in my bedroom as it prevents them from interfering with what I do at my bank.

The term classical liberalism no longer means anything to

most people. It is not a term that has been used in any popular literature since soon after the Second World War. So rather than insist on its use, and to educate a population about something lost to some degree of obscurity, I believe we can have more fun and impact using those divisive terms in American politics, conservative and liberal, in a way that will subvert the very division they have for so longed helped to maintain.

In that spirit, I'd like to suggest not that we try to popularize the term classical liberalism as the name of modern political school of thought most closely aligned with the Constitution, but that we go with conservative liberalism, which is just as good a name, and has the added benefit of directly subverting our current division-inducing, perception-limiting political tribes.

Conservative liberalism is liberal because it demands the freedom of individuals to express themselves how they wish, religiously, sexually, racially and culturally. It is conservative because it recognizes that those freedoms can only be safeguarded if all types of intrusion—whether by other individuals or government—are rejected. It is liberal because it recognizes the value of social equity, in the sense of impartiality and justice. It is conservative because it demands that people be allowed to enjoy economic equity, which empowers them to make their own choices so as to maximize their utility. It is liberal because it emphasizes that opportunity should be equal. It is conservative because it recognizes that opportunity should be equal—and that forced equality eliminates opportunity and is at odds with justice. It is conservative precisely because it rejects the moral privilege of the religious right to impose through law their social or sexual morals on anyone, and it is liberal for the same reason. It is liberal because it rejects the moral privilege of the socialist left to impose their economic morals on anyone, and it is conservative for the same reason. Classical liberalism, in its original meaning, or conservative liberalism, as I call it here, is both conservative and liberal, but it is neither Conservative nor Liberal.

I've already said that when it was written, the Constitution, in raising the individual as the seat of all political power, making him more powerful than a king, was a highly progressive document. It was truly liberal. Indeed, it was written to liberate. But many of the Founders thought of themselves as conservative. They were declaring independence in an attempt to conserve what they understood to be their traditional English rights in common law, and an English democratic tradition that ran back to 1215 and beyond, trampled by a power in the mother country that did not respect them. In the 20th century, it was Churchill, a conservative, who did more for the survival of liberal politics against those who would defeat it than perhaps anyone in the world. The point here is that there is precedent that some of the greatest achievements of liberalism have been simultaneously some of the greatest achievements of conservatism.

Accordingly, I offer this label, conservative liberal, for anyone who sees the value in replacing current political divisions with the one that truly matters, having been drawn a long time ago by the original classical liberals, and just now, in Chapter 2 of this book. That is the division between the idea that the individual knows what is best for himself (moderate Left and moderate Right, today), and the idea that some group knows what is best for everyone (socialist Left and neo-con Right).

It was Bill Clinton, the Democratic President, working with a Republican Congress, who established what many commentators have called one of the most effective reforms in modern American politics—the workfare reforms that reduced welfare dependency and saved tax dollars. The reforms involved expecting more of people, rather than giving more to them. They made work more profitable and gave the poor more dignity. They simultaneously reduced poverty and reduced total welfare payouts. The benefits of this reform are still being felt today.

What Clinton and the Republicans showed was that good policy depends on right intentions of policy up front and right outcomes of policy after implementation. Concentrating on one only one of these two pieces invariably leads to bad outcomes. In the example of Clinton's welfare reforms, the left's intention to reduce poverty and positive outcomes for the poor were realized by rethinking much of the approach to welfare that had until that time been supported by the left.

The general lesson is this. If you hear a policy you like, withhold judgment for a few years until you see if it has had the intended effects. A law is as likely to be bad because its consequences are not as intended as it is because the intentions that motivated it were bad.

Such suspension of judgment is an act of political humility. From that perspective of humility, look again at America's birthright—its Constitution. No other nation has such an excellent philosophical and practical road-map for tackling the deepest issues with which a society must grapple. It is a conservative liberal document that defaults to preventing policy that aggresses against people economically or socially.

In that spirit, let the moral burden of American politics be on those that would use the power of the state—through statute or taxation—to force their good intentions on anyone's choices regarding their religion, sexuality, property, relationships, charity, money or anything else at all. Government may always be about compromise, so give the politician who would take from Peter to give to Paul a hearing—but require him to tell you what would, in the long-run, indicate that his policy was a success, and that this success could not have been achieved without aggressing against Peter. Require him to tell you how the policy would be rectified should it fail to deliver. Require him to tell you under what provision of the Constitution, his proposed course of action is legal. If he complains that the Constitution is too restrictive, invite him to make the case to amend, and support him if you agree with him. (Remind him too that his complaint is worthless since he took an oath to uphold the Constitution without reservation.) All the while, realize that left and right are just constructs, that whatever the media are telling you is likely either to be simply false or to miss the point. Make cause not with those who would impose a will similar to yours on American society, but with those who would balk at imposing anyone's will, including their own, on anyone at all. The only thing each of us has in common with every other American, except our humanity, is our Constitution. Fortunately for us, it's just about the best thing anyone has ever had to share with 300 million other people. It is a point of commonality that, properly understood and exploited, will enable us to debate with each other without dividing ourselves against each other along lines that do little other than appeal to some rather primitive parts of the brain.

Magna Carta for Our Time

This book has been about breaking through and breaking down our paradigms—the paradigms that prevent us from seeing what is being done to us and in our name, yet often without our consent, and at odds with our basic liberties. Seeing our own paradigms and stepping out in front of them helps us to stand on our shared common ground as Americans and human beings, and thereby to unite against Power and corruption as necessary to defend our natural rights and well-being.

The success of such a defense depends on the defenders' not dividing themselves against each other. That means not losing sight of the big tasks because we cannot get everything we want. It means not letting the perfect be the enemy of the good.

The Constitution that was written to specify a form of governance that would favor the utterly shared ground of life, liberty and the pursuit of happiness was born out of an Anglo-tradition of Constitutional liberty that began one millennium ago in about 1014, with the Anglo-Saxon charter, which was the first document to be signed by a Head of State, King Ethelred II, to limit his power.

The one milestone in the Anglo-tradition of liberty that some hold in higher esteem than even the founding of our nation is the Magna Carta, sealed by King John at Runnymede in England exactly 800 years ago last year. Some of its provisions, as we have seen, are still statute in England—and Magna Carta is still referred to in courts throughout the Anglosphere.

In the spirit of this anniversary, in recognition that only the People can ultimately protect their rights by actively defending them, and in the spirit of many of the documents that the representatives of the People have formulated since that time to re-assert their rights against an overbearing government and establishment, I offer one for our time—a Remonstrance that I believe speaks for all of the People.

A Remonstrance of the People of the United States of America

Whereas our Rights, enumerated in our Constitution, have been won with blood against tyrants for one thousand years;

Whereas that to secure these Rights, Governments are instituted among Men, deriving their just powers from the consent of the governed;

Whereas whenever any form of Government becomes destructive of these ends, it is the Right of the People to alter or to abolish it;

Whereas, when a long train of abuses and usurpations evinces a design to reduce those Rights, it is the Right, it is the duty, of the People to throw off such Government;

Whereas, under the Patriot Act and other legislation, even free speech has been criminalized and security of personal property is denied;

Whereas, under the National Defense Authorization Act and other legislation, the privacy of the People is violated daily;

Whereas, under the aforesaid legislation, the basic Rights of due process and habeas corpus have been abrogated, even to the extent that the government asserts an unnatural privilege to kill American citizens;

Whereas our police have been turned into a domestic paramilitary force, directed against those who pay them and whom they serve;

Whereas our sons and daughters have been sent to die in wars not fought to protect our nation from immediate threats, all in the name of the People, but often without our consent, or even the consent of those who represent us;

Whereas the People are criminalized by a tax code so complex that no one can possibly comply with complete accuracy and are therefore liable to punishment;

Whereas millions of fellow Americans languish in prison cells for so-called "crimes" that did no harm to anyone in either person or property;

Whereas our political system has been corrupted by a political duopoly of Republican and Democratic parties that has legislated to deny fair access to the political process by those who do not promote the agendas of either of those two parties;

Whereas those same parties empower themselves at the expense of the People by gerrymandering to ensure that most elections are foregone conclusions without any possibility of unseating the incumbent;

Whereas institutions of the Federal government, such as the Central Bank, transfer the wealth of the People to selected entities without specific authorization by the People or their Representatives;

Whereas unelected executive agents make rules with the force of law without the approval of the People or their Representatives in Congress;

Whereas it has become the habit of our Presidents to collapse the necessary divide between the Legislature and the Executive by using executive orders not in support of legitimate executive duties but by directing the aforesaid executive agencies to enforce against the People rules that have not been established in law;

Whereas our politicians accept money from entities that, not being People, have no democratic standing, and create legislation in the interest of those entities despite harm done to the People;

Whereas our entire political system has become a means of imposing the world view of some of the People on the others using the force of government, rather than a means of protecting our Life, Liberty and the Pursuit of Happiness, which is its only function and justification;

Whereas the final protection of our liberties—the right of jury nullification by which a jury may judge not only a defendant but also unjust legislation by which he is convicted—is hidden from the People;

Whereas each Representative has sworn an oath to uphold the Constitution, and not the narrow interests of any organization—political, economic or cultural;

Whereas almost all Representatives are in violation of their oath and therefore wield delegated power without legitimacy;

Therefore, We the People, in whom all power resides, revoke that delegation of power, and demand, consistent with the duty of the People, made explicit in our Declaration of Independence, the following.

- All laws that seek to limit those Rights of the People that are codified in the Bill of Rights shall be repealed. In particular, the Patriot Act, National Defense Authorization Act Sections 10.21 and 10.22, and the Federal Restricted Buildings and Ground Improvement Act shall be repealed.
- Where it is necessary for covert operations to be conducted in defense of our nation, those operations shall be governed according to principles that are publicly known and set in Law. And those servants of the People who are tasked with covert operations shall be individually criminally liable for failing to act according to said principles. And a body with the sole mandate of protecting the natural Rights of the People shall be established with access to all information held by the government about People on whom no warrant has been served and who have not been charged with a crime. That body shall also have the power to

investigate the procedures used by our covert agents and shall be given authority to publicize their findings and initiate terminations when violations are found.

- The Federal government shall not require from State or local law enforcement agencies shared jurisdiction for any reasons whatsoever, including but limited to, the receiving of resources, such as military equipment and manpower.
- No government agent shall threaten lethal force against any U.S. citizen except in response to an imminent threat of the unlawful use of force against human life.
- No American shall be held criminally responsible for any tax that cannot be calculated by an individual with a typical high school education. The individual tax return shall not exceed one page in length. Income tax shall not be garnered from salaries paid by employers except with the consent of the payer or when the payer has been found guilty of tax evasion. No American shall have to divulge the whereabouts of any of his assets, within or outside the country, unless he has been found criminally guilty of tax evasion or other property crime. All contrary legislation shall be repealed or amended.
- No action without an identifiable victim shall be a Federal crime. Accordingly, no American shall be incarcerated for actions that do not violate the

natural Rights of another. All contrary legislation shall be repealed.

- To debates held between candidates or their representatives for public consumption shall be invited all candidates of any or no party who are on the ballot and have the theoretical (rather than statistical) possibility of winning the election in relation to which the debate is being held.
- No person who has been voted to political office with the official or financial support of any party shall be allowed to directly participate in redistricting. Redistricting shall be conducted by a politically independent body in each state, according to a method that shall be published and opened for public consultation. No information about historical voting patterns may be used in the process of redistricting. Redistricting with the purpose of giving a political party an electoral advantage shall be a criminal offense.
- The country's central bank shall be audited. All transactions shall be publicized within one year of their being made.
- The Constitutional authority of Congress to make legislation shall not be given in any form to any agency under executive control. Should any such agency seek to impose a rule that shall in any way limit the actions of any of the People, they must submit that rule to Congress for a vote. It shall become enforceable only when it becomes law.

- The President shall sign no executive order for a purpose other than enabling him to conduct the affairs of his office. He shall claim no authority to abrogate or change any legislation passed by the People's representatives. All powers and authorities possessed by the President, any other officer or employee of the Federal Government, or any executive agency, as a result of the of any declaration of National Emergency, of which more than 30 are concurrently in effect, shall be terminated within 90 days, unless each House of Congress shall meet to consider a vote on a joint resolution to determine whether each emergency shall be terminated. All future National Emergencies will automatically terminate within 6 months without Congressional joint resolution and will not be eligible for renewal by the President without said resolution. The legally required condition for such Emergencies, that there be "unusual and extraordinary threat to the national security", will be applied with its intended strict definition: any pro forma application of these words will nullify the National Emergency created.
- Only American citizens can vote. Organizations, including but not limited to corporations, charities and unions, are not citizens and cannot vote. Only citizens who may vote for a candidate or ballot initiative may contribute material resources to that candidate, his or her campaign or any political

organizations that seek to affect the outcome of an election involving that candidate or a vote concerning the initiative.

- All legislation passed by Congress shall specify that part of the Constitution that authorizes the legislation. The Commerce, General Welfare, Necessary and Proper and Tax and Spending Clauses shall be applied only in their original meaning.
- Juries in Federal criminal cases shall be informed of their right to nullify the law under which the defendant is being tried; that is to say that a jury will be informed of their duty to find a defendant not guilty if the legislation under which he would otherwise convicted is contrary to natural justice and common law. There shall be no garnishment of assets by any Federal authority or agency from anyone who has not been found guilty of a crime.
- Fraud is a deception deliberately practiced in order to secure unfair or unlawful gain. Accordingly, Federal representatives shall be personally and criminally liable for failing to honor their oaths of office.

To Which End, We the People declare that those in office who purport to represent us no longer do, and shall not be deemed to do so until they consent to the demands herein, and express their sincere intention to use their political office to fulfill these demands. Until then, we leave our political servants with the words of a former President as they consider the weight of their responsibility and the precarious position of our nation.

> *Those who make peaceful revolution impossible make violent revolution inevitable.*
>
> —John F. Kennedy.

Should those who borrow the power of the People continue to use it against the People's Rights, whose protection is the only justification for the delegation of said Power, We the People shall hold them entirely responsible for the consequences.

—Witness Our Hands, this fifteenth day of June, in the year 2015.

CPSIA information can be obtained
at www.ICGtesting.com
Printed in the USA
FSOW02n0605210616
21747FS